DIVERSITY AND DEVELOPMENT OF HIMALAYAN ECONOMY

THE AUTHORS

Dr. M.C. Sati (b. 1967) obtained his MA in Economics with first position in 1988 and PhD in Agricultural Economics in 1994 from HNB Garhwal University, Srinagar (Garhwal). Currently, a Reader in the Department of Economics at his alma mater, he has more than two dozen articles in many national and international journals and is also the editor of the popular book *Uttarakhand Statehood: Dimensions of Development*. Dr. Sati is the key professional working on various issues, e.g. elementary education, health, community empowerment and human development in the Indian Central Himalaya Region. He is also associated with various research projects and training programmes of National Institute of Administrative Research, LBS National Academy of Administration, Mussoorie. He has also supervised 8 PhD scholars in different aspects of mountain development. He has actively participated in a number of national and international conferences, seminars and workshops.

Dr. Anil K. Dimri, PhD in Economics, is currently working as Deputy Director in Indira Gandhi National Open University (IGNOU). Prior to joining IGNOU, he was Research Officer at the Centre for Micro Planning and Regional Studies, Lal Bahadur Shastri National Academy of Administration, Mussoorie, India. He has also served as Joint Chief in the Institute of Applied Manpower Research (Planning Commission), GOI, New Delhi. He has published more than two dozen papers in national and international journals and also prepared and submitted several research reports pertaining to different Ministries/Institutions and organizations. His areas of interest are Decentralized Planning and PRI Institutions, Participatory Learning and Action (PLA) and Distance Education. He has also supervised 3 PhD in Applied Economics.

DIVERSITY AND DEVELOPMENT OF HIMALAYAN ECONOMY

Horticulture in Perspective

M.C. SATI

ANIL K. DIMRI

ZENITH BOOKS INTERNATIONAL

DELHI - 110092 (INDIA)

DIVERSITY AND DEVELOPMENT OF HIMALAYAN ECONOMY

First Published 2008

ISBN 978-81-906069-1-2

Published in India by
ZENITH BOOKS INTERNATIONAL
B-1, ABC Complex, 20 Veer Savarkar Block,
Shakarpur, Delhi-110 092
E-mail: zenith_book@yahoo.com
visit us at: www.zenithbooksintl.com

Printed at: R.K. Offset, Delhi.

Contents

Foreword

Himalayas has been known since times immemorial for its rich social, religious and cultural diversity that uses many wild and domesticated plant species as sources of livehood/sustenance, e.g. food, fodder, fuel, medicine etc. Crop diversity in this region is one of the famous strategies for reducing risk in the future harsh and highly variable climate. Mountain soils are highly variable and frequently stony and thus support varied type of crops on terraced fields. The agricultural research community has generally neglected mountain farming in comparison to plains which have greater food production potential and are often more densely populated and richer. Also due to remoteness and inaccessibility, the genetic resources from most of the off-routes and farflung areas of Himalayan region have not yet reached to the hand of conservationists or plant breeders. The most important task ahead is to cover entire area and to collect, conserve and document our unexplored greater diversity.

In the context of the Uttarakhand state, agriculture and horticulture sectors have played a vital role in the sustainable livelihood. Production of organic crops, fruits and vegetables has socio-economic significance. The state has tremendous potential to draw the attention of investors to take advantage of liberalization and globalization. Horticulture and related micro enterprises can open the avenues of employment and income generating opportunities. This will ultimately help boost the economy of state.

On the other hand, medicinal plants and floriculture are two subsidiaries of horticulture sector, which can also play significant role in the development of the region. Floriculture has gained impetus in the recent time, primarily due to ever increasing international demand for the cut-flowers. Uttarakhand is in advantageous position so far as the suitability of the climatic conditions are concerned. The varying climatic conditions are suitable for cultivation of cut-flowers. The significance of Valley of Flowers cannot be ruled out, similarly Doon valley and

Shivalik foothills have suitable climatic conditions for cultivation of a number of species of cut-flowers of utmost economic importance.

Uttarakhand hills are well suited for growing a wide variety of horticultural and subsidiary crops. The potential is yet to be fully exploited to reduce poverty level in the region. The situation could be improved by adopting integrated approach towards horticulture development through the supply of quality seeds and planting material. There is ample potential for horticultural development particularly fruit and vegetable production and processing enterprises in the zone where conditions are ideally suitable. However, in spite of favourable soil and climatic conditions horticulture has not been paid due attention in this region. The transportation, communication and marketing system are also very poor in the region. Some of the other constraints to the growth of horticulture are also identified in the present study.

To give further boost to the development of horticulture and its processing, government should encourage establishment of more processing industries through simplified procedures. In view of huge investment and uncertainty of their full use and profitability the private agencies are reluctant to invest in infrastructural facilities. Government should encourage their development in joint and cooperative sector. The post-harvest losses in agri-horticultural crops are relatively more in remote tribal and hilly regions. Besides the above, these activities will help in improving income and open new employment opportunities in the region.

I am glad to find that Dr. M.C. Sati and Dr. Anil K. Dimri have ably addressed some of the important issues regarding development of horticulture in Himalayan economy in general and Uttarakhand in particular. In this book horticulture related issues are valuable which reveal a wealth of data and information about horticulture, floriculture and medicinal plants. The findings are based on the analysis of empirical primary data and field visits. I am sure this book will prove of great help to policy-makers, practitioners, researchers and all those who are concerned for sustainable mountain development.

Prof. S. P. Singh, FNA
Vice-Chancellor,
H.N.B. Garhwal University,
Srinagar (Garhwal), Uttarakhand

Preface

India has varied agro-climate zones, with highly favourable climatic conditions for growing a large number of horticultural crops such as fruits, vegetables, root tubers, aromatic and medicinal plants and spices and plantation crops like coconut, cashew and cocoa etc. Presently, horticulture occupies about 13 per cent of gross cropped area, producing 177.41 million metric tonnes of horticulture produce (2005-06). India is the second largest producer of fruits and vegetables in the world. The total production of fruits has been estimated at 52.85 million metric tonnes from an area of 5.34 million hectares and vegetables has been estimated at 108.20 million metric tonnes from an area of 7.05 million hectares during 2005-06. India is also the largest producer of mango, banana, sapota and acid lime. About 39.5 per cent of the mangos and 11 per cent bananas are produced in India. Similarly grapes have the highest productivity per unit area in the world. India is next only to China in area and production of vegetables and occupies prime position in the production of cauliflower, onions and cabbage.

The Himalayan region of India has rich biodiversity of flora and most horticultural species traced here are in use in various forms for hundreds of years to meet the needs of the people. Though majority of the people of the region are engaged in agricultural activities, however, agriculture never been economically profitable venture due to hilly terrain, low fertility and high labour absorption and other reasons. Agriculture cannot fetch enough income for the survival of the people of the region. Therefore alternative economic activity, which may yield more income, is essentially required for the planned economic development of the region.

During the past few decades the importance of horticulture sector has been realized in the Himalayan region. Promotion of horticulture is included in the national priorities of most of the countries of the region. National Horticulture Mission (NHM) has emphasized on the area-based development of the sector. There are also opportunities for the development of ancillary horticultural crops such as floriculture, medicinal plants etc. because of the suitable agro-climatic conditions.

With the increase in production of horticultural crops, especially fruits, vegetables, and potatoes, marketing has become a serious problem in the Himalayan mountains. The markets are far away from the production areas and the produce has to pass through different types of climates before reaching the market. Marketing of horticultural produce includes not only the commercial transactions of buying and selling but also physical distribution. This physical distribution includes all the handling and forwarding activities such as harvesting, collecting, grading, packing, storing and subsequent dispersal through the markets to the consumers. In addition, there are various other auxiliary functions of marketing such as pre-harvest information, market finance and administration, marketing intermediaries, market training, and extension and research.

Considering the issues raised above the book is divided into nine chapters. In introduction, broad prospective of horticulture sector is analysed in detailed and some useful studies carried out in the similar socio-economic setting were also reviewed. This is followed by the general discussion on the methodology of the study. Uttarakahnd has varying socio-economic and geo-physical conditions, which has certain impact on any kind of study. Therefore in the second chapter these issues are discussed in detail. The availability of infrastructure such as road network, health status, electrification are analyzed and gaps therein are also identified. The chapter also analyzes the growth and distribution of population, sex composition, rural-urban composition and the literacy position. Education is another aspect which play important role in the development of the region in general and human resources in particular. As such crucial issues related to education are also studied.

The traditional agriculture of the Himalayan region exhibits a great deal of variability in crop diversity, crop composition and crop rotations etc. along the altitudinal transect due to corresponding variations in a number of factors, as a result the region can be divided into three agro-climatic zones along the elevation gradient. According to traditionally accepted criteria of agricultural land in the region is identified either as the rain-fed (*ukhar*) or the irrigated (*sera*). Irrigated land is often confined to the river valleys and along the lower altitude and some times in the small chunks as terraced agricultural fields in middle altitude where water is available. Mainly the spring fed rivers and small rivulets provide the irrigation water. In Chapter 3 issues related to area, production and productivity of various crops are dealt in detail. Also crop rotation, crop diversity, agro-climatic zones and status of irrigation facilities as well as potential and prospectus of agriculture are highlighted .

Chapter 4 is based on the primary data collected in Joshimath, Porkhri, Chamaba, Pratapnagar, Purola and Bhatwari blocks. Profile of orchard owners and position of orchards in relation to accessibility to road head is also analysed. Chapter further focuses on the general profile of the orchard owners including age, educational qualification, sex, main and subsidiary occupation and size of land holding etc. Analysis of both agriculture as well as horticulture crops is also made with respect to the sample orchards to find out comparative advantage in replacing Agriculture crops with horticulture crops to fetch more cash income. In chapter-5, indepth analysis of secondary data is carried out in order to assess the potential and prospect of horticulture in the region and to identify the areas which have suitable climatic conditions for the cultivation of a particular fruit and vegetable crop. To. exploit the potential of horticulture in state, government has developed infrastructure under the department of horticulture and food processing, availability of the infrastructure for the overall development of horticulture sector is also analysed in this chapter.

Agrarian system is well adapted to the rural mountain environment, and most of production is locally consumed. Although availability of infrastructure makes positive impact on the agricultural productivity but its importance is considerably higher for horticulture. Like subsistence agriculture, subsistence horticulture, traditionally prevailing in the area may do without additional infrastructure but commercial horticulture needs strong foundation of necessary infrastructure. Therefore, subsistence nature of prevailing economy is semi-self-reliant and hardly there is any scope of produce and import of inputs. Similarly, areas of horticulture production are generally poor road and market accessibility and technical support is also not available in time. Horticulture produce is highly perishable and fragile which means that in order to maintain it in a suitable cool state over time and distance, the biological changes to which it is subjected, must be thoroughly known. This state of affairs raises problem of balance between supply and demand, which make the market for horticultural produce specially sensitive not only at the level of individual producer, but also at regional, national and even international levels. Therefore, in Chapter 6 issues related to marketing, transportation, storage etc are deliberated.

Moisture, microorganisms, enzymes etc are major factors responsible for spoilage of fruits and vegetables. To avoid the spoilage of consumable items preservation is essential to store material in perfect condition for a longer period. Fruit and vegetables are available as a seasonal surplus in production areas and large quantities is wasted due to the absence of facilities, poor technical know-how. A massive amount of perishable fruits and vegetables produced during a particular season result in a glut in the market and becomes scare during other seasons. Neither can they be all consumed in a fresh condition nor sold at economically viable prices. Only adoption of improved storage facilities and processing facilities can help to increase life of perishable commodities. Therefore, in chapter 7 all these issues occupy prominent place as development of horticulture requires reasonably good production as well as proper planning for processing the produce so that it can be marketed in most efficient manner.

In chapter 8 and 9 potential and prospects of medicinal plants and cut-flowers are analysed. The region is rich in high commercial value of medicinal plants and cut-flowers. Exploitation of medicinal plants ensuring the balance in biodiversity can also become important economic venture in the region. The medicinal plants with high medicinal gradients has significantly higher demand in the international market. Similarly cut-flowers from the region are also in the great demand. Uttarakhand government is also committed to harness the sector as it has tremendous potential and can be proved important employment and income generating venture in future.

The study was supported and funded by the Indian Council of Social Science Research (ICSSR), New Delhi through the project "A Study of Income and Employment Potentialities through Horticulture Development in Garhwal Himalaya". The authors gratefully acknowledge financial support from the ICSSR. We are deeply indebted to Prof. S.P. Singh, FNA, Vice-Chancellor, HNB Garhwal University, Srinagar (Garhwal) for providing excellent academic environment to the university and also for contributing a Foreword to this volume. We extend our sincere thanks to Prof. N.S. Bisht, Prof. P.L. Bhatt, Prof. H.C. Pokhriyal,

Dr. R.P. Juyal, Dr. B.P. Chamola and Dr. R.P. Mamgain for their valuable comments, suggestions and help. We also express our gratitude to our departmental faculties for their intellectual support. We are also thankful to our friends whose constant, direct and indirect support has been our inspiration throughout dealing with the task. Last but not least, we are thankful to our parents, brothers, and our wives for their constant encouragement.

M.C. Sati
Anil K. Dimri

Glossary

Baranaza—A combination of 10-12 traditional crops grow simultaneously in one field in a monsoon season.

Doon Valley—Lies in district Dehradun belongs to Ganga and Yamuna river systems and bounded by Shiwalik Hills in the South, and the outer scrap the Himalayas in the north.

Gool—Indigenous canals through which water reaches to fields from the source for irrigation purpose.

Khals—Place where two ridges meet. Wind blows there at very high speed.

Madua—A coarse grain, rich in nutritious value, is grown in hills' rainfed land.

Nali—A local measurement unit of area, prevalent in Garhwal and Kumaon. One nali = 196 sq. mt or 51 nali = 1 hectare.

Sera—Flat cultivated areas mostly in river valleys with perennial source of irrigation.

Talaon—Irrigated land.

Tola—Hemlet.

Ukhar—Rainfed cultivate land.

Upraon—Cultivable unirrigiated land.

1

Introduction

India has made significant progress in the field of agriculture since Independence as a result it has become sufficient not only in production of foodgrains but also produces in surplus. However, due to regional disparities a significant segment of the population is deprived of the access to adequate nutrition and basic amenities and services. On the one hand the official statistics claims reduction in the number of people living below poverty line, however there are areas, particularly in the rural and remote areas including Himalayan region where concentration of poor people is relatively high and the level of development is significantly low. Therefore, the labour migration from these pockets for economically productive areas is an ever increasing phenomenon for better employment opportunities. In the hilly areas particularly in Uttarakhand this phenomenon is relatively more as compared with the other parts of the country.

Sustainable economic development delineates more than enhancing capital and labour flow. It is about people deciding themselves how to use their valuable assets and scarce resources, for which markets they wish to produce and which services they need to achieve their goals. Enhancing people's income may lead to enhancing people's autonomous development. Therefore, in the context of Information about markets, their long-term perspectives and risks determines to a large extent, when and how producers respond to opportunities is very vital. A conducive environment is needed to development understanding in terms of legislation, taxation and communication, to create a dynamic exchange of goods, services and capital among main stake-holders including producers and traders. Consequently, this warrants a new role for the government in this arena of globalisation and liberalisation. A government that stimulates rather than regulates, and provides services that meet the demands of the productive and commercial stakeholders is essential to meet the new challenges. With the opening up of economy this phenomenon is likely to catch momentum in the time to come. Redefined the role of government which provide conducive environment to face the challenges of liberalisation and globalisation in the Indian context is essential particularly to pace the rhythm of development.

India is bestowed with a varied agro-climate zones, which are highly favourable and suitable for cultivation a large number of horticultural crops including fruits, vegetables, root tuber, aromatic and medicinal plants and spices and plantation crops like coconut, cashew and cocoa. It is estimated that horticultural crops occupy about 13 per cent of the total gross cropped area of the country producing about 177.41 million metric tones of horticulture produce during the year 2005-06. As far as cultivation of fruits and vegetable is concerned it is the second largest producer of fruits and vegetables in the world. The total production of fruits has been estimated at 52.85 million metric tonnes from an area of 5.34 million hectares and vegetables production has been estimated at 108.20 million metric tonnes from an area of 7.05 million hectares. It is also estimated that India is the largest producer of mango, banana, sapota and acid lime producing roughly 39.5 per cent of the world's mangos and on the other hand 11 per cent of world's bananas are produced in India. India occupies an important place in the world market in production of grapes as its productivity per unit area is highest in the world. It is important to note that we are next only to China in area and production of vegetables and occupy significant place in the production of cauliflower. As far as onions and cabbage production is concerned India occupies second and third place respectively in the world.

Cut-flowers trade has also gained significant momentum in India considering its export potential. As a result there is noticeable increase in the production of cut flowers. India has produced 669000 metric tonnes of loose flowers and 27.23 million cut flowers during 2005-06 and the total area under flower cultivation was reported to be 1.40 lakh hectares. India plays significant role in spice trade as it is the largest producer, consumer and exporter of spices and spice products in the world. The total estimated production of spices during 2005-06 was 4.86 million metric tons and the area under cultivation was 3.20 million hectares. Similarly India is also largest producer and consumer of cashewnuts and the total production of plantation crops during 2005-06 was around 10.39 million metric tonnes from an area of 3.11 million hectares.

Though India has made significant and incredible contribution in the production of horticulture crops and it has tremendous potential to play a leading role in the world market in the export of certain species however, the sector has not developed to its full potential. The emphasis for horticulture development is mainly focused through the developmental programmes of the Department of Agriculture and Cooperation such as the National Horticulture Mission, Technology Mission for Integrated Development of Horticulture in North-Eastern States, Sikkim, Jammu and Kashmir, Himachal Pradesh and Uttarakhand; Development of Commercial Horticulture and Capital Investment Subsidy Scheme of the National Horticulture Board (NHB), and Integrated Development of Coconut including the Technology Mission on Coconut. Further, new initiatives on micro-irrigation, National Bamboo Mission, the establishment of the Central Institute of Horticulture, and the promotion of bee keeping through the National Bee Board in India.

National Horticulture Mission

The Centrally-sponsored National Horticulture Mission (NHM), launched during 2005-06, was continued during 2006-07 for the holistic development of the horticulture sector in India, with an outlay of Rs 1000.00 crore. Eighteen States and two UTs were covered under the NHM during the reference period. The thrust of the NHM is on an area-based regionally differentiated cluster approach for the development of horticultural crops, having comparative advantage. Under NHM, 259 districts have been taken up under the cluster approach and this includes 32 new districts added during 2006-07. In order to coordinate the activities of various states, State Horticulture Mission have been set up for various states and union territories. Therefore, the activities for the states and UTs are carried out through the State Horticulture Missions of various States and UTs. Further, some components of the NHM are being implemented through various national-level agencies such as the National Committee on Plasticulture Applications in Horticulture (NCPAH), which coordinates and monitors activities relating to precision farming and hi-tech horticulture. Others include the National Horticultural Research and Development Foundation (NHRDF), the IFFCO Foundation, the National Seeds Corporation (NSC), and the

State Farms Corporation of India (SFCI), for implementation and monitoring programmes relating to vegetables and quality production of vegetable seeds and planting material. The Directorate of Cashew and Cocoa Development (DCCD) is involved with the programmes relating to cashew and cocoa, and the Directorate of Arecanut and Spices Development (DASD) for implementation and monitoring of the programme relating to arecanut and spices. The programme is being monitored regularly through field visits, using Teleconferencing to interact with the state level agencies, visits by joint inspection teams and area officers. A web-enabled monitoring system has also been designed and put in place to monitor the physical and financial progress on a monthly basis. An amount of Rs. 771.86 crore was provided to the State Horticulture Missions (SHM) and national-level organisations during 2006-07. Funds have also been approved for the establishment of 1158 nurseries, bringing an area of 4.86 lakh hectares under new orchards and rejuvenating 0.64 lakh hectares orchards, taking up organic farming in 0.49 lakh hectares, promoting IPM in 1.87 lakh hectares, and protected cultivation in 0.08 lakh hectares. Funds have also been approved for setting up 2281 cold storage facilities and 1083 markets.

Central Institute of Horticulture, Medziphema, Nagaland

Recognising the importance for institutional support for development of horticulture, the Government of India approved the establishment of a Central Institute of Horticulture in Nagaland in January 2006, with a financial outlay of Rs 20.00 crore spread over a period of five years. The Institute is being set up at Medziphema in an area of 43.50 hectares. The objectives and the identified programmes of the Institute are as given below:

- Capacity building by training of trainers, extension officers, farmers, entrepreneurs, processors and exporters.
- Demonstration of improved technologies such as use of improved varieties / hybrids, adoption of INM/IPM practices, Hi-tech farming, precision farming, protected cultivation, post-harvest technology, etc.
- Follow-on extension support in the field of horticulture.
- Promotion of organic cultivation of horticultural crops.
- Establishing convergence and synergy among programmes in the field of horticultural research and development.

- Monitoring of centrally-sponsored programmes in the area of horticulture.

Micro Irrigation

The Centrally Sponsored Scheme on micro irrigation was launched in January 2006 under the Tenth Plan for implementing drip and sprinkler irrigation in an area of 6.2 lakh hectares. The scheme envisages achieving greater water use efficiency resulting in enhanced productivity and better quality of produce. Under this scheme drip and sprinkler irrigation is being promoted on a large scale. Assistance is provided to all categories of farmers at the rate of 50 per cent for drip/sprinkler system implementation and at the rate of 75 per cent for training and demonstration in each district of the State for both horticulture crops as well as non-horticulture crops. Further, training and demonstration is being imparted by the Precision Farming Development Centres (PFDCs) at 17 locations through the National Committee for Plasticulture Applications in Horticulture. During 2006-07, the annual action plans of 16 States have so far been approved for implementation as per the guidelines and a sum of Rs 337.00 crore has been released to these States till December 2006 to cover an area of 3.31 lakh hectare.

Technology Mission for Integrated Development of Horticulture in Uttarakhand

This Centrally Sponsored Scheme was launched during the Ninth Five- Year Plan. The scheme during the Tenth Plan was also under implementation in the state of Uttarakhand along with the States of Jammu and Kashmir and Himachal Pradesh. The Tenth Plan outlay for the scheme was approved at Rs 845.00 crore for implementation in the aforesaid 11 states. The Small Farmers' Agri-Business Consortium (SFAC) is involved in coordinating the scheme. State government submit the yearly proposals/plans which are approved by the State-Level Steering Committee constituted under the chairmanship of the Chief Secretary for the release of funds from the centre. During the year 2006-07, an amount of Rs 157.00 crore was released, of which an amount of Rs 81.86 crore has been released to the North-Eastern States and Rs 75.63 crore to the hilly states of Jammu and Kashmir, Himachal Pradesh and Uttarakhand. This is against the overall allocation of Rs 278.40 crore consisting of Rs. 150.00 crore for the North-Eastern States and Rs 128.40 crore for other hilly states. As a result an additional area of 117872 hectares and 25373 hectares, was brought under various horticulture crops in the North-East States and three hilly states respectively, including fruits cover (54973 hectares and 18925 hectares), vegetables (20979 hectares and 4658 hectares), spices (26950 hectares and 898 hectares); plantation crops (5252 hectares), medicinal plants (1652 hectares and 170 hectares), aromatic plants (4027 hectares and 135 hectares) and flowers (4039 hectares and 537 hectares). The increase in area under horticulture crops in the North-Eastern States over the pre-mission period (2000-01) was 34 per cent. Among the North-Eastern States, Sikkim and Mizoram recorded a maximum increase of 72 per cent and 71 per cent followed by Manipur (34 per cent), Nagaland (32 per cent) and Arunachal Pradesh (30 per cent).

Attempts have also been made to encourage women to be self-reliant and taking the scheme as an opportunity to diversify their economic activities. Therefore several initiatives have been taken, important among them are:

- Organisation/identification of women groups which would act as a network for channelising the horticultural support.
- Need-based assessment of women farmers in terms of the horticulture support such as input support, technological support and extension support.
- Prioritising the activities of individual women groups on the basis of the needbased assessment.
- Providing adequate organisational and financial support to the women groups for themselves with SHGs.
- Providing technical training in horticulture and allied areas to women farmers.
- 18593 women entrepreneurs have been trained on different aspects of horticulture under this Mission.

The NHB focuses on the development of high quality horticulture farms in identified belts across the country and in making such areas vibrant with horticulture activities as development of hubs for commercial horticulture, development of post-harvest infrastructure, strengthening of market information systems and horticulture data base to capture the attention of traders globally. In addition, the NHB provides assistance for research and development programmes to develop products that suited for specific varieties with improved methods and horticulture technology, provides training and education to farmers for skill development and industry personnel for improvement of agronomic practices and purchase and implementation of new technologies. Therefore many innovative schemes launched by the NHB during the Ninth Plan have been made more broad-based and entrepreneur-driven and friendly. It has been revealed that an outlay of Rs 100.00 crore has been earmarked for implementing these programmes during the financial year 2006-07. The major schemes of the Board are now supported by capital investment subsidy schemes.

The Himalayan region is known to possess the richest flora in the world. Most horticultural species have been in use in various forms for hundreds of years to meet the needs of the people particularly in this region. It was in the last century that, with the increasing pressure of population and the consequent need for more food, greater emphasis was given for growing more cereal crops. Extensive deforestation caused by the unplanned and haphazard landuse resulted in serious soil erosion and soil degradation. Now, due to excessive abuse of land, its fertility has depleted to a great extent and agriculture has become unsustainable in large part of the Hindu Kush-Himalayan region. Though majority of the people of the region are engaged in agricultural activities, yet, agriculture has never been economically profitable venture due to hilly terrain, low fertility, high labour absorption and high cost. In fact, agriculture cannot fetch enough for the survival of the people of the region. Therefore alternative economic activity, which may yield more income, is essentially realised for the planned economic development of the region.

During the past few decades the importance of horticulture crops has been realized in the Himalayan region. Promotion of horticulture is included in the national priorities of most of the countries of the region including India. In addition to refurbishing the mountain economy, horticulture also helps to promote environmental conservation in the region along with sustainable economic development. Mountain horticulture also supplements the national food requirement by providing fresh and processed fruits, vegetables and nuts. However, due to the lack of a proper infrastructure including transportation communication network, difficult terrain and lack of technical knowhow the desired result could not be achieved. Therefore concerted efforts are required to make the region economically sustainable and viable.

Some horticultural crops have very specific soil requirements. Therefore, cultivation is limited to certain areas only. The Hindu Kush-Himalayan Region has climatic conditions that are favourable for the development of certain horticultural crops only. There are some crops which have greater adaptability and can be grown in various locations, provided the basic requirements are met wholly or partially, either naturally or artificially.

The region has monopoly in cultivation of temperate fruits because they can only be grown under temperate conditions and therefore do not compete with the kinds of fruit grown cn the other parts of the country particularly in the plains. Sub-tropical and tropical fruits have the additional advantage of maturing later because of the lower temperatures and, therefore, the farmers fetch better economic return as they can be marketed once the fruit supply is scarce. It is also observed that hill fruits have a better colour and taste.

There are opportunities for the development of ancillary horticultural crops in the Hindu Kush-Himalayas because of the suitable agro-climatic conditions. In India, floriculture and mushroom cultivation have been given some priority and, in certain areas, they have become popular, although the cultivation of these crops has yet to gain impetus in other countries of the region. However, the cultivation of spices and medicinal plants and the practice of apiculture are carried out all over the region with varying degrees of success. There is need to develop technologies on different aspects of these undertakings before they can be launched commercially and the role of NHM is very important and crucial in supporting these aspects.

With the increase in production of horticultural crops, especially fruits, vegetables, and potatoes, marketing has become a serious problem in the Himalayan mountains. The markets are far away from the production areas and the produce has to pass through different types of climates before it finally reaches the destination. Marketing of horticultural produce includes not only the commercial transactions of buying and selling but also physical distribution. This physical distribution includes all the handling and forwarding activities such as harvesting, collecting, grading, packing, storing and subsequent dispersal through the markets to the consumers. Due attention is required before the produce reaches to the consumer in order to fetch the high price of the products. In addition, there are various other auxiliary functions of marketing including pre-harvest information, market finance and administration, marketing intermediaries, market training, extension and research.

Due to the high risk involved in marketing a large number of farmers, mainly small and marginal farmers, are discouraged from growing horticultural crops. The initial heavy investment required and long crop gestation periods also discourage them to opt for this venture. The amount of investment required to produce apples, oranges, vegetables, potatoes and ginger clearly indicates that, without institutional credit assistance, small and marginal farmers will not be able to establish and maintain horticulture cultivation. In certain regions, along with other facilities, horticultural loans are made available on easy terms at subsidized interest rates and this has encouraged the farmers mainly marginal and small farmers for cultivation of horticulture crops. However, the success experienced by farmers in such regions can be demonstrated throughout the region and it can be replicated elsewhere. Nevertheless, due to small land holdings in the mountains, the farmers face difficulty to find alternative sources of income particularly during the long gestation periods.

The cultivation of off-season vegetables has increased near the townships in the mountains and in areas primarily due to accessibility to transportation and communication facilities as seeds can be supplied easily to the plains when temperate vegetables are not available. The climatic conditions in the mountain sites are also suitable for growing the seeds of vegetables that do not set in the plains because it require a temperate climate. Remote areas that are suitable for vegetables, but are inaccessible, can cultivate seeds, which have high value and low volume, as a result these can be transported easily. These areas are ideal for growing hybrid seeds because cross-pollination with other varieties or species can be avoided in the new areas by suitable combinations of crops which are not compatible with each other. Specific distance is required for each crop to eliminate cross-pollination hybridization programme.

In the mountain region the yield per unit area is relatively low in comparison to the other parts of the country. There are variety of reasons including strains, quality and yield capacity of earlier used varieties and resistance to pests and disease found in new varieties. It has also been realised that there was no research back-up programmes to address the various problems that have encountered such as brown rot in potatoes, scab disease in apples and die-back in citrus fruits. However with the establishment of research units across the region, it is expected that these problems will be addressed effectively in future and high quality seed and planting material will be produced not only to meet the demand of the region but also the other parts of the country. In the mean time, the industry can import modern technology to meet the existing requirement in order to sustain the pace of horticulture development.

The Present Study

In Garhwal Himalaya, agriculture is characterized by the dominance of cereal crops, which is unable to meet the needs of villagers. Most of the farms of the region are either small or marginal. Limited per capita land and poor irrigation facilities restrict the work potentialities of the arable land. Although foodgrain crops like paddy, wheat, maize, millets, pulses and oilseeds are grown across the region, neither the production of these crops is sufficient to meet the total food requirements of the people, nor is it capable of giving full employment to absorb the people of this region. Therefore, low production and seasonal employment in agriculture has an adverse impact on the economic development of the region resulting in migration of a large number of people to the other parts of the country in search of gainful employment to enhance their income.

Horticulture-based small scale industries can bridge industrial gap, reduce poverty, out-migration and increase the opportunities of employment and income in Garhwal Himalaya and can provide good scope for development. At present a substential amount of fruits and vegetables are being produced in the region. Besides other bottlenecks, lack of processing, storage and marketing facilities have not allowed any substantial economic benefit to the producers.

Therefore, considering the prospects and potential of horticulture development in the region an attempt is being made to carry out an in-depth study taking various factors such as coverage, production and employability into consideration, which in turn may contribute substantially in reduction of inequality and poverty. The out-migration in terms of a large number of workable people has always been a cause of concern for the planners and policy-makers of the region. Therefore diversification towards horticulture may provide platform for initiating gainful economic activities, thereby creating employment opportunities not only in production sector but also processing and trading. Taking above factors into account an attempt is made to assess the potential of income and employment in horticulture sector.

Realising the potential in horticulture an emphasis was laid on overall development of this sector during the fifth Five Year Plan. As a result this region was recognized as a potential area for production of fruits which were viewed as a major factor that may lead to its development, but due to failure in planning the region could not produce fruits even for its local needs. Nevertheless the objective was to diversify the economy as it provides scope for establishing ancillary activities but due to low production the objective could not be achieved. It has been estimated that a well-maintained orchard of one hectare can generate more than five times cash income than the foodgrains grown in the same piece of land. Therefore, the cultivation of horticulture crops has comparative advantage over foodgrains.

Objectives of the Study

The study primarily deals with the identification of potential employment and income generating activities in horticulture and allied sectors such as floriculture and medicinal plants. Since the state has limited potential in agriculture due to small and marginal land holdings, horticulture provide subsistence economic base to the people. As such the other objectives of the study are enumerated below:

- To analyse the present status and potential of horticulture in the study areas.
- To assess the potential of medicinal plants and floriculture as income generating venture.
- To find out the present economic status of the workers engaged in horticultural activity.
- To identify the areas where horticulture-based industries can be established.
- To find out the present trade links and marketing scheme and

make an analysis of the same in order to plan policies for strengthening and/or simplifying the existing process.

Apart from these major objectives, the study will be helpful in formulation of a suitable horticulture policy for the all hill regions in respect to optimum use of the available natural resources.

There is dearth of relevant literature on horticultural development in the Himalayan region. Although official publications have made appearance about the region's prospect in horticulture during British period where J.M. Clay, the first Dy. Commissioner of Garhwal, rightly remarked, 'nothing but food-grains are grown owing to prohibitive cost of grain, yet with the arable land at all altitudes a great variety of valuable fruits, spices are also being grown.'

It may be noted that the individual researches have made sincere attempt to analyze various issues related to horticulture development in the region. Singh (1993) highlights the problems of marketing and storage of apple crops in UP hills. Seth (1993) has touched the issues related to planting material, extension supports, financial assistance to support growers, production and marketing facilities. Similarly Pant (1935), Dhyani (1977), Bist (1981) Nand N. & Kumar K. (1989), Swarup, R. (1993), have also touched the issues of production, productivity, processing and trading, besides attempting case studies. Some scholarly doctoral dissertations, e.g. Juyal (1984), Pokhriyal (1984), Sati (1994), Dimri (1996) have also given place for horticulture development as a main pursuit for overall development of the region. Though these works primarily deal with the overall economic backwardness of Himalayan districts and raises issues related to development of this area, however no specific work on the horticultural development of the Uttarakhand as a whole has appeared till now.

On the other hand a series of studies have been conducted on the problems and prospects of medicinal plants sector. Nautiyal and Nautiyal (2005) in their paper based on collaboration between farmers, research institutions and industry, experiences of Picrorhiza Kurrooa Cultivation at Ghese Village in District Chamoli, Uttarakhand have deliberated that with increasing demand for herbal medicines in the modern pharmaceutical industry and growing faith in herbal based health care, diagnosis and treatment of almost every disease, ISM has gained tremendous prominence in the recent past. India, having a large repository of medicinal plants and a rich tradition of herbal medicine, has certainly become a centre of attention for its health care traditions and the supply of raw material. It is estimated that the world demand for medicinal and aromatic plant products is growing at the rate of 7% per annum and if this trend continues it is expected that by 2005 AD India's export would be of the value of Rs 5000 crore. In Uttarakhand approximately 500 plant species are being traded. However nearly 160 species have been identified as threatened, and if these are not saved, nearly 10% reduction in the present turnover can be expected during the next five years. Furthermore, according to cumulative estimate, Uttarakhand has nearly Rs.1.5 billion per annum trade through the hidden market, as most species collected from the wild are already banned, and there is no proper trade price controlling authority. The main concern is therefore to conserve these plants in the wild and to identify means for their sustainable utilization.

Uttarakhand has very little fertile land, with an average land holding capacity of less than 4 nalis/family, and its topography and environment would never sustain large industrial setups in the hilly regions of the state. It is therefore necessary to fine tune our planning with our natural resources and develop climate based policies in order to conserve our natural wealth for present prosperity and sustainable management in the future. The medicinal and aromatic plant sector is recognized as a potential booster in strengthening the economy of the state. It can generate employment options and find substitutes for low yielding traditional crops, which will do better in infertile soil and different kind of climate. Paper focuses that the collaborative arrangement have benefited both the growers and traders, however the possibility of exploitation of farmers cannot be ignored.

Purohit (2003) in his paper states that beginning in 1930, the collection and marketing of all minor forest products including MAPs was done by villagers and the State use to collect Tax / Octroi on all wild harvests which were traded. Gobind Ballabh Pant, the first Chief Minister of Uttar Pradesh State of India, had realised the importance of medicinal plants for livelihood and health security of the people of Uttarakhand region soon after independence of India. He emphasised that sustainable and scientific extraction of medicinal plants from wild should be done by the local communities to provide them employment and make available pure medicinal plants for industry. Subsequently, since early 1960s, the then State government had put emphasis on promotion of cultivation of medicinal plants besides sustainable and scientific extraction of medicinal plants from forests for livelihood and health security of the people of the region. However, Uttar Pradesh did not have a written policy on medicinal plants but has taken several policy decisions from time to time to promote cultivation and commercialisation of medicinal plants.

K J Collins in his paper, 'A Model of New Industry Development in Horticulture,' gives important premises of new crops research in horticulture is that biologically successful new species can lead to successful new industries. Success in a biological sense is a necessary but insufficient condition because successful new crop industries are driven by economic and social factors as well as biological factors, and in practice these three sets of factors interact as a system. How to model any one of the biological, economic or social sub-systems is reasonably well understood, but modelling the dynamics of the whole system is more problematic. This paper presented a descriptive model that may be a first step towards understanding the many pathways that new horticultural industries follow, some towards success and others towards failure. The model adopts the view that the biological and environmental science of developing a new crop species must be considered in the context of new industries as emerging social systems with economic objectives. It argues that the multiple developmental pathways of a new industry reflect the principle of growth through discontinuous change, or punctuated equilibrium. The structure of the model is based around four linked phases, each described in terms of the activities of the actors within that phase. Punctuations of equilibrium can occur within or between phases, with either negative or positive consequences. In this way multipie pathways of development become possible. New crop examples drawn from horticulture are used to demonstrate the features of these various pathways in practice. With caution, it is concluded that the model could be used as a diagnostic tool to indicate future developmental pathways for a new horticultural industry, or to help to identify approaches to intervening in a new industry's development to enhance the likelihood of its success.

K. Mahindra and A.S. Sandhu in their paper 'Development and Dissemination of Horticultural Technologies by the Punjab Agricultural University, Ludhiana' has been assigned the responsibility to generate technologies in the field of Horticulture i.e. cultivation of Fruits, Vegetables and Flowers. These technologies are disseminated to the farmers through extension scientists of the PAU and the State Department of Horticulture. The research projects are formulated in the concerned departments, on the basis of field situations and the scientists keeping in view the objectives of the projects generated the data. The data are critically evaluated at the departmental research committees and was sent for consideration to the Research Evaluation Committee (REC) of the University headed by the Director of Research. Keeping in view the conclusions drawn, necessary recommendations were made to the extension scientists to test the performance of these technologies at the farmers' fields. The data so generated by the extension scientists is resubmitted to the REC for its consideration and making conclusions. After the REC's approval, the technologies were discussed at a wider scale in the Horticultural Officers' Workshop, wherein the scientists and the extension scientists of PAU and State Department of Horticulture discuss it critically. The innovations approved in the Workshop, were included in the Package of Practices/Recommendations. Thereafter, the technologies are disseminated to the farmers of the state through the extension network for adoption. Necessary provision of inputs required for the adoption of these technologies is made by the State Department of Horticulture. The shortcomings faced by the farmers in adoption are brought to the notice of the scientists through the extension workers. This feedback is further refined by the research system of the University to find out the solutions. The modified technologies are processed for recommendations to the farmers in the same manner at various stages as explained earlier. This is a never-ending process.

L.R. Sharma in his paper 'Marketing and Trade of Indian Apple' describes the status of internal and export marketing of Indian apples. There has been an appreciable improvement in the marketing efficiency at domestic level. The export marketing has shown a dismal performance. Based on observed pattern of trade, the country do not possess comparative advantage in apple export. International competitiveness in future, will largely depend upon the ability to develop the comparative and competitive advantages. The main constraints in pushing up apple exports are volume insufficiency, low productivity, quality deficiencies, technological deficiencies, high production and transport cost and lack of post-harvest infrastructural facilities. In view of the increasing domestic and export demand, rates of growth of output need to be stepped up.

Growth must be promoted in the backward hilly tracts of non-traditional areas to increase the supplies and cool down domestic prices. To achieve the breakthrough in exports, the areas of efficient production needs to be demarcated and strategies devised to ensure an efficient apple based farming systems. Farmers will have to be trained about better production of quality through increased investments in R & D efforts. Quality standards as expected by foreign markets will have to be observed. In order to harness export potentials information on consumer preferences, psychology, power, needs to be generated through market surveys to identify the thrust products and thrust markets.

Sati (2004) emphasized fruit cultivation and its development in the mountainous area particularly in the Alaknanda Basin of Uttarakhand Himalaya. The study deals with the present potential of horticulture under the presence of favourable geographical conditions. The contribution of the governmental agencies and people's interest towards its cultivation is also elaborated in this book. The basin is divided into different fruit zones according to climatic conditions, soil texture, ample water supply and uses of modern technology. Research and technology in the field of fruit cultivation are discussed in detail. A broad based conclusion has been done after the study and suggestions have been made for the steady development of the hilly terrain

G. Fox Wilson (2001), narrates that pests cause revere injury to horticultural crops in various ways, direct as well indirect. A classic in its own subject—this book contains necessary scientific information useful for recognizing the many symptoms of pest damage to horticultural plants and describes the different control measures: cultural, mechanical, physical, biological and chemical. The introductory chapter briefly describes the types of pests, their life histories, feeding habits and the general types of damages caused by them. Emphasising upon the fact that every part of a plant is apt to be attacked by one or more species of insect or related pest, the major portion of the book is divided into eight chapters corresponding to the main parts of the plant, bulbs, corns and tubers, roots, stems and shoots, buds, foliage, flowers, fruit, and seeds. The rigours of attack which may be found on that particular part of the plant are described under various sections, alongwith control methods. A set of indices (containing host plant index, Pest index and general index) has been provided in the book, so as to assist the reader in the diagnosis of damage.

Malik's (2000), is a collaborative academic exercise undertaken by a group of leading agricultural scientists (many of international repute), aiming at putting together and reviewing the available scientific information on various aspects of horticulture. After in introductory chapter, it discusses systematically the topics like the development and structure of flowers and fruits, plant metabolism, vegetative and floral growth of plants, advanced methods of crop improvement, plant tissue culture, environmental impact on plants, etc. Not only that, the state of the art developments in areas likes establishment and management of gardens; insect, pest and disease management, and floriculture and lands was also discussed.

Skaria's (2007) *'Aromatic Plants and Scope of Aromatic Plants'* deals with the importance of aromatic crops and their close association with human health and beauty care from time immemorial. History of development of cultivation and aroma-based industries in different regions of the world is described to emphasize their significance, scope and role in increasing the quality of human life. *Classification of aromatic plants* based on their climatic requirement, growth habit and floral morphology elaborated in succeeding chapter will be of great interest to students, researchers and farmers. Chapter on *'Extraction of aroma principles'* describes traditional as well as modern techniques employed for efficient extraction of volatile oils and resins from different plant materials and equipments employed for the purpose. Quality of oil is found to vary significantly with ecotypes, season, time of collection, crop maturity and weather conditions prevailing during the growth period, extraction method and duration of extraction process. Conditions and duration of storage also have a bearing on quality of essential oil. The development and imposition of appropriate quality standards in trade has also been discussed. These aspects are covered in fourth chapter on *'Quality assurance of essential oils'*.

Aromatic oils and their derivatives and combinations occupy a covetable position in holistic medicines such as aromatherapy. Chapter on 'Aromatherapy' details the use of essential oils in human health care, techniques employed, aromatherapy massage, aromatic bath, facial care, hair care etc. Information on aromatic oil's widespread application to relieve stress and rejuvenate body are also included.

Sharma (2000) deals with Retrospect and prospects of developing Himachal horticulture in to a world class horticulture industry, Horticulture

Vision 2000 and Beyond. Bees in pollination of horticultural crops, approaches for optimising productivity of horticultural crops with special reference to apple, vegetable development: an overview, water harvesting technology, prospects of wild fruits, greening wasteland through horticulture, problems and constraints of vegetable production in hilly areas, role of co-operatives in organising production and marketing of horticultural produce: a case study, role of co-operative banks in the development of horticultural industry, plasticulture: an innovation for production of horticultural crops and fruit wines production technology: an overview are some of the topics covered in the book.

The other topics included are agro-forestry systems: an overview, protected cultivation of flowers, sustainable fruit farming: issues in apple orchard management, identification of flower species for different agro-climatic zones, horticulture: progressive trends and future strategies need for high powered policy formulation and management coordination committee for horticultural development, Galgal and Drunj: the natives of Himalaya, Planting materials for landscaping and their utilisation in hills, combating drought in horticulture, nutrient management in temperate fruits, transgenic plants: a wonder of genetic engineering, olive: past, present and future, progress of fruit processing industry, transfer of technology for the development of horticulture, floriculture: opportunities, constraints and strategies, tea industry, varietal status, improvement and future strategies in temperate nut crops, women and horticulture, management of potted ornamental plants, varietal status, improvement and future of temperate fruits, diversification of fruit crops, potato—an overview, survey, collection and scope of floriculture germplasm, strategies for the development of fruits in Himachal Pradesh, Kiwifruit: a promising fruit for Himachal Pradesh, recent trends in Agaricus bisporus research in India and terminator gene technology and its implications.

The book also covers modern horticulture industry, Himachal horticulture: historical perspective, need for research for improving the quality of fruits and vegetables for processing industry, Hill lemon (Galgal): a promising fruit, studies on the utilisation of wastes from processing plants: with special reference to apple pomace, need of a census of agro-horticultural produce, premature leaf fall in apple: symptoms, causes and cure, apple scab forecasting and management, present status of diseases of sub-tropical fruits and their management, disease management of vegetable crops, post-harvest disease management in temperate fruits and vegetables, diseases of ginger and their control, disease management of commercial cut-flowers, status of pesticide residues in food, management of key pests of vegetables, revolutionary advancement in packaging of horticultural produce, fruit processing: past, present and future, insect pests of sub-tropical fruits, pest status of temperate fruits and their management, advances in fruit tree propagation, apple nursery production technology improvement, participatory processes in water harvesting technologies, human skin reactions to plants, domestication of selected medicinal plants, profitability and growth of horticultural crops: an economic analysis, pears of future for temperate region, status of nut crops, management of soil moisture, harvesting, grading and post-harvest handling of cut-flowers, improvement of Bulbous plants, past, present and future of cut-flowers, seed production of ornamentals, indigenous flower species, seasonal flowers for commercial uses and floriculture related industry, drip irrigation and vegetable cultivation for village economy and status of women, management of pollinisers for sustainable apple production, sweet cherries under high density plantations: a new look, ginger production technology, model nursery and European red mite: an emerging problem of apple. Horticulture is fast changing, both in area and production but the pace of development in this field has been very slow. This is the only field which can make the agriculture sustainable in the country, particularly in the hills. This book Horticulture Technology: Vision 2000 and Beyond in two volumes is a treatise of past and present position of this branch of practical science connected with life and economy of the people. This book also throws light on the things to come in the future along with some very useful suggestions and strategies for speedy development in various fields of horticulture.

Singh (2006), has presented two volumes, containing 86 papers presented at a national seminar on horticulture for sustainable development and environmental protection, jointly organised by the department of horticulture, Nagaland University and Department of Horticulture, Government of Nagaland to analyse different dimensions of horticultural development in India, in general, and NEH region, in particular. Focusing on advances in horticultural practices, fruits and ornamentals, volume one discusses at length the soil and water management, crop diversification, nutrient and plant bioregulators, pest management, post-harvest management, productivity and employment generation. Volume two deals with the production technology, export diversification of production system, product diversification and marketing strategies for vegetables, spices, plantation crops, medicinal and aromatic plants as well as their produce.

Gopalkrishnan's (2007) Vegetable science is advancing fast with development of varieties and hybrids which are high yielding, resistant to pests and diseases and suited to specific purposes and situations. Progress in the field of crop production and protection is also remarkable. The book 'Vegetable Crops' contains latest information on scientific crop production practices of more than 70 vegetables right from nursery to marketing in 16 chapters. Classification of vegetables based on their cultural requirement is followed for presentation. Basic principles of vegetable production, systems of classification, special systems of vegetable production including high-tech production, organic farming and biofertilizers are also dealt in the book. This is oriented for undergraduate and postgraduate programmes in agriculture and horticulture and gives a comprehensive picture on the production scenario of vegetables in the country.

Rahda and Mathew's (2007) book Horticulture series Vol. II Fruit Crops is a comprehensive and need oriented volume encompassing the latest and balanced information about various aspects of fruit culture (tropical and subtropical). The important topics covered in the book included chapter on fruit industry which deals briefly with production statistics, social, nutritive and industrial relevance and importance of fruit production. Second chapter provides a complete overview of all principles and practices associated with orchard planning, layout and management in a very abridged manner. The third chapter on classification of fruit crops includes botanical, horticulture and environmental grouping in a very precise but meaningful manner.

It also gives a detailed account of different aspects including origin, distribution, botany and varieties, classification, climate and soil requirements, propagation, cultivation methods, flowering, harvesting, post-harvest methods and crop protection of different fruit crops coming under each group such as tropical, subtropical and arid and semi-arid fruits, tropical fruits - Banana, Guava, Mangosteen, Papaya, Pineapple and Sapota, ten major subtropical fruits - Avocado, Citrus, Grapes, Litchi, Loquat, Mango, Olive, Passion fruit, Persimmon and Pomegranate, and semi-arid fruit crops namely, Aonla, Ber, Custard apple, Date, Fig, Jack, Jamun and Phalsa. Apart from these major fruit crops, comprehensive account of a large number of under- and unexploited fruit crops of tropical and subtropical parts of the world and well-known minor fruits and a list of other very less known fruit species, which can be made the subject of detailed study for further utilization and information generation. Information provided in this compilation will be of use to students, teachers, scientists, extension workers, orchardists and others interested in fruit culture.

Desh Raj's (2005) book, *Floriculture in Hills* is designed to serve as key guide to the flower growers of hilly areas, students, researchers, teachers, amateur gardeners, policy makers and traders involved in various activities of floriculture in hilly areas. In this book special emphasis is given on off-season cultivation of commercial flowers in hilly areas, seed and planting material production, dried ornamental plants and marketing of the floricultural products. The book mainly deals with floriculture industry components, off season flower production, nursery management and plot perfumer, marketing of horticultural products and persons and organization associated with horticulture.

Mudgal et al. (1999). The first volume in this series contains valuable information on different recognised groups of non-flowering plants and Gymnosperms. Volume II and III are devoted to the Biodiversity of flowering plants occurring in different Phytogeographical regions of India. These volumes capture the enormous floristic diversity, their utility and status. Numerous illustrations and coloured pictures have been added to enhance the scientific utility of the volumes.

Pande et al. (2006), in their book, *"Folk Medicine and Aromatic Plants of Uttarakhand"* give an account of folk medicinal plants used in human and animal healthcare in Uttarakhand. The main text deals with 1338 ethnomedicinal plants and 364 ethnoveterinary plants followed by diversity of MAPs, MAPs available in Uttarakhand used in Indian System of Medicines (ISM), biologically active MAPs, rare and threatened MAPs, ethno-medico-zoological wisdom and alternative systems of therapies prevailing in Uttarakhand. In addition the book includes nine appendices pertaining to patenting, medicinal plant gardens and nurseries, cultivated MAPs, herbalists, ethnobotanists, glossary of medicinal terms. Indices of botanical names, zoological names and vernacular/local names are also provided. This book will act as a ready reckoner for academicians, policy makers, researchers, Ayurvedic physicians and general readers.

In the First Five-Year Plan, the Government of India has stated that little is known about the primary factors shaping present regional horticultural structure and that it has remained a "Neglected area". It has been stressed by the Govt. of U.P. in several development plans that no serious attempt has so far been made to study the potentialities of horticulture in this region and no integrated approach to develop horticulture has been proposed. Horticulture specifically has not got its proper place in the regional economy. Therefore, present study attempts to fulfil the existing gaps in available knowledge and an attempt will be made to point out the inadequacy of horticultural development.

At the macroeconomic level, India has created an increasingly liberal economic policy since 1991. In turn it has precipitated an unprecedented expansion in Indian exports, among which horticultural exports have been important (APEDA, 1998). However the sector has witnessed strong growth and policy support. Kaul (1996) comments that the trend observed since 1991 is that the horticultural sector has gradually moved out of its rural confines as a traditional agricultural activity into something approaching corporate enterprise. This trend has led to the adoption of improved technology, greater commercialisation and professionalism in the management of production and marketing. However horticulture in India continues to be troubled by constraints such as major plant diseases across commodities, low yields compared to other producer countries and in particular, poor post-harvest practices. All this leads to low final product quality. Quality management is thus a major concern for export marketing where standards are high and punitively enforced. It would appear therefore that improved productivity, post-harvest management, hybrid development, and product diversification are all challenges which horticultural science is to face if it is to continue to play a strategic role in sector development. Furthermore, these efforts will need to be supported by an adequate market infrastructure and policy environment, together with relevant mechanisms for articulating the technological needs of producers and processors to scientists, which in turn must be linked to efficient mechanisms for technology transfer (Kaul, 1996).

Methodology

The study of this kind cannot be done only through secondary data. Secondary sources of data are found to be both inadequate and unreliable. Since the study is geared to address the cultivators, traders and the general administration, each segment's perceptions need to be analysed and integrated into a coherent framework. It was felt necessary to approach the issues in a participatory manner as well as through structured schedules/questionnaires. As it was not possible to cover all the blocks and villages within the stipulated time, it was decided to concentrate on a few selected types of blocks where concentration of fruit orchards is more and from which generalizations could be drawn.

Sample Choice: Technique of multi-stage random sample was adopted in selection of villages and households. On the other hand selection of blocks was purposive.

Selection of Blocks: The study was primarily conducted in Uttarkashi, Tehri Garhwal and Chamoli districts of Garhwal Himalayan region. There are six blocks in Uttarkashi district, ten blocks in Tehri Garhwal and eleven blocks in district Chamoli. On the basis of fruit belts, Bhatwari and Purola blocks in Uttarkashi, Chamba and Pratapnagar blocks in Tehri Garhwal and Joshimath and Pokhari blocks in Chamoli district have been selected.

Selection of Villages: While selecting the villages attributes such as altitude of fruit belt, slope, aspects (wet and sunny), types of fruits cultivated in the belt and production of fruits were taken into consideration. Out of the total villages falling in the fruit belt, 5% villages were selected. Therefore total 87 villages were selected for the study.

Selection of Household: Among the sample villages, household-having orchards with at least 100 fruit trees was taken into consideration. Attempt was also made to give due weightage to each section of the society while selecting the households. Out of these, 10% was from a random sample by lot. Thus this constituted a random sample obtained from a purposive group and will remain relatively small in size but fairly representative. The final approximate sample size was 435 household in 87 villages (Table 1.1 & 1.2).

Table 1.1. Blockwise Distribution of Sample Size in Study Area

District/Block	*Total Villages*	*Sample Villages (10% to total)*	*Sample Households*	*Final Sample Size*
Joshimath	95	10	05	50
Pokhri	252	25	05	125
Chamba	223	23	05	115
Pratapnagar	126	12	05	60
Purola	77	08	05	40
Bhatwari	94	09	05	45
Total	876	87	05	435

The researchers also covered all the sampled villages by following procedure.

(i) The villagers belonging to different interest groups, namely landless labourers, marginal farmers, small farmers, landlords, harijans were gathered at a common meeting place.

(ii) The purpose of village meeting was introduced to them.

(iii) They were explained the importance of village meeting and importance of problems being identified by them related to horticulture development.

(iv) They were asked to identify the problems associated with various issues of horticulture development in the region.

(v) They were also asked to identify the problems associated with cultivation, extension, storage and marketing of horticulture produce in their village.

(vi) The identified problems were prioritized with the help of the villagers, while prioritizing the problems proper consideration was given to the problems identified by disadvantaged groups such as SC, ST, and economically backward people.

(vii) Their suggestions were also invited for addressing the problems identified.

Such meeting was also conducted separately with the women of the villages. Similar procedure was followed with the women folk also. It was noticed that a large number of women participated in the meeting and discussed the problems of horticulture development in their villages. Attempt was also made to conduct such meetings separately in SC *tolas* or hamlets. This methodology has been tried successfully in all the surveyed villages of the district.

Table 1.2. Blockwise and Road head Distancewise Distribution of Sample Size in Study Area

District/Block	*Sample selection at Road head side*		*Sample Selection with in 1-3 km. from road head*		*Sample Selection more than 3 km. from road side*		*Final Sample Size*	
	No. of Villages	*No. of Households*	*No. of Villages*	*No. of Households*	*No. of Villages*	*No. of Households*	*Total Villages*	*Total Households*
Joshimath	04	20	03	10	03	15	10	50
Pokhri	09	45	08	40	08	40	25	125
Chamba	08	40	08	40	07	35	23	115
Pratapnagar	04	20	04	20	04	20	12	60
Purola	03	15	03	15	02	10	08	40
Bhatwari	03	15	03	15	03	15	09	45
Total	31	155	29	145	27	135	87	435

Also the researchers visited Dehradun, Pauri, Chamoli, Pithoragarh, Almora and Nainital districts of Uttarakhand during August 2001 to May 2003. Researchers primarily interacted with the key researchers of various research institutes, government officials, NGOs and individuals involved in the field of horticulture, medicinal plants, floriculture in Dehradun, Srinagar, Chamoli, Gopeshwar, Ranikhet, Kosi, Almora and Pithoragarh. The objective of the visit was to understand horticulture and allied sector and problem and its prospect in shaping the economics of the region. During the visit relevant literature was also collected from the cross-sections of researchers and Government functionaries.

The issues raised were discussed in detail and short field visits were also organized to Tugnath, Gopeshwar, Chamoli, Joshimath, Tapovan and Mana to verify the facts and to collect secondary data and the profile of the farmers so that a suitable sample could be drawn for future research. Besides interacting with the researchers, academicians and government officials in Dehradun, Srinagar, Gopeshwar, Chamoli and Joshimath, farmers were also interviewed in Tapovan and Mana villages. A series of discussion sessions were held at the end of each day to synthesize the information collected and to give a shape to the findings. Based on the experiences gained during the three phases the researchers decided to conduct a similar type of field visit to Munsyari block, district Pithoragarh of Uttarakhand state. Accordingly a field visit was planned to cover the cultivators of Munsyari areas. As a result, government officials, NGOs, farmers, small traders, and local villagers were interviewed in Munsyari, Darkot, Laspa, Bela, Malla Dummar, Sarmoli, Fapa and Ucheti villages. The villages in and around Munsyari area are low altitude villages and winter habitats. There are also high altitudes villages in Johar Valley which include Milam, Martoli, Laspa, Pahcu, Ganghar, Mapa, Tola etc.

The researchers interviewed cross-sections of researchers, academicians, administrators, NGOs, cultivators, traders (retailers as well as wholesalers), local leaders and common people during the course of field visit. The research team was divided into smaller groups and attempted to cover the different interest groups and individual farmers in the villages. The discussion on the findings of the day was a regular feature in order to share the findings of a particular day and attempt was made to synthesize the findings on regular basis.

2

Profile of the Study Area

Physiographically seven districts of Garhwal region of Uttarakhand state viz. Uttarkashi, Chamoli, Tehri, Pauri, Rudraprayag, Dehradun and Hardwar forms the extreme north- western part of Indian Himalaya and has been accepted as a development planning unit. The area is spread over 32448 sq km. accommodating over 49.16 lakh persons as per census of 2001 which constitute 59.97 percent population of the state of Uttarakhand. Geographically, the region is located between 77' 33" to 80' 6" longitude and from 29° 31' 9" to 31° 26' 5" N latitude (Nand and Kumar, 1989). The boundaries of the region are spread in the north from the high Himalayas, touching international border with Tibet to the river Yamuna which also separates the region from the Himachal Pradesh in the west. The region is bounded in the south by the river Tons and Saharanpur and Bijnore districts of Uttar Pradesh and in the east by Almora, Nainital and Pithoragarh Districts of Uttarakhand. The snow line is about 150 kms., from the foothills and the horizon is dominated by high peaks amongst which Nanda Devi is by far the highest at 7818 meters above MSL, revered by people of the region as the supreme goddess of the Garhwal Himalayas.

Traditionally this region has been a tract of Bawani meaning having Bawan or 52 forts. At one point of time, the region was under the control of 52 chiefs, each having his own Garh or fort, (Mishra 1989), deriving its name from the Hindi word Garh, which means fort. Subsequently, the region acquired Garhwal as its name during the fifteenth century after Raja Ajai Pal earned the credit of amalgamating fifty-two small principalities (Garhs) into a single kingdom with Srinagar as its capital. Later in 1815 the British took full possession of Chamoli and Pauri. The region was also invaded by the Gorkhas before the

British took possession of the region. There was an agreement between the raja of Garhwal and Britishers, as a result Tehri was declared as a sovereign state with its legal and administrative system under the direction of the British. Under this system, both the parts of Garhwal progressed somewhat in matters of education, health, communication, etc., which the British considered necessary for their effective and efficient rule.

Forest administration, conservation and protection were accorded priority in British Garhwal followed by Tehri Garhwal, where Forest Department was established in 1885 (Bond, 1988). Land settlements in both parts were undertaken simultaneously. It was during this period that the region became more known to other people outside. But the pace of economic development and social change remained slow (Dilwali and Pant 1987) as the interest of the British was quite different and their primary focus was to exploit the natural resources of the region rather to focus on the overall development of the region. The most convenient route to Tibet being through Niti and Mana passes in Garhwal was also of special interest to the British who did not intend to extend their rule over Tibet but were equally apprehensive of Russian influence over Tibet. It could possibly endanger security of India, which at that state was their responsibility, and slightest relaxation in the matter could jeopardize their authority over the country. With this aim, the British maintained very friendly relations with the people of Garhwal as well as with those of Tibet.

The native state of Tehri Garhwal merged into Indian Union in 1949 when it was declared as a separate district of Uttar Pradesh. On February 24, 1960 there was a major reorganization of the hill districts of the state resulting in creation of two districts Uttarkashi and Chamoli broadly carved out from Tehri and Pauri districts respectively. Till 1968 the four districts of the region viz. Tehri, Pauri, Uttarkashi and Chamoli were part of Kumaon Division while Dehradun district was part of Meerut division. In 1968, a new Division of Garhwal was created and all the five districts viz-a-viz Dehradun, Tehri, Pauri, Uttarkashi and Chamoli were included in it.

Physical Structure

Physiographically the region has unique characteristics as on the one hand it has several snow peaks and other hand a significant proportion of the area is spread in the valley areas. The holy rivers originating from the glaciers with perennial water flow also make the region different from other parts of the country. The high snow peaks included Nandadevi (7817m), Comet (7755m.), Manapeak (7439m), Trisul (7273m), Dunigari (7066), Chaukhamba (7138m), Kedarnath (6940m), Gangotri (6672m.), Shivling (6543), Narayan (5965m) etc. are world renowned peaks. Lower Himalaya ranges are widely spread over Garhwal division forming gorges and deep river valleys. The region is also fed with perennial holy waters of Yamuna, Bhagirathi, Bhilangana, Alaknanda, Dholi, Nandakini, Pinder and Mandakini rivers. These rivers are flowing in deep valleys within steep rock. In the foothill of this region some plain areas known as doons and dwar valleys surrounded by low Sivalikas are very fertile and famous for cultivation of Basmati rice and Litchi. The soothing climate of the valley has also attracted a large number of people all over the county to settle there permanently.

A significant variation has been noticed while analyzing the rainfall data of the region. As evident among the all districts Dehradun receives considerably higher rainfall averaging 2200mm annually whereas Pauri Garhwal districts receives relatively lesser rainfall. The average rainfall of the district was recorded 1250 mm. annually. In other districts the average of annual rainfall lie between 1300 mm to 1500 mm. Due to non-availability of permanent snow peaks in Pauri and Tehri Garhwal the average rainfall is lesser.

Like all other parts of Himalayas, Garhwal is also heterogeneous in several matters. It has four major topological features including Tarai Bhabar or sub-mountain, the valleys, the mountainous and the Trans-Himalayan or the alpine areas which mostly remain covered under snow throughout or at least for a large part the year. Broadly speaking, ruggedness and steepness of the area increase with an increase in the elevation. The differences in elevation induce wide climatic differences as well as the soil and other natural factors including flora and fauna also vary considerably. Such dissimilarities have significant influence over human activities. It may be noted that the life at the high elevation is extremely difficult. The high altitude villages which are predominantly inhabited by the Bhutias who migrate to low altitude villages during extreme winter seasons. The region remained neglected because the policy-makers in the erstwhile UP government due to lack of practical knowledge to the climatic and other conditions of the region. But the fact is that the specificity of hills with the abundance of natural resources there is tremendous potential to harness it for the overall development of the region in general and country in particular.

This is a narrow strip of land known as tarai bhabar or sub mountainous tract which is about 95 kms. in length and 3 kms. wide stretching along the foothills which mainly lies in district Pauri. In this region the rivers from the hills disappear for a considerable and reappear above the surface once they reach further south. Therefore, cultivation is carried on only by irrigation through canals, which tap river water before it goes underground. Formerly the entire Bhabar was covered with forests, however, the remains of a fort and a tank at Mawakot indicate that this area was also inhabited sometimes in the past. There are a few villages just outside the hills below Patlidoon, where limited cultivation was carried out in the past, however, intensive cultivation was introduced two decades back only. This tract was very valuable for forest produce including minor forest product, wildlife and livestock grazing, however over a period of time wild animals have reduced considerably with the expansion of agricultural and commercial activities.

The valleys of the region play significant role in shaping the economy of the entire Garhwal region. Doon valley is considered most suitable place for human settlement. Doon valley is the largest and most known in the region. Other valleys of the region include Ganga, Alaknanda, Ramganga and the Nayar.

The Doon valley, a single largest valley of the region belongs to two great river systems, those of the Ganga and the Yamuna. It is bounded by the Shiwalik Hills in the south, and the outer scrap of the Himalayas in the north. As its name indicates, it lies in district Dehradun wherein the entire valley forms a Tehsil of the district Dehradun. It is an irregular parallelogram in shape with a length of about 75 kms, and about 25 kms. wide. Its existence is supposed to be due to the presence of Shiwalik hills, as a well-marked range extending along the entire south- western border of the Doon. It is believed that the Shiwaliks are the obstacle which confines the detritus swept down by torrents from the mountains in the north.

The valley has very fertile soil on which the famous *Basmati* rice is grown and the grain carries the name of the valley. Tea gardens and orchards of Litchi are the other specialities of the valley. The valley is known for its moderate soothing climate for which reason the proportion of retired persons settled here is largest in the state. It may also be for this natural gift that the two towns of Dehradun and Mussoorie could have a number of institutions of research, education, technology and administration of national repute.

Table 2.1. Doon Valley: Area With Varying Height

(Area in Sq. Kms.)

Height in Feet	*Shiwalik*	*Himalayan*	*Total*
1000-1250	19	19	38
1250-1500	30	72	102
1500-1750	69	91	160
1750-2000	63	85	148
2000-2500	54	206	260
2500-3000	13	51	64
3000-4000	—	37	37
4000-5000	—	30	30
5000-6000	—	21	21
6000-7000	—	18	18
7000- above	—	6	6
Total	248	636	884

Dehradun valley located within 29°, 55' and 30° 30' north latitudes and 77° 35' to 78° 20' east longitudes in the area of lesser Himalaya in the north and the Shiwalik in the south, with the holy rivers namely Ganga in the south-east and the Yamuna in the south-west bordering the valley transversely. The valley is situated in the north-western region of U.P. It is bounded on the north by Chakrata tehsil of district Dehradun and Tehri Garhwal. In the south by Saharanpur district and at its extreme south by districts Bijnor and Hardwar. The eastern boundary of the tehsil Dehradun of district Dehradun underwent a slight change in 1956 because of the transfer of two villages Tapoban and Dhalwala to the district Tehri Garhwal.

The valley is characterised by three distinct altitudinal belt with the height of 303 mtrs to 1818 mtrs. The low altitudinal valley ranges from 303m to 909m. It covers an area of 644.8 sq. km in SW and SE

Shiwalik hills and 1362.4 sq. km. in Valley proper and Ganga, Yamuna, Suswa and Asan river terraces. Piedmont colluvial belt is spread in 909m to 1818m, covering an area of 228.8 sq. km in NW and NE lesser Himalaya, whereas lesser Himalayan belt covers an area of 62.4 sq. km. in NW and NE in lesser Himalayan range. A study carried out by Prof. P.B. Saxena indicates that the gradient from the valley bottom to the mountain uplands, varies from 35' to 3000' per km. The hydrographic curve indicates that the maximum area, e.g. 74.7 per cent lies below 3000' consisting of the hilly terrain clad with vegetation, 14.3 per cent is between 3000' and 6000' covering the arable land. On the north and north-east the horizon is bounded by the Mussoorie ranges which is opposite to Dehradun valley. The important peaks on this range are Bhadraj (2229m), Gunhill (2124m), Lal Tibba (2277m), Deok Tibba (2347m) and Top Tibba (2615m).

Prasad and Verma (1974) concluded that the inclination of form of slope is controlled by mass movement in the valley. While Shukla (1974) pointed out that the slope in the valley is the function of lithostratigraphy. Whereas Anantharaman (1981) says that the slopes have been created by weathering followed by mass wasting, running water and structural control.

Table 2.2. Doon Valley: Area-Altitude Relationship

Altitudinal Zones	*Height in Mtrs*	*Area in Sq. Km.*	*% of the Area*	*Nature of the Marpho unit*
Lesser Himalayan Bhadraj, Nagtibba High Altitudinal Hill Tracts Zone	1515-2424	117	6.18	NW, NE Structural Hills
Submontaine Piedmont Hill Tract Zone	909-1515	174	7.06	NW.NE Colluvial Terraces
Shiwalik Moderately High Altitudinal Zone	606-909	174	7.06	SW,SE, Shiwalik Structural and Denudational Hills
Low-Suswa-Asan River Tract Zone	303-606	1833	79.7	Valley River Terraces

There is a central ridge covered with Suswa-Asan terraces. The western part of the valley slopes towards NW and eastern part is inclined towards SE. The Nagsidh structure is discordant rise, otherwise there is flat landscape. NW and NE parts exhibit high angled slopes

(32°) and south-west and SE part exhibit comparatively low angled concave slopes (8°-16°). Flood plains and terraces possess flat, gentle and moderate concave slopes (2°-8°). The piedmont hill tract colluvial terraces have convex form with steep slope (16°-32°). Escarpments show high angled extremely steep slope (36°). Alluvial terraces along Suswa form concave-convex slopes. Shiwalik along the Asan exhibit gentle deep slope.

Table 2.3. Doon Valley Regionwise Slope, Gradient and Angle

Slope Regions	*Gradient*	*Angle*
Extreme Steep Slopes Lesser Himalayan Hills	303-757m/1.6 Km.	32°–64°
Steep to Extreme Steep Sloped Piedmont Colluvial Hills Tract (NW, NE)	151-303m/1.6 Km.	16°–32°
Moderate to Steep Sloped Shiwaliks (SE, SW)	60.6-151/1.6 Km.	8°–16°
Gentle to Moderate Slopes Asan-Suswa Terraces	15.5-60.6m/1.6 Km.	8°–2°

The Ganga valley commences from the confluence of rivers Bhagirathi and Alaknanda near Birahi. It is a narrow belt up to Byasghat in Pargana Barhasyum and a strip along the northern part of Pargana Ganga Salan. At places where the valley is relatively wider, is well cultivated by its hard working people. In Pargana Ganga Salan, the land is rugged, and the villages are thinly populated with only scattered patches of cultivation. The Alaknanda valley includes the two valleys of Panai and of Srinagar. It enjoys the privilege of embracing the road to the holy shrines of Badrinath and Kedarnath to which places lakhs of pilgrims visit every year for their salvation. The upper portion of the valley is covered with forests of oak and pine while the lower parts are cultivated.

The valley of Ramganga is called Patlidoon. It is about 20 kms. long and 2 to 3 kms. wide with rich grass cover. Two ridges of low hills separate it from the Bhabar in the South. Since long its vast areas are under the jurisdiction of forest department. The area is rich in wild fauna which find this as their natural habitat owing to the nature of the area. The river Nayar has two branches, western Nayar and eastern Nayar. The valley formed by the former is fertile and therefore the people are well off. The valley of the other branch of Nayar is more known for grass and other forest products. Forest roads cross through this area and are mostly used to move various products from here and bring in merchandise needed by people in upper areas.

Mountains

This can be sub-divided into two—lower hills having an elevation up to about 1600 meters above MSL, and those above this and up to the snow line. Both portions, by and large, are identical except their elevation with which the ruggedness of the terrain, sparseness of population and coldness in temperature increases. The lower hill portion has an approximate width of 75 kms. and is separated from the Doon valley by the main boundary fault. Plateau-like features characterize these areas. The high hill areas extend up to the snow line. This has temperate climate offering healthy conditions for growth of a large number of forest trees. The numerous streams and rivulets provide good humid environment which turn harsh during winters. This can also be termed as the greater Himalayan zone. In the upper parts of this, not more than one crop can be raised during any year. In practice, all crops irrespective of their affiliation to seasons known at lower elevations are sown together as a mixed crop and harvested or picked in accordance with their maturity. The foodgrains produced here are coarse millets and beans of several types. The productivity is relatively low because of limited manure inputs, which means only the farm yards manure is used and no chemical fertilizer is put in to increase the yield. Temperate fruits, virus free potato, off-season vegetables, seeds and several other high value products have tremendous scope to grow.

The Trans-Himalayan Zone

This covers the northern most part of the region with a general elevation up to about 3500 meters. This being a rain shadow area, is factually also called snow desert. The population density is too thin and the developmental activities are too expensive. It has large areas of pasture where the people graze their herds of livestock, particularly sheep and goat flocks. This area received special attention after the Chinese aggression of 1962.

Before Chinese suzerainty over Tibet, there used to be a big trade with Tibet through the passes of Niti and Mana of this area. Now a trade pact has been executed between the two countries but the trade is supposed to be carried on only through the Lepulekh pass of Kumaun. Thus, the people who were traditionally traders have been forced to adopt some other vocations. However, with the recent opening of the area to foreigners, the increasing number of trekkers particularly has provided very good opportunity of employment to local inhabitants as guides and porters, the jobs they are naturally most competent in. The people of the area have also started collection and cultivation of medicinal plants.

Nitya Nand and Kamlesh Kumar (1989) have divided the entire Garhwal region into three zones such as: (i) Shiwalik or outer Himalaya, (ii) Himachal or Lesser Himalaya, and (iii) Himadari or Greater Himalaya. This is based on physiography of the region, as observed by the two geographers. The sub-regions given above are from the point of view of agricultural economist. However, there is no fundamental difference between the two.

Climate

The physical diversities of the region bring in wide variations in its climate. As a result there are many micro-climatic pockets in Garhwal. These may partly be due to uneven distribution of human settlement and livestock and their increasing pressure. Disturbances to natural resources such as forests, water, soil, minerals etc. also contribute to climatic change and its variations. The important factors determining the climate of a place in hilly areas are elevation, slopes, directions of mountain ranges and their position in relation to the snow peaks and the foot hills. Thus, the climate in mountain area is determined mainly by relief and altitude rather than the latitude and situation with respect to sea. Compared with low lands, in mountains due to decrease in atmospheric pressure, temperature and humidity increases. The region also experiences heavy rainfall upto certain height.

There are fundamental differences in the intensity of sunshine through the thin and clear atmosphere above the snow line where it is much greater than that received through a considerable thickness of the atmosphere in the plains. During day time there is often reversal of wind direction as that of the night when the flow of cool wind is generally down the mountains slopes and valleys. Owing to the establishment of temperature inversions during the colder months and at nights, temperature may be higher on mountain summit and diverse and annual ranges of temperature on middle and higher latitudes may thus be lesser. Ranges of temperature, however, vary considerable in valley bottoms, and are much greater on plateau than on mountains of the same height. There are great contradictions in terms of temperature between sunny and dappled slopes.

Another important attribute of hill climate is winds. During day time wind flow from valleys upwards and flow downwards at night, there flow being determined by the direction and degree of slope in the valleys. When nights are relatively shorter, during summers, the local winds caused by the flow of air during the day time in valleys and mountain slopes continue throughout the night at the foothills. Around the snow-covered area, the air cools down considerably and flow rather viciously. Local winds are observed through passes called *khals* locally. Khals are the places where two ridges meet and the speed of the wind is fierce at the these places. Khal is an important and bountiful source of renewable energy, which deserves to be harnessed in the mountain areas.

Other illuminating phenomena of Garhwal, and almost all hill areas, are prevalence of snow, hail, rain, frost and fog during the different seasons. It is very rare to get snow below 1650 meters while it may sometimes occur even in valleys of lower elevation at higher reaches. The life of the people is very hard and topographic conditions forced them to work hard in order to earn the livelihood. Badrinath, the famous Hindu shrine experiences at least 4 meters of snow every winter. At lower elevations, the coldest period is December to January when snow falls. Hailstorms are mostly during autumn or after the spring season. This is the most dreaded phenomena and considered as a calamity by farmers particularly as it causes heavy damage to field crops and fruit trees. The hard work of the farmers is ruined by hail storm. Rainfall varies considerably with height and situation of the place with respect to the high ridges and peaks. On an average, the annual rainfall ranges between 92 cms. and 237 cms. in various parts of the region. It is reported that areas receiving higher rain have their maximum share during monsoons while those getting relatively lesser of it, receive lesser during the seasons. In valleys, frost is common in the months of December and January. Fog is the outcome of excessive humidity and is more commonly observed in upper valleys. The valley of Srinagar gets fully covered with thick fog during winter nights reducing the visibility to very short distance.

There has been a general lack of climatological data for the Garhwal region as a whole. The situation in this regard is improving certainly though slowly. Therefore, the above presentation gives some idea of the existing climate of the region. On the basis of these, a year in Garhwal can be divided into the following seasons:

(i) Spring- March to mid April
(ii) Summer- Mid April to mid June
(iii) Rainy- Mid June to mid September
(iv) Autumn- Mid September to mid November
(v) Winter- Mid November to February.

Rivers and Lakes

Broadly speaking, Garhwal region is drained by the Ganges and its numerous tributaries, including the Yamuna, which joins the Ganga at Allahabad forming the holiest of the many holy confluences. The Ganga assumes this name at Deoprayag where Alaknanda joins Bhagirathi. This river is sacred not only to the people of this region but also to all the Hindus. The origin of Ganga was Gangotri glacier at the time of Vedas but now it is the representative site only. The glacial source has reduced 19 kms. further to Gaumukh (Gurmeet & Thukral 1989) on the other hand the Yamuna originates from Yamnotri. Alaknanda, Bhagirathi, Mandakini and Ramganga are the important rivers that join the main river Ganga. Several other smaller rivers, rivulets and streams, join these rivers in turn. Each of them is held in great esteem locally because each of them supplies water, which is life-saving for the crops, livestock and the people. All these water carrying courses are natural originating from the stocks of snow in the north.

Alongwith so many other pieces of eternal beauty and utility, Garhwal is no less known for its lakes located at high altitudes where they enjoy the locational advantage of providing mirror images to the peaks around them. The epic *Skanda Purana* mentions about 66 lakes available in Garhwal, each one carrying interesting tales. Hemkund is one of them. This is a lake of ice approachable only during the four months of June to October every year. Surrounded by high peaks including Nanda Devi, it is situated at 4150 meters elevation. Both Hindus and Sikhs worship this lake with equal reverence. To the

Hindus, it is better known as Lakshman Kund where an ancient temple is believed to be of Ramayana period. For the Sikh, here is the highest Gurudwara called Hemkund Sahib where Guru Govind Singh is believed to have done penance in his earlier birth. Other lakes worth mention are Deoria Tal, Rupkund, Gaurikund, Kakbhushandi, Sahastratal, Dodital, Vasukital and Kedartal.

Glaciers of Garhwal are invaluable natural as well as renewable resources that keep the twin river systems of Ganga and Yamuna flowing throughout the year. The largest glacier is that of Gangotri with an estimated volume of about 20 km, and nearly 200 km as its surface area. There are three main glacial systems in this region: those of Alaknanda, Bhagirathi and Dhauli.

The soil is one of the basic factors conducive to the agricultural prosperity of a region. It is a direct outcome of land and lies over the land surface, either deep or shallow, rich or poor. Every soil is a natural body of mineral and organic constituents, differentiated into horizons, which differ among themselves as well as from the underlying mineral in morphology, physical makeup, chemical composition and biological characteristics. In the simpler way soil is the result of soil formation process representing an intricate exchange of energy and matter, a complex of prolonged interaction between lithosphere (soil forming rocks), biosphere (the organic world) and the environment including topography parental material, climate, geographical solution (space and time).

Thus, such a basic resource like topsoil represents a considerable diversity and its knowledge and proper utilisation can only be achieved on the basis of its functions, formation and classification.

The functions of soils are: (i) to act as a physical support to the vegetation. (ii) to reserve as a medium for storing water to be used by roots of the plants; (iii) to supply small but essential per cent of minerals which are converted into plant food by photosynthesis [Manchanda and Dutta, 1984].

Soil

The soils of all characteristics and composition are found in this area. The land in the rugged and often rocky hills are usually of an inferior quality. The soil is often porous and water drains away. The fields of good loams, good clay, such as found in Dun are rare in Jaunsar-Babar except near the water courses. The soil of the region depends upon the underlying rocks and vegetation cover. The northern slope usually bearing dense growth of oak forests have a thick layer of soil cover with humus and high moisture. The soils of this tract can be divided into four distinct genetic types.

Red loam is usually found in hill slopes and along the ridges. A series of parallel ridges having red loam soil is the noticeable feature of the area, the profiles are generally sandy in nature. The sites of this nature occur at places which receive maximum solar radiation and are always dry on account of their situation on the ridges and slopes. These soils are mostly brownish, grey, loamy to loamy sand with plenty of under composed organic material.

The whole region is well covered by forest. The formation of brown forest soil is generally found in greater part of the division. These are highly organic finely granular clayey and clayey loam containing plenty of under growth.

Pedsol is found in sandy places on mild slopes and gentle gradients. These are loamy, some times mixed with single grained sand or with sandy cementation of clayey hard soils.

Meadow Soil: The profile development of meadow soil is usually met with near water streams, cool and low lying sandy places. Because of the high water level the soil remains moist and during winter thick matting of frost covers the soil. These are dark grey, granular, sandy loam and sandy soils at greater depth.

The soil in Doon valley varies from place to place mainly loam, clay sandy and gravel-sandy soils are found in the area. The researcher conducted various surveys with regard to the land utilization and soil types. Participatory Rural Appraisal technique was adopted to find out the soil types.

Goyand is a very good clayey fertile soil which has no pebble and stone. This is the soil deposited below the spur in the fields where Basmati rice or vegetables are the cherished crops. They are like "Ghurtti" soil of western U.P. plains. It is a priced soil of Dehradun. It is mainly found between the Suswa and the Song river basin which cover the villages such as Majra, Niranjanpur, Sewala Kalan, Sewala

Khurd, Harbhajwala, Harbanswala, Brahmanwala in Nyaya Panchayat Sewala Khurd of Raipur Block, Dudhali, Nagal Jwalapur, Nagal Bulandewala, Simlasgrant of Nyaya Panchayat Markhamgrant and Bhaniyawala and Majri Grant of Bhaniyawala Nyaya Panchayat.

Rausli is a medium soil consisting of some pebbles and Baisari. It is sandy in nature, supporting poor crops, Dakra, is also good soil without pebbles with 20 per cent to 30 per cent clay sustaining the paddy crops. It is like Dumet and Dhora of the central U.P.. These are coarse in texture and brownish in colour as compared to the finer and greyish subdued colour in U.P. plain. In the low land it is puddled easily when it is wet, and on drying it gets hard in clots in water logged situation. This type of soil is found in the patches in the entire valley.

Sankra is the infertile soil in the Dun. In such soil the development of a horizon is found incomplete, mostly the land is covered with grass, weeds and shrubs. The local hard-rock topography favour the formation of hydromorphic or holomorphic soils known as kallar and papper which are not rich yielding soils in the Dun. Many of the Dun soils are extremely sandy and are responsible for the nomenclature of the villages located therein, such as Bhur, Barkot in Langha and Bhurpur village lying at the left bank of river Asan.

Vegetation

The Garhwal Rajas derived a considerable revenue from the Dun forests in pre-British days, mainly through excise collected at posts erected at the passes of the Shiwaliks. In the early years of the British rule no attempts were made at forest conservation. The district abounded in fine trees 100 and 200 year old or more. For the first time in 1844 the British authorities stopped to leasing the forests and kept the collection of dues in their own hand till the establishment of forest department in 1855 [Atkinson, 1884]. Since 1864 regular forest operations were commenced, but it took 13 years to properly demarcate the forests. Although, in 1878 the Forest Act had become a law, it was not till 1887 that the first working plan for the forest of tehsil Dehradun could be prepared and the scientific management of forest started.

The forest in hilly regions were neglected until 1860. No restrictions were placed upon their utilisation by surrounding villages (Majumdar, 1956). The rules were more stringently enforced following the appointment of Conservator of Forests for the north-western provinces in 1868. In

1872 demarcation of the forests into three classes was carried out. The first class, measuring about 6360 hectares was dominated Government forests, which consisted mainly Deodar. The second class was open Government forests, including mixed trees spreading over an area of 30972 hectares. The villages were allowed right of fuel and grazing and on certain conditions building timber and cultivation. The third class measuring about 66005 hectares was made over entirely to the villagers for their own use.

The third class or the village forests of Chakrata tehsil have greatly diminished. So far there is no working plan for this class of forest in which villages have got unlimited rights. Every year a large number of trees are alloted to the villagers for their own use, because right from the British period they are allowed to get certain numbers of trees under the Maphi Act.

The forest in region scattered in the north-west and south and are surrounded by cultivation, but greater part of the forests form a compact belt. Some of the distinguishing features of the division are as under:

- the division contains some of the finest patches of spruce and fir forests;
- Kail forests are found only mixed with other coniferous species;
- there are luxuriant ban forests over a large area which are still much spoilt;
- the quantity of chir is very good over a considerable area;
- the content and quantity of deodar forest is very high;
- the fir and spruce forests are conspicuous by the absence of natural regeneration of fir; and
- the division has some substantial patches of good kharsu forests mixed with fir and spruce.

The important type of forest in the hilly region are as under:

- Dry Shiwalik Sal Forests
- Northern Dry Mixed Deciduous Forests
- Khair-Sissoo Forests
- Dry Deciduous Scrub
- Sub-tropical Pine Forests
  Sub-tropical Himalayan-Chir-pine Forest
  - o Himalayan Sub-tropical Scrub

  - o Sub-Tropical Dry Evergreen Forest Kau Scrub Forest
- Himalayan Moist Temperate Forests Lower West Himalayan
  - o Temperate Forests - Ban-Oak Forest:
  - o Moru - Oak Forests:
  - o Oak Scrub Forests:
  - o Moist Deodar Forests:
  - o Western Mixed Coniferous Forests:
  - o Moist Temperate Deciduous Forests
- Upper West Himalayan Temperate Forests
  - o Kharsu Oak Forests
  - o West Himalayan Upper Oak Fir Forests
  - o Himalayan Temperate Parkland
  - o Himalayan Temperate Pastures
- Edaphic Types of Himalayan Temperate Forests
  - o Cypress Forest
- Seral Types of Himalayan Temperate Forests
  - o Alder Forest
  - o Lower-level Blue Pine Forests.

Important species consists of sal, sain, bakli, pipal, dhaman, chamror, harsingar, semal, khair, kunja, bahera, amaltas thingan rohini, gentni, khinni, mandra, siris, sandan, kachnar, kanra, mahua, kharik, banj, ayar, burans, kaula churur, bhadroi, kasakmal, bekot, gingau, emroi, akhrot, utis and deodar. Important growths are dhaula, gandhela, jharberi, bindu, kandai, dias, kashmoi, kumeria, suina, tachla ringal, ninawa, kakhisar, ennsohi, kaknoi, bhutnoi, kandheru, chamanbai, bhankoi, marroi, kalahisar, taknoi, bhutnoi, kanderu, kandai and kimoi. Important grasses are baib, grola, bambo, kans, kumeria, mirchgandha.

The forest of valley taken over by the forest department on July 1, 1952 as the consequence of the enforcement of the U.P. Zamindari Abolition and Land Reform Act, 1950. These forests were brought under scientific management since 1955-56 when the first working plan was prepared for these forests. The recommendations of working plan carried out by trained officers and subordinate field staff. Poorly stocked forests, grassy banks and forest of low economic value is being replaced by plantation of fast growing species which are of industrial importance. The scientific management of reserve forests of the district have raised plantation over grassy blanks and in open or poor type of forests. The species of plantation are mulberry, semal, tun, khair, sissoo, pulla, bahera, eucalyptus and bamboo. The important forest types in Valleys and Shvaliks are::

- Moist Shiwalik Sal Forests
- Moist Bhabar Doon Sal Forest
- Gangetic Moist Mixed Deciduous Forest
- Low Alluvial Savana Woodland
- Sub-Montane Hill Valley Swamp Forests
- Dry Shiwalik Sal Forest
- Northern Dry Mixed Deciduous Forests
- Dry Deciduous Scrub Forests
- Khair Sissoo Forests
- Sub-tropical Shiwalik Chir-pine Forests
- Sub-tropical Himalayan Chir Forests
- Himalayan Sub-tropical Scrub Forests
- Ban-Oak Forests
- Himalayan Temperate Secondary Scrubs.

Important species are bakli, sain, dhauri, chamror, jamun, machlus, listsea, sissoo, chinensis, sal, siris, bahera, jhingan, buras, kharpat, sites, qutel, jamun, banj, tun, safed, kathber, piyal, kachnar, quiral, padal, semal, khair, kanju, khanni and mandlana. Important underwoods are rohini, amaltas, nal, aonla, sandan, dhaman, kakraunda, cameli, gaujand, vasica, jharberi, bindu, condida, harsingar and gadhela. Important under growths are karaunda, gandhela, bindu, dhaula, vacica, kans, gorla, munj, jharberi, karaunda, baib, gorla and vasinga.

Demography

The regional economy of an area is the expression of the correlation between resources and population. The level of the development of the regional economy, therefore, is determined by socio-technological efficiency as applied to the development. The source base both physical and human, provides the basis on which the structure of the economy is built. Among the several indicators of diversification of economy the relevance of human resource is paramount. Owing to this overwhelming importance of the human resources it is necessary to study various aspects which have direct bearing on it [Bhende and Kanitkar, 1978]. Generally population distribution and growth pattern conditions differ from area to area. The population of Garhwal Himalaya is mainly concentrated in Doons, Bhabar and lower levels of the valley of the lesser Himalayan rivers. As per the census of 2001, the Garhwal region accommodates 49.16 million people in 8660 villages and 80 big and small towns. A considerable variation has also been noticed in the density of population in the region as only 37 person per sq. km. was reported in Uttarkashi against highest 612 persons per sq. km. in Haridwar district.

While analyzing the distribution of population it is revealed that out of the total population of the region more than 50 percent reside in Dehradun (26.02 percent) and Haridwar (29.38 percent). On the other hand the proportion of people residing in Rudraprayag (4.63 percent) and Uttarkashi district (5.98 percent) is significantly low. This indicates that the concentration of population in the region is primarily in valleys and plain areas. Inclusion of Haridwar district has also influenced the population distribution of the region to a great extent. Settlements are in district Dehradun. On the hill slope the settlements are located landslide debris'. (Pant B.R., p. 26) (Table 2.4)

The Garhwal Himalayas has registered tremendous growth of population the last hundred years. The population has increased by 257.6 percent since 1901 to 1991 in Uttarakhand as compare to 254.6 percent in whole country during the period of 1901-1991 (Pant B.R., p. 26).

Table 2.4. Garhwal Region: Distribution of Population (2001)

Districts	*Area Sq. km.*	*Population*			*Sex Ratio*
		Total	*Male*	*Female*	
Uttarkashi	8,016	294179	151599	142580	941
Chamoli	9,168	369198	183033	186165	1017
Rudraprayag		227461	107425	120036	1117
Tehri Garhwal	4,421	604608	294842	309766	1051
Dehradun	3,088	1279083	675549	603534	893
Pauri Garhwal	5,397	696851	331138	365713	1104
Garhwal	30,090	3471380	1743586	1727794	990
Uttarakhand	53,119	8479562	4316401	4163161	964

Source: Census of India 2001 and Statistical Diary Uttarakhand, 2000-2001, p. 1.

On the analysis of district-wise growth of population during the decade 1991-2001 and 1981-199 it was revealed that Hàridwar district has recorded highest growth (26.30 percent) followed by Dehradun district (24.71 percent). The growth of population recorded in other districts were 22.72 percent in Uttarkashi, 16.15 percent in Tehri 3.89 percent in Pauri and 13.51 percent in Chamoli Garhwal. The decennial growth of population has decreased substantially in the region. Relatively low Decennial growth rate in Pauri Garhwal can be attributed to a number of factors including the vastness of the area and migration of a large number of male population to the other parts of the country in search of employment (Dimri 1994) (Table 2.5).

Table 2.5. Growth of Population (1991-2001)

District/ State	*1991-2001*	*1981-1991*
Uttarkashi	22.72	25.54
Dehradun	24.71	34.66
Tehri	16.15	16.69
Pauri	3.87	9.05
Chamoli	13.51	21.97
Rudraprayag	12.44	17.51
Garhwal	26.30	28.44
Haridwar	19.68	25.50
Uttarakhand	19.20	24.23

Source: Census of India 2001 and Statistical Diary Uttarakhand, 2000-2001, p. 2.

Districts like Pauri. Chamoli have witnessed population growth below the average growth rate of the entire state population growth.

Sex-Composition

Sex composition is the basic characteristic or biological attribute of any biological group and affects not only its demographic but also its social and economic structure. The sex composition influences and is influencing birth and death rates, migration etc. Sex composition is an important aspect both in economic and rural sector planning. The region has peculiar sex composition and is different from the other mountain states. Change in the sex composition largely reflects the underlying socio economic and cultural pattern of a society in different ways. The sex ratio is mainly the outcome of the inter play sex differentiate in mortality, migration and at a time the sex differentials in population enumeration (Table 2.6).

Table 2.6. Districtwise Decennial Variation in Sex Ratio Since 1901-2001

State/District	*Sex Ratio (Females per 1000 male)*										
	1901	*1911*	*1921*	*1931*	*1941*	*1951*	*1961*	*1971*	*1981*	*1991*	*2001*
Uttarkashi	1015	1026	1035	1017	976	993	964	899	881	918	941
Chamoli	1028	1033	1080	1066	1073	1092	1103	1035	1020	982	1017
Rudraprayag	1061	1067	1105	1092	1084	1144	1169	1169	1121	1094	1117
Tehri	1006	1016	1025	1007	967	1122	1196	1179	1081	1048	1051
Dehradun	733	696	656	673	644	715	766	770	811	843	893
Garhwal	1031	1035	1083	1069	1076	1137	1163	1119	1091	1058	1104
Pithoragarh	977	971	1000	998	1010	1020	1052	1033	1027	992	1031
Champawat	928	924	946	947	961	956	929	955	947	945	1024
Almora	989	983	1012	1011	1023	1060	1114	1100	1095	1099	1147
Bageshwar	936	931	959	957	969	1008	1024	1057	1031	1055	1110
Nainital	780	753	706	693	689	699	715	837	847	881	906
U. S. Nagar	812	785	737	723	720	731	726	774	841	863	902
Hardwar	864	823	818	820	802	806	796	803	817	846	863
Uttarakhand	831	907	916	913	907	940	947	940	936	936	964

Source: Census of India 1981, 1991, 2001 and Juyal, R.P. & Sati M.C, 2002, *Colonial Legacy of Migration in Uttarakhand*, (In Press).

As evident from the Table in Chamoli, Rudraprayag, Tehri Garhwal and Pauri per thousand females are more than males. The region has no scope for employability, therefore able-bodied youth and elderly people in a large number move out of the region in search of employment. It is also pointed out that in the region when choice between the male and female child for education outside the region is decided it is the former who generally gets preference. This also influences the male-female composition in the region. This phenomenon is more prevalent in the hilly districts except Uttarkashi. Whereas on the other hand Dehradun and Haridwar has more per thousand male than female.

Rural and Urban Population

The stage of socio-economic development of any society is often view by level of urbanisation attained by a particular society in a specified space and time. The growth of urban population in the region of this newly created State has been steadily upwards since 1901.

The people of the region predominantly reside in the rural areas. As noticed in the Table 72.60 percent people in the Garhwal region has reported rural areas as their place of settlement, which is marginally lower than the state average (74.04 percent). On the analysis of table it is also revealed that Dehradun district is most urbanized in the state of Uttarakhand as more than 50 percent population live in the urban areas. It is pertinent to note that after independence the population of Dehradun Urban Agglomeration has become more than doubled (increased 143 per cent in a span of 40 years i.e., from 1951 to 1991) whereas the area has increased only 40.80 per cent. The above referred disproportionate growth of area and population is more alarming because of the fact that the ultimate burden of the population growth is largely on the urban centres of the district. Likewise, the villages on the immediate periphery are de-facto urban, as a significant portion of their land is used up or is being used for non agrarian purposes like housing, paramilitary troops, education institutions and developing posh colonies [Dimri and Juyal, 1995].

Nevertheless the strategic location of the district (i.e. in the transit-zone of plains of Uttar Pradesh and Garhwal Himalayas) amidst the fertile arable land, orchards, lush green forest and position in relation to its connectivity with major centres of industry, trade and commerce and surplus production of northern India. Because of this locational advantage, scores of settlers throng the valley and continue to make it the centre of their activities. Important among these were Sri Guru Ram Rai and his followers, who settled and made his abode (Dera) in the village "Khurbura". The town derives its nomenclature from this specific incident of settling a Dera (abode) in a valley (Doon). Later, a Gurudwara was built here around which the town got nestled. The missionaries with the objective to spread Christianity in the district were established. Mr. Culvert brought about 200 scheduled caste people from the neighbouring district to convert them into Christians, who were later settled in Vikasnagar, Clement Town, and Dehradun [Williams, 1874].

After the annexation of the Himalayan region to the British Empire in 1815, the district received a special favour from imperial rulers because of its soothing climate; consequently physical activity in the district got momentum. Gradually local self-administration was introduced and cantonments, institutions of eminence, centres of administration got established with the improving mode of accessibility and communication.

After Independence, the prominence of the district increased many

Table 2.7. District-wise Population, Decadal Growth Rate, Sex Ratio and Density 2001

India and State/ Union territory/ District*	*Population 2001*			*Decadal growth rate*		*Sex ratio*		*Density*	
	Persons	*Males*	*Females*	*1981-91*	*1991-01*	*1991*	*2001*	*1991*	*2001*
1	2	3	4	5	6	7	8	9	10
Rudraprayag	227,461	107,425	120,036	17.51	13.44	1,094	1,117	106	120
Tehri Garhwal	604,608	294,842	309,766	16.59	16.15	1,048	1,051	128	148
Dehradun	1,279,083	675,549	603,534	34.66	24.71	843	893	332	414
Garhwal	696,851	331,138	365,713	9.05	3.87	1,058	1,104	124	129
Pithoragarh	462,149	227,592	234,557	14.11	10.92	992	1,031	59	65
Champawat	224,461	110,916	113,545	34.22	17.56	945	1,024	107	126
Almora	630,446	293,576	336,870	9.43	3.14	1,099	1,147	198	205
Bageshwar	249,453	118,202	131,251	14.92	9.21	1,055	1,110	99	108
Nainital	762,912	400,336	362,576	30.01	32.88	881	906	149	198
Udhamsingh Nagar	1,234,548	649,020	585,528	44.46	27.79	863	902	332	424
Hardwar	1,444,213	773,173	671,040	28.44	26.30	846	868	485	612
Uttaranchal	8,479,562	4,316,401	4,163,161	24.23	19.20	936	964	133	159

Source: Census of India 2001 and Statistical Diary Uttarakhand, 2000-2001, p. 2.

folds, as institutions of national eminence and repute continued to be established and expand in for the affluent. The present day district Dehradun has many institutions and agencies of national and international repute. To name a few these are the Oil and Natural Gas Commission, The Wild Life Research Institute, the Central Soil Research Institute, the Survey of India, the National Remote Sensing Agency and many other besides scores of schools and colleges drawing students from across the nation and even from abroad.

Simultaneously the abundance of non-metallic minerals like lime-stone, marble, dolomite and phosphate deposits in the lower Himalayan ranges, ushered in mineral based industrialisation of the district. After sixties, about 184 limekilns, one cement factory, one calcium carbide and one calcium carbonate and six other chemical factories were established in and on the periphery of the Agglomeration. Likewise the erstwhile Govt. of Uttar Pradesh, provided many financial incentives to hotel industries to promote tourism in the Himalayan region.

On the other hand the urban population of the other districts, particularly predominantly hilly districts of the region is considerably low. As furnished in the Table, district Rudraprayag has only 1.93 people living in the urban areas and Uttarkashi and Tehri Garhwal has 7.79 percent and 9.67 percent urban population respectively. On the basis of urban-rural composition of population all the districts of the region can be grouped into three categories such as highly urbanized moderately urbanized and least urbanized. This indicate that the rural economy of the region still plays major role (Table 2.8).

Table 2.8. Rural and Urban Population of Uttarakhand

Districts	*Area Sq. km.*	*Population*			*% Rural of total Population*	*% Urban of total Population*
		Total	*Rural*	*Urban*		
Dehradun	3,088	1279083	601965	677118	47.06	52.94
Uttarkashi	8,016	294179	271255	22924	92.21	7.79
Tehri Garhwal	3,796	604608	546133	58475	90.3	9.67
Pauri Garhwal	5,230	696851	606629	90222	87.05	12.95
Chamoli	7,626	369198	319613	49585	86.57	13.43
Rudraprayag	2,334	227461	224740	2721	98.81	1.19
Haridwar	2360	1444213	998550	4455663	69.14	30.86
Garhwal	32448	4915593	3568885	901045	72.60	27.40
Uttarakhand	53119	8479562	6309317	2170245	74.04	25.59

Source: Census of India 2001 and Statistical Diary Uttarakhand, 2000-2001, p. 2.

Scheduled Caste and Scheduled Tribe Population

The total population of scheduled castes in the region was reported 14.98 percent as per census of 2001 which is marginally less than the state average (17.52). Among the eight districts of the Uttarkashi has higher proportion of SC population (22.77 percent), whereas in Dehradun the proportion of SC population is lowest (13.40 percent). From the Table it is evident to note that no significant variation was noticed in the distribution of SC population in all the districts of the region. On the other hand out of the total population of the state 3.01 percent was recorded as ST population. The proportion of ST population was reported highest in Dehradun (8.20 percent) followed by Chamoli (5.76 percent). In other district of the State the schedul tribe population was significantly low (Table- 2.9).

Table 2.9. SC and ST Population of Garhwal Region (2001)

Districts	SC	ST
Dehradun	1,37,464 (13.40)	84,076 (8.20)
Uttarkashi	54,594 (22.77)	2,300 (0.96)
Tehri Garhwal	68,364 (14.20)	487 (0.20)
Pauri Garhwal	92,261 (13.5)	1,502 (0.18)
Chamoli	62,643 (13.71)	10,148 (5.76)
Rudraprayag	30,979 (17.27)	128 (0.07)
Garhwal Region	4,46,305 (14.96)	98,641 (3.30)
Uttarakhand	12,35,546 (17.52)	2,11,739 (3.01)

Note: Figures in parentheses indicate percentage to Total.

Source: Census of India 2001 and Statistical Diary Uttarakhand, 2000-2001, p. 2.

Literacy

Educational achievement of a society and its overall development are reciprocally related. It is often the level of educational development that determines the levels of development of other sectors and vice versa. For instance, it has been theorized that a highly developed health sector may yield in poor results unless its development is coupled with that of the education sector. Similarly, adoption of technological innovations in agriculture is dependent upon education levels among the rural masses. Development process is accelerated with the expansion of education and literacy. Modern theories of economic development accept human resource development as on of the potent factors of progress.

Literacy is the base of the educational pyramid and forms an important indicator of development in underdeveloped economies. However, the experience of total literacy in Kerala has shown that in spite of a near hundred percent literacy in the State, problems such as malnutrition, unemployment, poverty, etc. continue to exist. Thus, literacy is a first step in achieving the goal of universal elementary education and not an end in itself.

Therefore, an attempt has been made to assess the situation of literacy rate in the region. While analyzing the literacy data of the Garhwal region of Uttarakhand state it is revealed that among the various districts of the region Dehradun has attained highest literacy rate (78.98 percent) followed by Pauri Garhwal. In general literacy rate of males as well as females of the region is considerable higher than the state and national average. Among the various districts Tehri and Uttarakashi districts have marginally lower literacy rates. This phenomenon is also persisted in male-female and urban-rural literacy rates. A significant gap has been noticed on the analysis of male-female literacy rates of the region, and the gap is much wider in case of certain districts, i.e. in

Table 2.10. Literacy Rate in Garhwal Region (2001)

Districts	*Total*	*Male*	*Female*	*Rural*	*Urban*
Uttarkashi	66.58	84.52	47.48	64.70	87.46
Chamoli	76.23	89.89	63.00	74.17	88.95
Rudraprayag	74.23	90.73	59.98	74.14	81.67
Tehri	67.04	85.62	49.76	64.82	86.67
Dehradun	78.96	85.87	71.22	71.42	85.35
Pauri Garhwal	77.99	91.47	66.14	76.41	88.28

Source: Census of India 2001 and Statistical Diary Uttarakhand, 2000-2001, p. 5.

Pauri Garhwal significant gap of about 25 percent has been recorded. Wide gap between female-male literacy is an indicator of backwardness and unbalanced economic development as seen in the case of Uttarkashi and Tehri (Table 2.10).

On the other hand, rural literacy was reported highest in Pauri Garhwal (76.41 percent) and lowest in Uttarkashi (64.70 percent). On the other hand urban literacy is highest in Chamoli (88.95 percent) closely followed by Pauri (88.28 percent). It may also be noted that literacy in the urban areas of the region is relatively higher and it is more than 80 percent in all the districts.

Infrastructure Facilities

Properly developed infrastructure fastens the pace and the stage of development in any region. Unfortunately the availability of various infrastructure facilities are relatively poor in the state of Uttarakhand in general and Garhwal region in particular. Though concerted efforts were made to ensure the availability of these services, however, the targets achieved were not very encouraging. Therefore an attempt has been made to analyse the various indicators of electricity in respect of the state of Uttarakhand. As evident from the Table 76.14 percent villages were reported electrified in the state. Proportion of the villages reported electrified was highest in Dehradun district followed by Uttarkashi. The number of villages reported electrified was lowest in Pauri Garhwal.

It may be pointed out that the region is rich in terms of water resources, however concerted efforts are required to exploit the source to its full potential. Proper planning will not only provide employment opportunity to a large number of the youth of the region but also enhance the living conditions. Therefore there is need to establish small hydroelectricity project in the region which may not only generate electricity to meet the requirement of the region, but the surplus can be sold to the outside region, fetching handsome revenue to the state, resulting in increase in the employment opportunity (Table 2.11).

An analysis of the above table reveals that 76.14 percent villages of the region are electrified. However the consumption of was electricity reported highest in industrial use followed by domestic use. While analyzing the inter-district variation it is interesting to note that domestic consumption is significantly higher in the predominantly hilly districts i.e. it was reported more than 80 per cent to total use in Chamoli and Uttarkashi. Whereas the consumption of electricity in industrial use was reported highest in Dehradun District. The proportion of electricity used for agriculture is relatively higher in Dehradun and Uttarkashi districts.

Table 2.11. Position of Electricity in the Region

Particular	Dehradun	Pauri	Tehri	Uttarkashi	Chamoli	Garhwal
Total No. of villages	746	3205	1959	678	1596	8184
Number	744	2168	1458	635	1226	6231
	(99.73)	(67.64)	(74.43)	(93.66)	(76.82)	(76.14)
For Domestic Use	48392	28916	19380	8840	13699	119227
	(16.11)	(52.50)	(26.06)	(80.51)	(80.00)	(26.03)
Commercial Use	18298	7795	20600	410	2011	49114
	(6.09)	(14.15)	(27.70)	(3.73)	(11.74)	(10.72)
Industrial Use	204965	7540	26450	730	778	240463
	(68.22)	(13.69)	(35.57)	(6.65)	(4.54)	(52.51)
Public Light	3772	412	140	80	330	4734
	(1.26)	(0.75)	(0.19)	(0.73)	(1.93)	(1.03)
Agriculture	20390	2847	550	920	145	24852
	(6.79)	(5.17)	(0.74)	(8.38)	(0.85)	(5.43)
Water Work	4609	7569	7250	—	160	19588
	(1.53)	(13.74)	(9.75)	—	(0.93)	(4.28)
ALL	300426	55079	74370	10980	17123	457978

Source: Statistical Diary Uttarakhand, 2000-2001.

Transport and Communication: The means of transportation and communication are the lifelines of any region. An increase in the ability to transport goods and people comfortably, safely, efficiently and economically is a good index of the stage of development and particularly of the technological progress attained. Likewise, the various means of communication provide the great facility of enabling news and views to reduce distance between places. Poor facilities in this regard are a great handicap to all activities strengthening development.

In general transportation is mostly carried through railways and roads. Better means of transport are helpful in adding place utility to goods efficiently. The whole region has 70.5 km of railway line—all broad gauged. Of this length, 64.5 km. is in district Dehradun while the remaining 6 km. in Pauri. Thus the region is almost devoid of this facility. The very terrain of the region is such that the laying of railway lines is extremely expensive, and its operation as well as maintenance is costly rendering the activity uneconomic for a very long time.

In such a situation, the only alternative left is that of roads. Several departments of Central and State Government are responsible for the road network in the region, and amongst these the Public Works Department (PWD) alone accounts for about three-fourths of the total road length in the region. For the PWD, the district and rural roads are the most important in every district of the region. The roads under local bodies are in district Dehradun only. As stated earlier, the northern boundary of the region is international and for which reason there is a separate department of border roads.

Table 2.12. Position of Roads in Garhwal

Particulars	Dehradun	Pauri	Tehri	Uttarkashi	Chamoli	Garhwal
1-Under P.W.D	—	—	—	—	—	—
National Highway	241	310	64	90	64	775
State Highway	(0.19)	(0.14)	(0.05)	(0.12)	(0.06)	(0.12)
Main District Roads	1052	117	166	86	62	1483
	(0.81)	(0.05)	(0.14)	(0.12)	(0.05)	(0.22)
Others District &	—	1738	980	558	1021	4297
Rural Roads		(0.80)	(0.81)	(0.76)	(0.89)	(0.66)
Sub-Total	1293	2185	1210	734	1147	6549
2-Under Local Bodies						
District Board	54	1	—	—	—	55
	(0.11)	(0.03)				(0.09)
Municipal Board,etc.	434	32	45	3	—	514
	(0.89)	(0.97)	(1.00)	(1.00)		(0.91)
Sub-Total	488	33	45	3	—	569
3-Under other Depart-ments Irrigation	71	—	31	—	—	102
	(0.03)		(0.02)			(0.01)
Cane	—	—	—	—	—	—
Forest	180	323	24	—	—	527
	(0.08)	(0.13)	(0.01)			(0.06)
Border Roads	—	54	260	148	228	690
		(0.02)	(0.17)	(0.17)	(0.16)	(0.08)
Others	87	—	—	—	13	100
	(0.04)				(0.009)	(0.01)
Sub-Total	338	377	315	148	241	1419
All Roads	2119	2575	1570	885	1388	8537

Source: Statistical Diary Uttarakhand, 2000-2001.

Such roads form 8.7 percent of the total road length in the region. These are mostly in Tehri and Chamoli districts, and none in Dehradun. On the average, the length of all roads per unit of area is observed to be decreasing with the ruggedness of the terrain while reverse is the case per unit of population. This is both the cause and the effect of the increasing sparseness of population with the roughness of the area. When compared with the neighbouring Kumaun region, the situation is not much different the road length per 1000 km. of area is somewhat more (11%) in Kumaun but lesser by about six percent when calculated for the population (Table 2.12).

From the analysis of the table it is revealed that total length of the road in Uttarakhand is 17457 km. The length of the road was reported highest in Pauri Garhwal and lowest in Hardwar. It may also be noted that in Uttarakhand length of the road per thousand km. was 33 km. And the same was 30 km. Among the various districts the position of road per thousand sq. km is relatively better in Dehradun, Pauri and Hardwar districts where as in Chamoli and Uttarkashi the length of roads per 100 sq. km is very low. It may also be noted that these districts are the remotest districts of the region and badly lacking in the road network. Therefore due attention is required to be paid to improve the availability of roads in these districts, which will not only ensure the development of the region but will also improve the living condition of the people of this area. On the other hand while analyzing the length of roads per lakh population it revealed that in Uttarakhand total length of road was reported 248 km and the same was 236 km for Garhwal region. Among the various districts, it may be noted that the facility in Hardwar is better served districts whereas on the other hand Uttarkashi is poorly served district.

Educational Facilities

Social needs being the most persistent and demanding, facilities for education are indicators of social progress of a region. Schools are the formal institution for learning and these transmit values and beliefs. Another social function that schools are supposed to perform is to pursuade the young boys and girls to specific work roles. Village schools play a still more important role in the educational system, particularly in the otherwise backward regions. Organic unity with the community is a characteristic of these schools. Such institutions impose no new ideals, open no strange vistas, and are not much concerned about the future and hence do not bother to set new targets. In most cases, schooling grants sanctions to the student what is already regarded valuable by him or her because the student does not really think of taking any sharp departures from the family's occupation.

As stated earlier Uttarakhand State has very good literacy rate. The region is well served by the schools. As evident from the Table there are 11525 primary schools in the state of which 6696 were reported in Garhwal region. Among the various districts the number of schools are highest in Pauri and lowest in Rudraprayag districts. The teacher- pupil ratio of the state as well as the study area is better as it was 34.52 for the state of Uttarakhand and 33.80 for the study area. The ratio is much favourable in Pauri, whereas the Rudraprayag district is poorly served in teacher-pupil ratio. The position in other districts of the region is favorable. In Uttarakhand nearly 136 schools were reported per lakh population whereas in study area it is marginally less. In Hardwar the number of schools per lakh population is significantly better than the other districts of the region. The situation is poor in Pauri as one school serves about 235 lakh population (Table 2.13).

Table 2.13. Road Network in Uttarakhand

Name of the District	*Total Length of Roads*	*Lengths of Road per 100 Sq Km.*	*Per Lakh Population*
Chamoli	1530	17	336
Dehradun	1702	55	166
Garhwal	2372	44	347
Hardwar	1014	43	90
Rudraprayag	—	—	—
Tehri Garhwal	1635	37	282
Uttarkashi	1362	17	568
Garhwal	9615	30	234
Uttarakhand	17457	33	248

Source: Statistical Diary Uttarakhand , 2000-2001.

An attempt has also been made to analyze the number of primary school with respect to distance. As evident from the Table proportion of primary schools in within a distance of one km is highest in Uttarkashi district followed by Dehradun. On the other hand number of PS within a distance of three km is highest in Pauri followed by Chamoli (Table 2.14).

Table 2.14. Educational Facilities at Primary Level

Name of the District	*Junior Basic Schools*				
	Number of Schools	*Number of Teachers*	*Number of Students*	*Teacher-Pupil Ratio*	*Schools per Lakh Population*
Chamoli	824	45636	1318	34.63	118.25
Dehradun	1309	130419	3733	34.94	102.34
Garhwal	1634	101319	3656	27.71	234.48
Hardwar	696	110538	2802	39.45	48.19
Rudraprayag	405	28778	640	44.97	178.05
Tehri Garhwal	1301	108537	2878	37.71	215.18
Uttarkashi	529	29603	1045	28.33	179.82
Garhwal	6696	554830	16072	34.52	136.22
Uttarakhand	11525	943521	27913	33.80	135.92

Source: Statistical Diary Uttarakhand, 2001-2002.

It may be noted that children in the age of 6-11 years have to travel for having access to PS more in Hilly districts than in the valleys and plain area of the region. Still there are 34 schools in Tehri, 5 in Dehradun and 1 in Chamoli where children have to travel more than 5 kms to have access to primary schooling. While analyzing the position of secondary schools it may be noted that in the entire state 2480 senior basic schools were reported out of which 1573 were in study area. Among the various districts Pauri has highest SBS and Rudraprayag has lowest number such type of schools. Average teacher-pupil ratio of the state was 26.74 and the same was 23.63 for Garhwal region. Among the various districts the ratio is more favorable in Uttarkashi and Rudraprayag. On the other hand the region has 29.25 schools per lakh population. It may be noted that in the hilly districts the position is significantly good. This can be attributed to low density of population in the hilly districts of the region. On the analysis of the school facility in the state it is revealed that the region is better served by school facility at the junior and middle level (Table 2.15).

Table 2.15. Distance Wise Villages from Schools

Facilities	*Distance*	*Dehradun*	*Pauri*	*Tehri*	*Uttarkashi*	*Chamoli*	*Garhwal*
Total No. of Villages		725	3181	1945	661	1553	8065
Junior Ba sic Schools	At road head	558 76.97	1451 45.61	1237 63.60	545 82.45	1010 65.04	4801
	Up to 3km.	140 19.31	1641 51.59	628 32.29	111 16.79	515 33.16	3035
	3-5km.	22 3.03	89 2.80	46 2.37	5 0.76	27 1.74	189
	Up to 5km.	5 0.69	10.68	34 1.75	—	1 0.06	40

Source: Statistical Diary Uttarakhand, 2001-2002.

The figures bring out that the facilities for primary school are the maximum and these continue to shrink with a rise in the level of education. The factual situation is that even if more schools are provided, there may not be sufficient number of students to justify those. Till the beginning of the twentieth century, formal education was considered to be for the elite only who could well afford to educate their wards at the big educational centres. But with increase in population coupled with the marginal chances of more dependence on agricultural pursuits, formal education was needed as a qualifying tool for jobs in government departments. For the female education, it was generally regarded to be a wasteful venture as jobs outside were tabooed to them. The situation has however been changing after the political independence of our country. In the Garhwal region there is now a University at Srinagar in district Pauri providing educational facilities in a number of subjects. In fact the saturation point now seems to have been attained as indicated by the increasing number of unemployed educated persons in the region, as well as by the rush for admission at schools and college. At the same time, the rush for jobs is not necessarily because of the need to earn through service for a living; in a great measure it is the easy way of earning which attracts the young men and women towards jobs and that too in public sector (Table 2.16).

Table 2.16. Educational Facilities at Senior Basic Schools

Name of the District	*Senior Basic Schools*				
	Number of Schools	*Number of Teachers*	*Number of Students*	*Teacher Pupil Ratio*	*Schools per Lack Population*
Chamoli	164	11937	543	21.98	23.53
Dehradun	309	35749	1552	23.03	24.16
Garhwal	398	34493	1162	29.68	57.11
Haridwar	139	25682	712	36.07	9.62
Rudraprayag	108	6955	379	18.35	47.48
Tehri Garhwal	380	22324	1099	20.31	62.85
Uttarkashi	175	7282	745	9.77	59.49
Garhwal	1573	144422	6112	23.63	32.00
Uttarakhand	2480	267459	10003	26.74	29.25

Source: Statistical Diary Uttarakhand, 2001-2002.

Attempt has also been made to analyze the position of higher secondary schools in the region. As is evident from the table the state has 1456 higher secondary schools accommodating 538903 students. It may be noted that 59.75 percent higher secondary schools are in the study area. While looking at the district figure it revealed that the number of schools are highest in Pauri and lowest in Uttarkashi whereas enrolled students are highest in Dehradun and lowest in Rudraprayag district.

Facilities for technical education have been provided in each district of Garhwal but their utilisation is below the capacity, as indicated by the number of seats available and those filled. It is reported that the persons trained at these institutions look for salaried jobs which are not available so easily while the government claim is that the technical training is imparted so as to provide the trainees better skill for carrying on his/ her technical profession more efficiently.

It has been observed that during nineties the expansion of telecommunication facilities have taken place in a rapid way. The situation of tele-communication and postal facilities were significantly poor in the entire region. The total dependence of the people for the use of these services was on the post offices and sub post offices spread in remotest parts of the region. From the following table it is evident to note that the region has 1525 post office branches which are highest in Pauri and lowest in Rudraprayag district. Similarly, the region has 553 telegraph offices proportionally distributed in all the districts. It may also be noted that the region is well served with bank branches of different types and these branches are proportionally distributed in all the districts (Table 2.17).

Table 2.17. Position of Higher Secondary Schools

Name of the District	*Higher Secondary Schools*		
	Number of Schools	*Number of Teachers*	*Number of Students*
Chamoli	87	35395	1327
Dehradun	139	78032	2305
Garhwal	259	65171	3145
Haridwar	77	49586	1411
Rudraprayag	83	15138	973
Tehri Garhwal	158	50291	2161
Uttarkashi	67	21402	729
Garhwal	870	315015	12051
Uttarakhand	1456	538906	19223

Source: Statistical Diary Uttarakhand, 2001-2002.

The banking facilities available in the region also depict the same. Even though the average number of persons served by each branch is more in district Dehradun than in each of the four districts of the region, the area covered by each branch is much larger. It is learnt that the commercial banks hesitate and avoid, as far as possible, in opening branches in the remote areas because it is not economically feasible due to lack of trade activities and for reasons of people's general poor economic conditions.

Public distribution system plays very important role in supplying foodgrains in the region. It may be noted that the farmers of the region has marginal holdings and not is a position to produce much which can meet out their annual requirement. The situation is further worst in the villages, which are not served with irrigational facilities. Therefore, the role of PDS system is very crucial as it take care of the food security of the people by making foodgrain and other items available at subsidized rates. For this purpose, there are a number of fair price shops, which are licensed by the civil supplies department of state government who also arranges the supplies to the licensees. This facility is also available at quite some distance to a large section of the population. This is again due to the low density of population, which cannot be helped ordinarily, and therefore, has to be accommodated by the people. Moreover, this should not be considered too bad because this shop is supposed to be visited at least twice or thrice by every household.

Table 2.18. Facilities of Communication, Banking and Fair Price Shops

Particulars	*Chamoli*	*Dehradun*	*Pauri*	*Haridwar*	*Rudraprayag*	*Tehri*	*Uttarkashi*	*Garhwal*	*Uttaranchal*
Post offices	233	250	433	117	115	275	129	1552	2683
Telegraph offices	72	81	87	23		75	15	553	715
Bank Branches									
Nationalised	34	143	65	89	—	49	23	403	618
Rural	14	14	37	1	—	24	4	94	86
Other Banks	36	166	98	95	20	69	27	515	847
Fair Price Shops	825	604	916	482	—	1023	403	4253	7326

Source: Statistical Diary Uttarakhand, 2001-2002.

The region is poorly developed in terms of establishment of industrial units. The region has 27622 small scale industries engaging 84105 people. The number of such units in the Garhwal region was reported 16112 which is 58.33 percent. The number of small scale units were reported highest in Hardwar district and lowest in Rudraprayag district. On the other hand, there are only 165 large and medium industrial units. The concentration of such units is mainly in Dehradun district. As shown in the Table the 72 large and medium industrial units provide employment to 22829 people (Table 2.18).

The analysis of Khadi and village industries reveals that the state has 15186 such units accommodating 25018 people. It is also evident that the region has 9001 khadi and village industries which is significantly higher. Total employment provided by these units was 11349. Among the various districts the number of such units was highest in Dehradun and lowest in Uttarkashi. The analysis of industrial data reveal that the industrial units have not grown speedily in the state. In the recent times the Government of Uttarakhand has invited entrepreneurs to invest in the state, giving them certain incentives. It is therefore suggested that attempt should be made to develop the industries of small and medium size based on the availability of raw material (Table 2.19).

Table 2.19. Number of Industrial Units and Employment (2001)

Name of	*Small*		*Large and Medium*		*Khadi and Village*	
	No.	*Employed*	*Public*	*Private*	*No.*	*Employment*
Chamoli	2549	5993	-	-	1379	1605
Dehradun	2557	8829	50	14052	2890	2838
Garhwal	2656	8396	7	1187	1323	3044
Haridwar	3659	12984	7	7080	1317	16902
Rudraprayag	48	87	-	-	-	-
Tehri Garhwal	2576	8173	8	29	905	1088
Uttarkashi	2067	5609	-	-	887	1172
Garhwal	16112	50001	72	22829	9001	11349
'Uttarakhand	27622	84105	165	46345	15186	25018

Source: Statistical Diary Uttarakhand, 2001-2002.

Table 2.20. Health Facilities in the Region

Name of the District	*Allopathic*					*Ayurvedic*		*Homeopathic*	
	No.	*Beds*	*Health Centres*	*Number of Hospital Per Lakh Population*	*Beds per lakh Popu-lation*	*No.*	*Bed*	*No.*	*Bed*
Chamoli	73	536	110	5.71	41.91	59	228	7	4
Dehradun	108	1926	117	36.71	654.70	37	104	8	4
Garhwal	120	1009	156	19.85	166.88	39	128	7	—
Haridwar	53	862	25	7.61	123.70	17	40	5	—
Rudraprayag	—	—	—	—	—	—	—	—	—
Tehri Garhwal	68	374	105	29.90	164.42	59	112	9	4
Uttarkashi	36	262	65	2.49	18.14	39	152	4	—
Garhwal	458	4971	581	9.32	101.13	250	764	40	12
Uttarakhand	783	8533	1016	9.23	100.63	366	1252	60	16

Source: Statistical Diary Uttarakhand, 2001-2002.

An attempt is also made to analyse the availability of health facilities in the region. It is pertinent to note that the state of Uttarakhand has 783 allopathic hospitals supported with 8533 beds. The number of allopathic hospitals in the study area was 458 with 5971 beds. The region also has 581 sub centres. The number of allopathic hospitals was reported highest in Dehradun and lowest in Uttarkashi District The region has 9.23 hospitals per lakh population, which is significantly low. It may also be noted that only 100 beds in the hospitals are available for one lakh people.

The region is poorly served in terms of qualitative health services. Non-availability of doctors in the hospitals severely effects the health systems in the state of Uttarakhand. In addition, the hospitals are not fully equipped with medicines and equipments. The doctors posted in the remote area are not willing to serve there. In case they are force-fully posted in the remote and rural area the cases of absenteeism are noticed. Therefore there is need to have proper policy framework to bump up better health facility to the people of the region.

The region offers a fascinating scenario. It has a complex physiography and diversified relief features. It consists of succession of deep gorges, steep hillsides, sharp and irregular ridges and rugged terrain on the one hand and plain and fertile valley on the other. It has been well-drained by numerous rivers and perennial gads, khuds and raos. Soils are highly diversified and vary from valley down to predominantly hilly districts. The forest wealth is rich in quality and abundant in quantity. Peculiar landuse practice is followed in the district with maximum area under forest followed by net area sown. The settlements are widely scattered, small in size and sparsely populated. Therefore, the physio-cultural dimensions reflects distinctive character of the district which is incidentally our study area.

3

Agricultural Practices

The agriculture of this region owes its existence to the forestry sector due to its dependence on the forests and at times more directly because of the age old tradition of agro-forestry itself. Broadly, three basic farming systems have been identified in the Central Himalaya, of which this region is a part. All the farming systems are livestock-based and form a spectrum of economic activities ranging from nomadic (practiced by Gujjars), trans-humane (Bhotias) to settled agriculture which is practiced by a majority of the people (Singh et al., 1984). Settled agriculture, a mixed 'crop livestock' farming system predominating over a broad range of altitudes between 300m and 2500m is organised as terraced agricultural fields on steep slopes and some times without terrace on gentle slopes of higher altitudinal areas. Mostly the size of terraces vary between 0.01 and 0.1 ha. Except for the narrow strips of Bhabar in the foothills and Doon valley where modern agriculture is practiced on flat land under irrigated conditions and the Haidwar district where totally different crop practices are followed, in rest of the mountains only about 15 percent land is under irrigation which is significantly low. In earlier times, along the warm temperature areas of the Garhwal slash and burn agriculture locally called as *Katil, Kureel* or *Khil* was a large scale practice (Pauw, 1896). However, now this practice is restricted to a few localities only (Negi, et al., 1997; Nautiyal et al., 1998). As such, majorities of the farmers are marginal and possess less than 1.0 ha. of agricultural land and that too in the scattered form. Owing to small and often scattered land holding in the region, livestock supplement the income and are considered to be capital asset. Animal dung and bedding material is an important farmyard manure for the crops in traditional agriculture. (Swaroop, 1993).

The traditional agriculture of the Garhwal is closely linked with forests and therefore essentially needs a massive input from it. According to an estimate 1 unit energy from agriculture requires 12 energy units from the forest biomass energy (Singh et al., 1994). Further, it has also been estimated that annually one hectare of cultivated land requires 11.5 t fodder, 7.4 t fuelwood and 3.4 t bedding leaves in the Central Himalaya (Singh et al., 1994). Until recently the agriculture of the Garhwal Himalaya was sustainable largely due to a large resource base. However, in recent years, reckless destruction of forests in the name of development, population growth, fragmentation of land holdings, the accelerated soil erosion etc. have adversely affected the sustainability of the agriculture system. These problems coupled with rapid socio-economic change are leading to ever growing process of land abandonment (Negi and Joshi, 1995). Large scale migration of young people from the region in search of new jobs to earn their livelihood has obvious impact in this regard. To quote Khanka (1985), 'about 30 to 40 percent of the working age population (15-35 years) has migrated to the plains'. Apart from the above, 10 percent decrease in the livestock population between 1972 and 1986 further confirms the current situation of the agriculture of the Garhwal Himalaya (Swaroop, 1993).

Agriculture Practices

The traditional settled agriculture of Garhwal Himalaya exhibits a great deal of variability in crop diversity, crop composition and crop rotations etc. along as altitudinal transect due to corresponding variations in a number of factors. As such, the region can be divided into three markedly different agroclimatic zones along the elevation gradient (vertical zonation) viz., lower altitude, 500 to 1000m, middle altitude between 1000 to 1800m and higher altitude, 1800 to 2500m and above. According to traditionally accepted criteria agricultural land in the region is identified either as the rainfed (locally known as *ukhar*) or the irrigated (known as *sera*). Of the two, the former is predominant form of land use since only about 15% land falls in the latter category. Based on the location of the land vis-a-vis village, generally rainfed land is further divided into two segments, namely *Mullasari* (below the village or lower segment) and *malla sari* (segment above the village).

Irrigated land is often confined to the river valleys of the lower altitude and some times in the small chunks as terraced agricultural fields of middle altitude where water is available. Traditionally, water is channelled from the river through *gools* (not cemented canals) to the agricultural fields. However, in the recent past canal (cemented) irrigation has also made its appearance in the region through governmental support. Mainly the spring fed rivers and small rivulets provide the irrigation water. Owing to difficult topography and lack of planning skills, irrigation through snowed rivers could not been utilised in the region so far despite the rich potential. In the higher altitudes, agriculture on the terraced and some times unterraced gentle slopes despite availability of water is entirely practiced under rainfed condition.

Mostly there are marginal farmers (above 68 per cent) in the region whose land holding usually ranges between 0.02 to 1.0 ha. Small land holders possessing 1.0 to 4.0 ha of agricultural land represent about 29 per cent while the big farmers having the land holding between 4.0 and 10.0 ha constitute only 3 per cent of the farming community. The total agricultural land occupied by each category mentioned above is 56 percent (maximum) for small farmers followed by marginal, 23.5 per cent and big farmers, 20.5 percent (minimum). The per capita land holding in the region is around 0.19 ha (Swarup, 1993). Further, it is interesting to mention here that across the altitudinal gradient, the per capita land holding is often significantly higher at higher altitude than middle and lower altitude. It is because of low population pressure and sometimes due to the encroachment upon the forest land by the high altitude inhabitants.

The cropping patterns, upto 1800m and some times up to 2000m are built around two major cropping seasons viz., kharif (April-October) and rabi (October-April). Kharif season crops occupy about 63 percent while rabi season crops about 59 per cent of the gross cropped area of the region with the cropping intensity of 159.29 per cent (Swarup, 1993). Paddy, finger millet, barnyard millet, foxtail millet, maize and pulses are the main crops of kharif season while rabi season includes crops like wheat, barley, mustard, lentils and peas. From the rainfed agriculture generally 3 crops are taken in every 2 years, while from irrigated land 2 crops are taken each year. However, sometimes in some lower altitude localities (< 1000 m) a third crop (intermediate crop) of hog millet (*Panicum meliacium*) is also taken from irrigated land between April and July, though on a smaller scale. Owing to cold climate conditions in higher altitude, particularly above 2000m, the cropping patterns are different from the above cropping seasons as most of the crops are cultivated between March and October (summer season crops). Interestingly, a unique variety of wheat is cultivated in some specific high altitude localities which takes as much as 12 months (September- August) to harvest. Contrary to the rainfed agriculture of lower and middle altitudes, where the land under mixed crop of finger millet and pulses in the kharif season remains fallow during rabi season for 6 months, at higher altitudes (> 2300m). It remains fallow after rabi season crops and that too for longer (10 months) period. Figures given below provide an overview on the crop compositions, cropping patterns and crop rotations practiced along an altitudinal transect in the region.

The diversity in the crop in this region is very high and about 40 different species of crops comprising cereals, pseudo cereals, millets, pulses, oilseeds etc. and their number of varieties are cultivated throughout the altitudinal gradient. Rainfed agriculture plays a significant role in the maintenance of crop diversity and often 2-6 crops are cultivated in mixed conditions. Generally, the diversity in the crops is maintained through mixed cropping and crop rotations. In the lower and middle altitudes cereals and millets (paddy, wheat, maize, barley, finger millet, barnyard millet etc.) are generally cultivated while at higher altitude cash crops (potato, amaranth, kidneybean, millets and pseudo cereals) find more prominence. The farmers of lower and middle altitude (up to 1500m) traditionally maintain a number of multipurpose trees (which further enhance the agriculture diversity) on the margins of their rainfed agricultural fields. These trees not only provide green fodder during lean period but also provide fuelwood and fibre. The important traditional agro forestry species are *Grewia optiva* (Bhimtal), *Boehmeria rugulosa* (Geethi), *Ficus roxburghii* (Timala), *F. glomerata* (Gular), *Celtis australis* (Kharik) and *Bauhinia variegata* (Gwiriyal) etc.

All across the agroclimatic zones, the agriculture is operated by human and bullock power. The role of women folk is so crucial that they are considered to be the backbone of the hill agriculture. These women folk perform agricultural operations ranging from field preparation, sowing, weeding, harvesting to threshing etc. The role of menfolk is however confined to ploughing and maintenance work on agricultural fields. In the households where male family members are not available for ploughing the same is hired. It has been observed that weeding (particularly during kharif season) extracts more than 45 per cent of the total human labour as three sessions of weeding have to be carried out to ensure better productivity. Bullock labour is used in ploughing and seldom in threshing activities of certain crops.

As far as the economic conditions of the farmers of different altitudes are concerned, the higher altitude farmers are economically better off than their lower and middle altitude counterparts. The major reasons being low population pressure, bigger land holding, greater accessibility to natural resources and more importantly suitable niche for specific cash crops that have great market demands nowadays. The comparatively poor economic condition of the farmers of lower middle altitudes to the factors like higher population pressure, smaller land holding and lesser accessibility to natural resources. The agriculture in lower zones has further suffered due to the influence of modern techniques, which are necessarily not suitable as also owing to the migration of young people, which is more pronounced here. The migrated people generally hand over their cultivable land to other persons (lessee) who cultivate the land and in turn give half or one third of the grain production to the owner of land (lessor). In such situations, the lessee does not pay due attention to the maintenance to the lessor's land, and as a consequence of this land degrades gradually. In some instances the absentee owners of the land have given their rights in favour of the actual operators (Swarup, 1993).

Crop Diversity

While talking about agriculture one often visualizes monotonous mono cropping system totally devoid of bio-diversity and energy subsidized which are prone to many diseases and perturbation. The biodiversity contributes in a variety of ways in maintaining agro-ecosystem stability and resilience (Ramkrishnan, et al., 1994). Recently, Altierie (1995) has described in detail the role of biodiversity in its functioning agro-ecosystem's resilience and stability.

Garhwal Himalaya is well known as repository of many crop species and their numerous varieties (Maikhuri et al., 1997). These are nurtured through a variety of crop compositions and crop rotations. But in the recent years the crop diversity of region has declined to an alarming proportion. Of the many reasons responsible for this declining trend, the unscientific change in the cropping patterns, change in the food habits of the inhabitants, declined natural resource base and consequently low grain productivity, replacement of traditional crops by high yielding varieties in lower and middle altitudinal zones and horticultural cash crops in high altitudinal areas (> 1500m) etc. are specially noteworthy. Consequently, there are few isolated pockets left in remote areas of the region where farmers still rely on the traditional crops. These traditional crops in no way are inferior or less productive than the introduced high yielding varieties (artificial varieties) as long as the natural resources are optimally but carefully utilised. Moreover, the byproduct (used as fodder) yield of the traditional crops is always higher than the high (grain) yielding varieties. This becomes significant when the prevailing fodder crises in the region particularly up to middle altitudinal areas is taken in to account. It has been estimated that the by-product yield of the crops meets only around 33 per cent of the total fodder demand needed per year per hectare of cultivated land (Singh et al., 1994). These crops are well adapted in the local environmental conditions and possess the inherent qualities to withstand the sudden outbreak of diseases, pests and natural hazards. This adaptability has, in fact, protected the hill farmers from absolute crop failure since millennia. Many of these crops also contain medicinal properties and used by the local people to cure different diseases (Maikhuri et al., 1991).

Studies conducted in different areas of the Garhwal Himalaya indicate that the area under cultivation to the various crops has significantly decreased over the last two decades, consequently, *Perilla frutlescence* (Perilla), *Macrotyloma uniflorum* (horsgram), *Sataria italica* (foxtail millet), *Panicum meliaceum* (hog millet) and many other traditional crops species have already fallen in the threatened category (Maikhuri, 1994, 97). Fortunately efforts are now afoot, though still sporadic, by some governmental and voluntary organisations to conserve the agricultural genetic variability of this region. Jardhar village of Henval valley of Tehri Garhwal district can be cited as an example, in this context. Here, Vijay Jardhari and his co-workers (volunteers) are involved in the collection of seeds of various traditional crops from different parts of the region under their 'save the seed' campaign. They are also trying to revive the old traditional agriculture in the valley. Such efforts may go a long way in creating the mega diversity of crop plants thereby contributing towards the sustainable development of agriculture in the region. The obvious contribution to these efforts to Indian agriculture ultimately in the context of global food problem should not be undermined.

Evidently, appropriate measures need to be urgently introduced in the region if the sustainability of the traditional agricultural system alongside the natural resources base is to be achieved. One of the effective strategy to this end could be planning agriculture not just as production system but an ecological system as well (see Ramkrishanan, 1992). Fortunately, with the renewed global interest in traditional agricultural system a positive trend in this direction has already set in. Mixed cropping, otherwise practiced by the traditional societies throughout the world, and which is also common in the Garhwal Himalaya, is once again receiving due attention. Alongside being a tool to enhance per unit area production, the traditional agriculture is also significant for controlling weeds and pests and is effective for the recycling of biomass (see Altieri, 1995). In fact, mixed cropping, along with the strengthening of agro forestry, effective soil and water management, weed control, optimum use of unused biomass, rehabilitation of abandoned and degraded land through technological inputs based on indigenous knowledge of the people offer considerable potential for augmenting the agricultural production of the region on a sustainable basis.

Agriculture in Garhwal has promoted diversified approach since yore days. The tremendous biodiversity has forced the people of the region to lead a tough life. On the one hand plain and fertile land of Hardwar district, narrow strips of Bhabar and Doon Valley provide highly fertile land, on the other Alaknanda valley in the middle altitudes motivates the farmers to opt for cultivation. The high altitudes with varying climatic conditions make the agriculture more difficult and sometimes all the efforts put in by the farmers are wasted due to natural calamities. The handwork put in by the women on the farmland make the agricultural practices more challenging. It is challenging because of its crop diversity. Nevertheless, agriculture is the only source of survival of some of the households at middle and high altitudes and concerted efforts are required from the state policy makers to understand the gravity of the problem so that it can be made economically sustainable venture.

Land Use Pattern

Remarkably, on account of hilly and mountainous terrain 16.5 percent of the total area lies under permanent snow cover and 70.5 percent has been classified under forests. As per the latest records available with the state statistical department only 11.91 percent of the total area in Garhwal region is under cultivation; whereas in the hilly part of Kumaon, percentage of cultivated area is slightly higher (17.61 percent) that is, in Garhwal reflects the varying conditions of altitude, climate and soil. In spite of the steep and rugged terrain of the region, the tremendous difficulties of the environment have not been able to suppress the initiative and energy of man. On the other hand, they have induced a high degree of adaptive skill and uncommon physical vigor to cope with the inhospitality of the environment.

Table 3.1. Districtwise Land Utilisation (Area in Hectare) (2001-02)

District	*1*	*2*	*3*	*4*	*5*	*6*	*7*	*8*	*9*	*10*
Chamoli	644395	439420	103110	11311	20845	13644	22105	57	1010	32903
	100.00	68.19	16.00	1.76	3.23	2.12	3.43	0.01	0.16	5.11
Dehradun	304894	207400	1864	19941	12690	53	4447	2497	4999	51002
	100.00	68.02	0.61	6.54	4.16	0.02	1.46	0.82	1.64	16.73
Pauri	752728	444341	32777	16748	42489	41449	58940	139	17048	98767
	100.00	59.03	4.35	2.22	5.64	5.51	7.83	0.02	2.26	13.12
Hardwar	233506	72475	2044	26320	2107	49	281	3173	2554	124503
	100.00	31.04	0.88	11.27	0.90	0.02	0.12	1.36	1.09	53.32
Rudraprayag	202682	87314	58028	6366	11733	7680	12442	32	568	18519
	100.00	43.08	28.63	3.14	5.79	3.79	6.14	0.02	0.28	9.14
Tehri	574542	397199	12927	11647	77013	3015	24	60	8874	63783
	100.00	69.13	2.25	2.03	13.40	0.52	0.00	0.01	1.54	11.10
Uttarkashi	817621	726290	19736	6758	8911	13648	7478	43	3792	30975
	100.00	88.83	2.41	0.83	1.09	1.67	0.91	0.01	0.46	3.79
Garhwal	3530378	2374429	230486	99091	175788	79538	105717	6001	38875	420452
	100.00	67.26	6.53	2.81	4.98	2.25	2.99	0.17	1.10	11.91
Kumaon	2061983	1124008	64279	67233	148655	149402	111316	5256	28169	363665
	100.00	54.51	3.12	3.26	7.21	7.25	5.40	0.25	1.37	17.64
Uttarakhand	5592361	3498447	294756	166324	324443	228940	217033	11257	67044	784117
	100.00	62.56	5.27	2.97	5.80	4.09	3.88	0.20	1.20	14.02

Note: The categories of land included 1. Reported Area, 2.Forest,3, Barren and Unculturable land, 4. Land Under Non Agriculture Uses, 5 Cultivable waste Land 6. Parmanent pasture and other grazing Land, 7. Area Under trees & Groves un included in the net sown area, 8. Current Fallow Land, 9. Other Fallow and 10 Net sown area.

The hilly region of Uttarakhand follow peculiar landuse pattern. On an average 62.56 percent area of the state is under forest, the coverage is more in Garhwal region (67.26 percent) than in the Kumaon region. Inter-district variation has also been noticed as forest coverage was reported highest in Uttarkashi district and lowest in Hardwar district which is significantly higher in Garhwal region.

The percentage of cultivated area varies from 16.73 percent in Dehradun district to 3.79 in Uttarkashi district. On account of flat-bottomed structural valley (Doon) of Dehradun tehsil, its percentage of cultivated area is relatively high. Otherwise in Middle altitude of Garhwal, comprising Pauri and Tehri districts, it is 13.12 and 11.10 respectively. On the other hands the recently included Hardwar districts follow different landuse practices which are not comparable with the other districts of Garhwal region. In Hardwar more than 50 percent area is reported under cultivation, which is significantly higher when compared with other districts of Garhwal region. Among the other categories of land, in Chamoli the area under barren and uncultivable waste constitutes 16 percent which is considerably higher and can be attributed to the availability of proportionally high altitudes and inaccessible land covered with snow round the year.

High alpine valley and high hilltops are covered with rich pasture from four to six months. Bhabar grass from the Bhabar area is collected and supplied to the Star Paper Mill (Sharanpur). Other pastures are insignificant and whatever exists are being depleted by overgrazing. On an average 2.25 per cent of Garhwal's area has been classified as permanent pasture. On account of the highly rugged terrain of Garhwal, there is almost no scope for any extension of cultivated area in this region. However the region can make significant contribution in the field of forestry, livestock raising and horticulture.

Among the other categories of land a significant proportion of land was reported cultivable waste and barren land which vary significantly among the various districts of the region. On the other hand the region has insignificant fallow land.

During the British period, peaceful conditions were revived and the ravages of Gorkha rule were more than compensated. Depopulation and abandonment of villages and fields occurred on a large scale during the Gorkha rule (1803-1815). During the British rule the population increased about five times between 1841 and 1941 from 1,30,000 to 6,00,000. On account to this increase in population, cultivation was extended to steeper slopes, and pastures were eliminated. Deforestation and overgrazing were practiced on a large scale. It accelerated the process of soil erosion. Pattis such as Manyarsyun, Banelsyun, Kanwalsyun and Bangrsyun of Pauri Garhwal district have been so badly affected by soil erosion that the places between 1,825 and 1,900 meters and above have almost been abandoned for agriculture and after every eight to ten years a single crop is raised. Another example is the Kuriya Patti of Talla Salan Pargana where due to the abundance of soil erosion the land totally been regarded unfit for cultivation as a result the land is being utilised for cattle grazing.

After the World War II, the retrenched soldiers of the armed forces and some of the pensioners were allotted land for resettlement in the bhabar area. Forests were not cleared but the wasteland was utilized for this purpose. This land is technically known as *kham* land and was under the ownership of the government. Oilseeds and sugarcane, generally grown as cash crops, are raised in Papinsnda and Saneh circles of Garhwal Bhabar. Practically the whole of the present cultivation in this area is confined to the tract irrigable by canals taken from the Khoh and the main rivers and other streams. The retired and retrenched army persons were so energetic and industrious that they have tried to achieve maximum production out of every piece of land, wherever irrigation was available. They produce rice, wheat, sugarcane, tobacco, oilseed and potato on commercial basis. Agriculture in Doon and Bhabar has benefited most from innovation of the Development Department. This trend is likely to be maintained in the future also.

The cropping pattern has also undergone considerable change in the Doon and Bhabar tracts. With the introduction of canal irrigation commercial crops were grown in many places. During the post-independence period, a large number of Punjabi refugees were settled in the Doon after clearing sparse forests. Being energetic and industrious, they have been successful in the extension of sugarcane cultivation and also in producing its highest yields in the eastern Doon particularly in the villages within the vicinity of Doiwala and Shyampur. Some such villages are Chhidarwala, Daishwala, Bhaniyawla and Markhamgrant. A block-wise analysis of changes in the cropping pattern of Garhwal between 1966-67 and 1975-76 has revealed that rice acreage decreased by more than 25 percent in Joshimath and Nagpur blocks and increased by more than 10 percent in Devprayag, Pratapnagar and Thauldhar blocks. Wheat acreage increased by more than 15 percent in Nagpur, Jakhinidhar and Doiwala and decreased by more than 10 percent in Dasoli and Tharali. Increase in the acreage of wheat and rice is related to the change in the area of millets (madua and jhangora) which is cultivated in those blocks which are characterized by highly rugged terrain having meager irrigation facilities. Joshimath, Khirsu and Pabo recorded an increase of more than 15 percent in the area of millets. The decrease in the acreage of millets varied from 19.3 to 26.3 percent in the blocks of Pratapnagar, Tehri, Thauldhar and Thailisan.

There has been slight change in the crop acreage of certain crops during the last five years between 1975-76 and 1980-81. The percentage of cropped area of wheat has increased during this period from 28.4 to 31.1. The cropped area of rice, maize and barley has also increased from 17.3, 2.7 and 2.3 to 18.6, 3.5 and 4.3 percent respectively. The area under pulses and oilseeds had declined from 3.0, 2.0 to 1.5, and 0.9 respectively. It seems that the area has been under reported on account of mixed cropping pattern across the Garhwal region..

Rotation of Crops

The people of the region have been practising a very skilful rotation of crops to preserve the fertility of soil. Through centuries of experimentation, they have evolved various types of crop rotation to suit the varied environmental settings and agronomic requirements. Out of varied crop rotations, three main types can be identified which are widely prevalent and common in Garhwal.

Two-year Rotation of Four Crops: Under this rotation four crops are grown in two years. In the first year, rice in Kharif and wheat in Rabi is grown. In the second year, maize in Kharif and mustard or potatoes in Rabi are sown. This rotation is practiced in the Doon and Bhabar. But in those tracts where sugarcane is cultivated, particularly in the east doon, this rotation is not practiced. In such tracts the most common rotation is: for three years continuously sugarcane; fourth year wheat and *toria;* fifth year again sugarcane. *Talaon* lands of the Middle Garhwal also grow four crops in two years. Rice in Kharif and wheat or barley in Rabi are grown every year under this rotation.

***Two-year Rotation of Three Crops*:** In the middle lands of the Sub-tropical zone (900-1800 m) of Garhwal, peasants practice a standard two-year rotation of three crops. For the sake of this crop rotation, the cultivated area of the village is divided into two *sars* based on different crop rotation. In two years, the rotation is complete. *Sar* is method of cultivation and crop rotation in which the same crop is grown in a large compact area of contiguous plots. The village headman allots a definite rotation to each *sar*.

In the temperate zone (1800-2400 m), there is a slight change in the pattern of crops on account of low temperature, however sar system is also followed in this zones. At very high altitudes the major crops grown are Cahulai, ramadana, faphar, rajma and potatos. Due to sever climatic conditions mixed cropping pattern is followed. The cultivation starts once migratory households reaches at the high altitude. They remain their form mid May to mid October. The fields remain uncultivated during winter.

The average crop intensity of the Uttarakhand State comes out to 160.61 and the percentage of double cropped is proportionally higher in Kumaon (169.90) region than in Garhwal region (152.50). Among the various district Tehri and Rudraprayag have reported marginally higher crop intensity of 162.19 and 161.69 respectively over other districts. Even the crop intensity of Tehri district is higher than the state average.

Table 3.2. District-wise Crop Intensity (Area in hectares) 1999-2000

District	*Net Area Sown*	*Area Sown More Than Once*	*Gross Cropped Area*	*Crop Intensity*
Chamoli	32903	17255	50158	152.44
Dehradun	51002	27063	78065	153.06
Pauri	98767	52240	151007	152.89
Hardwar	124503	55269	179772	144.39
Rudraprayag	18519	11443	29962	161.79
Tehri	63783	39669	103452	162.19
Uttarkashi	30975	17799	48774	157.46
Garhwal	420452	220738	641190	152.50
Kumaon	363665	254536	618201	169.99
Uttarakhand	784117	475274	1259391	160.61

Ecological Zones of Agriculture and Their Cropping Patterns

Climate is one of the most important ecological factors and the altitude in Garhwal primarily influences it. From the ecological point of view, Garhwal can be divided into the following altitudinal zones with slight modification in S.D. Kaushic's scheme. These ecological zones offer favorable conditions for certain specific crops only. For example, rice, *kauni* and *jhangora* would not grow above 1950 m. *Kodo* grows upto 2400 m. Potato is both a summer and winter crop in different altitudinal zones. Wheat, barley and red beans are winter crops below 2400 m and summer crops above this altitude upto 3600 m, *Phaphra* or buckwheat is a very handy crop which can be grown even without irrigation upto 3600 m. *Chua* or *massa* is grown upto 2850 m. *Uva* or naked barley is a crop of cool-temperature and cold zone and is cultivated between 2100 m and 3600 m. Pulses are not grown above 1,800 m and their altitudinal limits are as follows: Urd (Red kindney bean)-1350; Arhar or Tor (*Cajanus indicus*)- 1,200 m; Gahath (horse gram)- 1,800 m. Bhat or Soybean - 1,800 m.

Table 3.3. Ecological Zones of Agriculture

Ecological Sub-regions	*Altitude in meters*	*Chief Crops*
I. Sub-tropical Zone	300-600	Wheat, Rice, Sugarcane
(a) Lower Doon and Bhabar		Wheat, Rice, Madua,
(b) Upper Doon and Lower Garhwal	600-900	Jhangora, Chua, Maize Wheat, Rice, Madua,
(c) Middle Garhwal	900-1800	Jhangora, Chua, Kauni, Potato, Barley, Gahath, Bhat, Chhemi (Rajmah)
II. Cool-Temperature Zone Upper Garhwal	1,800-2,400	Wheat, Barley, Potato, Chhemi, Phaphra
III Cold-Zone	2,400-3,600	Summer Crop Zone Wheat, Barley, Potato, Chhemi, Phaphra, Chua, Kauni, Ogal or Koto, Uva, Beans

Crop-Combination Regions and Cropping Pattern

Crop combinations have been identified on the basis of J.C. Welvers' method as modified by Kikulazu Doi. The principle of combination analysis has proved to be an important tool of statistical studies in various fields of Agricultural Geography. The concept of crop regions is not an end in itself. Such a study is essential and useful for demarcating more complex agricultural regions. Crops occupying less than one percent of the total cropped area have not been considered, since they occupy an insignificant acreage. The data refers to the year 1999-2000.

So far as the crop-diversification is concerned it is interesting to note that in the six surveyed blocks six different crop combinations are practiced. In general two crops are grown in a year. Crops are primarily combined with wheat, rice and millets. The crop combination with wheat includes wheat, barley, masoor and channa, whereas crop combination with Rice includes rice, Jhangora, Kauni and the crop combination with millets includes *kodo, naduwa, chua, ramdana* and pulses like kulath, moong, swanth, bhatt, soybean, rains, urad etc. It is noticed that more than 50 percent area is occupied by wheat and rice except Joshimath block and the same was noticed 77.46 percent in Bhatwari block. The table also reveals that no compact farming zone is witnessed in any block, however two crop combinations are followed in each block. Joshimath block is exception and no crop is reported as dominating crop in the block.

Table 3.4. Crop-Combination and Cropped Area in Surveyed Region (In Percent)

Name of the Block	*Total Cropped Area (ha)*	*Rank and Percentage of Crops*					*Crop Combi-nations*
		1st	*2nd*	*3rd*	*4th*	*5th*	
Chamba	10,772	W-38.3	R-24.0	M-11.8	J-11.6	PU-4.6	WRMJ
Pratapnagar	10,346	W-35.2	R-23.8	M-10.9	B-10.5	J-9.2	WRMB
Bhatwari	7,193	W-54.4	R-23.06	M-11.3	J-6.9	PU-5.7	WR
Purola	12,618	R-33.8	W-24.2	M-21.4	J-8.1	PU-5.2	RWM
Joshimath	5,175	M-18.7	W-17.0	P-13.5	J-9.8	R-8.0	MWPJR
Pokhari	10,966	W-21.3	R-24.6	M-23.7	J-2.7	P-2.1	WRM

Attempt has also been made to assess crop combination of different crops in all the districts of Garhwal region. It may be noted that crop combination of two crops is followed in the entire region except in narrow strip of Bhabar, Doon valley and Hardwar district. Wheat and Rice are the two leading crops and other crops are primarily combined with them in the hilly parts of Uttarakhand. Area under Wheat was reported maximum except in Dehradun and Uttarkashi districts. It is interesting to note that in all the districts different crop-combination is followed. As evident from the table, in Chamoli the combination is wheat-rice-barley- pulses-maize (WRBPM) whereas in Dehradun it was rice-wheat-maize-pulses-barley (RWMPB) and the crops are differently combined in other districts. Even dissimilarities has been noticed in the combination of Garhwal and Kumaon.

Garhwal has been divided into three first-order regions on the basis of first ranking crops and the second order sub-regions on the basis of first ranking crops. The region has dominance of three crops

Table 3.5. Area, Production and Productivity of Major Food Crops (1999-2000)

	Rice			*Maize*			*Wheat*			*Barley*		
	A	*P*	*Pro*	*A*	*P*	*Pro*	*A*	*P*	*Pro*	*A*	*P*	*Pro*
Chamoli	11927	15271	12.80	182	169	9.29	15090	17411	11.54	1330	1523	11.45
Dehradun	13597	27992	20.59	12614	16557	13.13	23241	33199	14.28	1644	1468	8.93
Pauri	28880	32536	11.27	2860	2907	10.16	42361	42950	10.14	7950	6238	7.85
Hardwar	25087	54886	21.88	2785	4263	15.31	47177	115914	24.57	111	265	23.87
Rudraprayag	8871	10801	12.18	171	178	10.41	9802	11356	11.59	1057	860	8.14
Tehri	16079	23277	14.48	2477	2790	11.26	33827	30761	9.09	2995	2835	9.47
Uttarkashi	12188	19897	16.33	517	506	9.79	15206	16270	10.70	395	522	13.22
Garhwal	116629	184660	15.83	21606	27370	12.67	186704	267861	14.35	15482	13711	8.86
Kumaon	185457	368317	19.86	13911	15112	10.86	199993	416314	20.82	11618	12167	10.47
Uttarakhand	302086	552977	18.31	35517	42482	11.96	386697	684175	17.69	27100	25878	9.55

Note: A—Area, P—Production, Pro.—Productivity.

Table 3.6. Area, Production and Productivity of Oilseeds (1999-2000)

	Mustard			*Til*			*Soyabean*			*Oil seeds*			*Sunflower*		
	A	*P*	*Pro*	*A*	*P*	*Pro*	*A*	*P*	*Pro*	*A*	*P*	*Pro*	*A*	*P*	*Pr*
Chamoli	529	441	8.34	44	5	1.14	120	50	4.17	164	55	3.35	0	0	0.00
Dehradun	1272	1049	8.25	548	95	1.73	2	1	5.00	784	293	3.74	8	10	12.50
Pauri	454	378	8.33	220	27	1.23	144	60	4.17	364	87	2.39	1	1	10.00
Hardwar	525	439	8.36	608	109	1.79	3	1	3.33	3680	2691	7.31	54	66	12.22
Rudraprayag	0	0	0.00	0	0	0.00	0	0	0.00	0	0	0.00	0	0	0.00
Tehri	827	689	8.33	941	60	0.64	331	138	4.17	822	198	2.41	0	0	0.00
Uttarkashi	828	690	8.33	809	100	1.24	100	41	4.10	909	141	1.55	4	5	12.50
Garhwal	4435	3686	8.31	2720	396	1.46	700	291	4.16	6723	3465	5.15	67	82	12.24
Kumaon	9019	7546	8.37	276	31	1.12	3057	1350	4.42	3386	1392	4.11	1928	2415	12.53
Uttarakhand	13454	11232	8.35	2996	427	1.43	3757	1641	4.37	10109	4857	4.80	1995	2497	12.52

Table 3.7. Area, Production and Productivity of Pulses (1999-2000)

	Gram			*Peas*			*Arhar*			*Masoor*			*Urad*		
	A	*P*	*Pro*	*A*	*P*	*Pro*	*A*	*P*	*Pro*	*A*	*P*	*Pro*	*A*	*P*	*Pr*
Chamoli	0	0	0.00	21	21	10.00	117	70	5.98	76	55	7.24	419	112	2.67
Dehradun	164	143	8.72	194	199	10.26	104	62	5.96	932	675	7.24	576	155	2.69
Pauri	66	58	8.79	28	29	10.36	526	313	5.95	903	655	7.25	3160	847	2.68
Hardwar	113	99	8.76	241	247	10.25	48	30	6.25	2583	1181	4.57	27	7	2.59
Rudraprayag	0	0	0.00	0	0	0.00	0	0	0.00	0	0	0.00	0	0	0.00
Tehri	21	19	9.05	213	218	10.23	702	418	5.95	1167	846	7.25	1422	381	2.68
Uttarkashi	3	3	10.00	111	114	10.27	183	109	5.96	402	291	7.24	703	188	2.67
Garhwal	367	322	8.77	808	828	10.25	1680	1002	5.96	6063	3703	6.11	6307	1690	2.68
Kumaon	812	719	8.85	1557	1616	10.38	121	73	6.03	10614	7696	7.25	2908	779	2.68
Uttarakhand	1179	1041	8.83	2385	2444	10.25	1801	1075	5.97	16677	11399	6.84	9215	2469	2.68

Table 3.8. Area, Production and Productivity of Commercial Crops

	Tobacco			Potato			Onion			Ground nut			Sugarcane		
	A	*P*	*Pro*	*A*	*P*	*Pro*	*A*	*P*	*Pro*	*A*	*P*	*Pro*	*A*	*P*	*Pr*
Chamoli	1	7	70.00	1756	40067	228.17	39	473	121.28	0	0	0.00	0	0	0.00
Dehradun	18	127	70.56	1350	30803	228.17	70	850	121.43	234	197	8.42	6374	389655	611.32
Pauri	7	49	70.00	361	8237	228.17	350	4251	121.46	0	0	0.00	1	59	590.00
Hardwar	87	522	60.00	531	11405	214.78	21	253	120.48	3069	2581	8.41	61827	3840446	621.16
Rudraprayag	0	0	0.00	0	0	0.00	0	0	0.00	0	0	0.00	0	0	0.00
Tehri	21	148	70.48	1464	33404	228.17	111	1348	121.44	0	0	0.00	0	0	0.00
Uttarkashi	22	155	70.45	2118	48326	228.17	21	255	121.43	0	0	0.00	0	0	0.00
Garhwal	156	1008	64.62	7580	172242	227.23	612	7430	121.41	3303	2778	8.41	68202	4230160	620.24
Kumaon	60	423	70.50	7637	174254	228.17	757	9194	121.45	53	11	2.08	44257	2764096	624.56
Uttarakhandl	216	1431	66.25	15217	346497	227.70	1369	16624	121.43	3356	2789	8.31	112457	6994258	621.95

such as rice, wheat, and maduwa. Most of the crop combinations are based on varying ranks of three crops of wheat, madua and rice. It is significant to note that *Jhangora* occupies the important rank. Wheat is a common crop on both *talaon* and *upraon* land, but rice generally flourish on talaon lands. Madua and Jhangora are grown on Upraon and Katil lands. The distributional pattern of each of these crops reflects differences in the availability of water, nature of terrain, altitude and method of cultivation.

Area, Production and Productivity

Agriculture production depends on many physical and socio-economic factors, such as - soil, irrigation, fertilizers, seeds and improved agro-economic practices. In Garhwal region as stated earlier a peculiar land use pattern is followed, which is primarily determined by altitudes which varies significantly from 300 metres in Doon Valley and Bhabar areas to 3600 metres in cold zones. As a result the crops grown also vary significantly. However, there are some crops which are grown at all the altitude with varying yield per hectare. In this section an attempt is being made to analyse the area, production and productivity of major crops under different heads.

Foodgrains: As stated earlier the region spread over a huge area with varying altitude. The productivity is determined by various factors. The average productivity for rice for Uttarakhand was reported 18.31 quintal per hectare which is marginally lower in Garhwal i.e., 15.83 quintal per hectare. Among the different districts the productivity of rice is relatively higher in Dehradun and Hardwar districts which is 20.59 and 21.88 quintal per hectare. The lower Song valley is gifted with fertile land, hence it records the highest yields of rice, wheat and sugarcane in the whole of Garhwal. Fertile and comparatively deep clayey-loam soils, abundant sources of underground and surface water and industrious peasants make it agriculturally the most productive tract of Garhwal.

The irrigated fertile lands of the lower Song Basin and the alluvial terraces of Ganga at Shaympur and Bhogpur villages produce 30 to 50 quintals of rice per hectare. In the irrigated talaon lands it ranges between 30 and 35 Q/H. In the upper Doon and upraon lands of middle Garhwal, the production of rice varies from 5 to 15 Q/H, depending on irrigation facilities. The average yield of rice for Garhwal is 15.83

quintals per hectare. The highest yields of wheat in Garhwal was recorded in the Lower Song valley and on the alluvial terraces of the Ganga, where the yields ranges between 30 and 40 Q/H. The second tract of high yields is about 20 Q/H. In other areas the yield varies from 7 to 15 Q/H and the average for Garhwal is 1 4.35 quintals per hectare. On the other hand the average yield per hectare accounts for 24.57 quintals for wheat. Hardwar district has recorded higher average yields for wheat, maize, rice and barley than the other districts of Garhwal. The average yields in Alaknanda basin for these crops is also higher. Madua is generally grown on unirrigated land with poor soils of uproan and katil lands, hence its yield vary considerably over the region. The highest yield of 13.5 Q/H is recorded in Chamoli district whereas the lowest yield of 6.6 Q/H is recorded in Dehradun District. The average yield for the whole of Garhwal is 9.99 Q/H. The yield of maize is quite low, 9 to 15 Q/H on the poor lands of upper doon; but it is quite high, 30 Q/H, on the talaon lands of Nagau village in Kalsi block. The average yield for Garhwal is 12. 67 Q/H.

Oilseeds: The important crops under oilseeds included mustard, til, soybean, oilseeds and sunflower. The average yield of mustard for the state of Uttarakhand was recorded 8.35 quintal per hectare with no significant variation in Garhwal and Kumaon regions and even the inter district variation is also not very high. On the other hand similar pattern has been witnessed for til, however, the variation is marginally higher as it was reported 1.12 quintal per hectare in Kumaon and 1.46 quintal per hectare in Garhwal. However inter-district variation is quite steep as it was reported 0.64 quintal per hectare in Uttarkashi and 1.79 quintal per hectare in Hardwar.

While analyzing the productivity of soybean it is revealed that it is primarily grown in the hilly districts of Garhwal. The high altitude climate and soil is more suitable for production of soybean, moreover it gets least preference in the plain and fertile doon valley, bhabar strips and Hardwar districts over other commercially viable crops. The average yield per hectare was reported 4.16 for Garhwal region which is slightly lower than the state average. While looking at the districts picture it is noticed that Dehradun district has higher yield per hectare. On the other hand sunflower is predominantly grown in Dehradun and Hardwar districts of the region with average yields of 12.50 and 12.22 quintals per hectare respectively.

Pulses: Important pulses of the region included gram, peas, arhar, masoor and urad besides *kulath, tur, moong, rains, rajma etc* which are widely produced and consumed in the region. The yield of gram, peas, arhar, masoor, and urad was recorded 8.77,10.25,.5.96, 7.24 and 2.67 quintal per hectare respectively. No significant variation has been noticed in the yields of various districts.

Commercial crops: Among the commercial crops sugarcane and potato are very important crops in the region. The average yield of sugarcane is 621.95 quintal per hectares. Sugarcane is primarily cultivated in three zones viz. Doon Valley, *Bhabar* strips and Hardwar district. The average yield for sugarcane was reported 611 and 621 Q/H for Dehradun and Hardwar districts respectively. On the other hand, the area is best suited for potato cultivation and *pahari potato* is in more in demand and can fetch more money to the cultivators. The average yield for potato was reported 227.23 Q/H and no much variation has been noticed across the state. Similar trend has been noticed for onion, nevertheless, the average yield for onion was recorded 121.41 Q/H.

Table 3.9. Districtwise Irrigated Area by Source in Garhwal Himalaya

District	*Canals*	*Tubewells*	*Private Tubewells*	*Other wells*	*Other Sources*	*Total*
Chamoli	1403	0	0	0	1126	2529
	55.48	0.00	0.00	0.00	44.52	7.69
Dehradun	9450	1950	419	89	12059	23967
	39.43	8.14	1.75	0.37	50.32	46.99
Pauri	3057	263	0	0	4670	7990
	38.26	3.29	0.00	0.00	58.45	8.09
Hardwar	16657	5483	76478	919	1756	101293
	16.44	5.41	75.50	0.91	1.73	81.35
Rudraprayag		0	0	0	0	0
	0.00	0.00	0.00	0.00	0.00	0.00
Tehri	1037	0	0	0	8241	9272
	11.18	0.00	0.00	0.00	88.88	12.98
Uttarkashi	3350	0	0	0	1887	5237
	63.97	0.00	0.00	0.00	36.03	16.91
Garhwal	34954	7696	76897	1008	29739	150294
	23.26	5.12	51.16	0.67	19.79	35.75
Kumaon	65353	15968	74675	18610	14794	189475
	34.49	8.43	39.41	9.82	7.81	52.10
Uttarakhand	100307	23664	151572	19618	44533	339769
	29.52	6.96	44.61	5.77	13.11	43.33

In Garhwal 35.75 percent of the net sown area is under irrigation which is fairly low in comparison to the Kumaon region (52.10 percent). Hardwar (81.35 percent) and Dehradun (46.99) have better irrigational facilities. Chamoli has only 7.69 percent area under irrigation. Among the various sources, canal irrigates proportionally large area in Chamoli and Uttarkashi districts. Whereas in Hardwar district private tube well is major source of irrigation. The overall situation of irrigation facilities particularly in the hilly districts is not very encouraging and no serious attempt has been made to ensure irrigational facilities in these districts.

Food Deficiency

Deficient agricultural production is widely known fact about the mountain environment. This deficiency is partly compensated by animal products. But in Garhwal animal products are also falling short of requirement for the growing population. Garhwal was subsistence-agriculture society till the country got freedom and motorable roads traversed the area. Surplus foodgrains were sold at pilgrim routes and in the mandis of Bhabar. Now with the increasing population the scenario has changed completely. The availability of foodgrains, pulses and oilseeds has been calculated per capita per hectare day after deducting ten per cent for seed and wastage. It may be noticed that per day average foodgrain available in Garhwal was reported only 267.50 grams. The situation is relatively better in Kumaon region.

Table 3.10. Food Availability Per Day in Grams (2001)

		Production in MT			*Availability per day /Grams*		
District	*Population*	*Food grains*	*Oilseeds*	*Pulses*	*Food grains*	*Oil-seeds*	*Pulses*
Chamoli	369198	32900	551.00	258.00	244.14	4.09	1.91
Dehradun	1279083	77797	1448.00	1234.00	166.64	3.10	2.64
Pauri	696851	78442	553.00	1902.00	308.40	2.17	7.48
Hardwar	1444213	175112	3306.00	1564.00	332.19	6.27	2.97
Rudraprayag	227461	22384	0.00	0.00	269.61	0.00	0.00
Tehri	227461	56877	1085.00	1882.00	685.07	13.07	22.67
Uttarkashi	294179	36722	977.00	705.00	342.00	9.10	6.57
Garhwal	4915593	479940	7920.00	7545.00	267.50	4.41	4.21
Kumaon	3563969	799792	12734.00	10883.00	614.82	9.79	8.37
Uttarakhand	8479562	1279683	20654.00	18428.00	413.46	6.67	5.95

Division which has improved the overall situation of availability of foodgrains in Uttarakhand. Among the districts of the region, Tehri Garhwal is better off in terms of availability of foodgrains, whereas situation in Dehradun is very poor. Which is probably due to rapid growth in the urban population which has acceeded rural population. While analyzing the availability of oilseeds and pulses in the region, it is surprising to note that only about 4 grams of oilseeds and pulses are available per day.

Availability of cereals is comparatively more favorable than that of pulses and oilseeds. Availability of pulses range from 1.91 gram in Chamoli district to 22.67 grams in Tehri district. Average per capita availability of oilseeds is 4.21 grams a day, which represents one-fourteenth of the requirement. Adjustment to the deficiencies of pulses can be found in non-vegetarian diets of people and the deficiency of oils is partly compensated by animal fats (ghee). Diminishing forest area has affected the number of livestock adversely. Such conditions are leading to overall deficiency of proteins and carbohydrates in the diets of rural people. Families, receiving regular money order remittances from migrant relatives can only afford to purchase pulses and oil from market.

Pulses and oilseeds also suffer from under-reporting on account of mixed cropping pattern in which only the main crops are reported in the statistics, and these are seldom grown as main crops. Probably oilseeds do not yield well under low temperature conditions, which has preference of farmers for other crops.

Except the rural area of the Doon, most of the hilly areas suffer from deficiency of foodgrains. In most of the villages in middle Garhwal, local production of foodgrains meets requirement for three to nine months. In Chakrata tehsil, rice is supplied through fair price shops and peak values are maintained from April to August. Similar pattern is observed in the case of Tehri district, but deficiency of wheat also prevails here as reflected in regular import of wheat after the rabi harvest. In the main valleys food deficiency is more than double that of its tributaries. There is general food deficiency in the vicinity of towns. Mid July to Mid September are very vulnerable months in the region when the stocks of the households is totally exhausted and bad weather conditions aggravate the problem. Therefore, a proper planning is required to ensure the timely supply of foodgrains through PDS systems during this period.

The increasing deficiency of cereal crops reveals clearly that self-sufficiency in the production of foodgrains is not feasible, more emphasis should be given to pulses, oilseeds, potato, marsa, beans, fruits, vegetables so that agriculture becomes more remunerative and diet is nourished. Cereal farming over steep slopes (above 24^0) should be replaced by horticulture for maintenance of ecological balance in the area. Existing and developing network of roads is leading to a satisfactory distribution of foodgrains through fair price shops.

Future Scope in Agriculture

The Garhwali peasants carry on their traditional agriculture in the face of problems created by mountainous terrain, poor soils, adverse climate and natural hazards. These problems are accentuated by their small uneconomic holdings. They take out only a meager living from their subsistence agriculture. The problem of land development differs from region to region. The agricultural development programmes need to be recast on an agro-climatic basis at micro levels. It should aim at utilizing micro-peculiarities of environment. This can be done by growing winter vegetables in plains during summers. Cultivation of mango in the lower valley may be quite beneficial. Tomato cultivation during rainy season may prove highly remunerative. Similarly, mushroom cultivation has been widely advocated. Area under *ramadana, cholai* need to be enhanced so that this may become a commercial crop. There is sufficient scope for the development of agriculture through intensive mixed farming where animal husbandry, dairy farming and horticulture are integrated with the economy of the small farm. There is also considerable room for the development of poultry as a subsidiary industry provided imported stocks are available and proper guidance in poultry farming is provided.

The energy of the villagers is spent merely in the bare struggle for survival so that all talk of development and increasing production sounds rather hallow. The overwhelming majority of the fields are not irrigated at all. The farthermost fields are not only very small but are also scattered widely. Proper terracing is seldom undertaken and soil conservation measures are neglected. The yields are low and important land management has become yet another factor in the vicious circle making for ecological disaster in the Himalaya. Excepting in Purola and Naugaon blocks of Uttarkashi district, villages in Garhwal do not have any marketable surplus in agriculture and animal husbandry or work as labours in the forest or in road construction project in their off-season. Bench-terracing with slight slope inward and contour-strip-cropping in which alternate rows of erosion permitting (cereals) and erosion-resisting (pulses and legumes) crops are grown must be encouraged on large scale as a soil-conservation measure. Over uproan land lift-cum-sprinkle irrigation may prove boon. It would be beneficial to keep fewer milch cattle of better quality and as the situation improves, to stall-feed rather than graze them.

4

Prospects of Horticulture in Uttarakhand

Uttarakhand constitutes a diverse geophysical, sociocultural, agro-economic and environmental entity. About 78 per cent of the people in the region primarily depend on farming as a primary livelihood. Unlike the plains that have witnessed the success of Green Revolution, mountain farming till date has remained at the subsistence level, still dependent on forest-based resources including fodder and fuelwood. The scattered land holdings with dominance of marginal farmers and poor irrigational facilities with rainfed farming, the agriculture production is also relatively low. As a result the agricultural produce does not fetch high returns and the output is not even enough to meet year-round food needs of the farmers and the surplus production is distant reality. The monsoon months are considered to be the months of greatest vulnerability primarily due to non-availability of work and poor food stock. This state of destitution instigate many of the men here migrate to the cities within the state and even outside state in search of job. Though agricultural production could be increased through external inputs, irrigation and new high-yielding varieties of crops, nevertheless the green revolution techniques are not appropriate for this terrain. Subsistence agriculture, organic production and diversification hold the key to sustainable economic reforms and development. However, practices that help this process include horticulture which include growing vegetables and fruits. The space farming may also enhance cash income to the farmers of this region, besides mushroom cultivation and medicinal plants, bee keeping and fruit and vegetable processing. The Himalayan environment is suitable for all these. Despite the huge potential for traditional and cash crop cultivation in small pockets, due attention was not paid to harness diversified agriculture practices to a full extent as a result the sector could not gain the required impetus.

India contributes nearly 10 percent to world fruit production. Temperate fruits like apple, walnut, pears, peach, apricot and plum are grown in Himachal Pradesh, Jammu and Kashmir, Uttarakhand and other eastern hilly states of India. This chapter presents the current status of fruits and vegetables production in Uttarakhand which has favourable climate for cultivation of different varieties of fruits including apple, pear, perch, plum, apricot, walnuts, mango, guava, lichi, grapes, banana etc., as well as vegetables such as potato, peas, tomatoes lady's finger and creeper vegetables which are commonly known as *bailwali* vegetables including bitter guard, pumpkins, guard etc. Besides, climatic conditions also favours cultivation of spices including ginger, garlic, turmeric, chillies, cardamom, coriander etc. Since horticulture is a major source of cash income, which enable them to complete the social and household commitment including the continuation of schooling of their children, participation in religious and social ceremonies and nutrient food and supply of food in the month of greatest vulnerability.

Area and Production of Fruits

Considering the importance of fruits and vegetables an attempt has been made to assess the spatial distribution in terms of area, orchards and production of fruits across the region. Apple is the predominant temperate fruit crop of India which accounts for about 10 per cent of the total fruit production of the country. At present these Delicious group mainly includes Star King Delicious and Red Delicious which constitute nearly 80 per cent of apple trees. Although India ranks 10th in world production of apple, yet the decreasing trend in productivity of its orchards, in the last decade due to changing climatic conditions has caused a serious concern to the fruit growers and planners of the country. Several factors like inadequate pollinizer proportion, reduction in natural population of pollinating agents, inadequate winter chilling, occurrence of spring frosts, hails and gales, nutrient deficiencies, droughts etc. are the main factors leading to poor fruit setting in Delicious. More than 70 per cent of orchards have less than 20 per cent pollinizer proportion, whereas a minimum of 25 per cent is required in our agroclimatic conditions for good fruit cultivation. Moreover, there is lack of diversity in pollinizing cultivars as mainly Golden Delicious and Red Gold are being predominantly used which have attained biennial bearing tendency and their bloom seldom coincides with the flowering period of Delicious cultivars. The population of natural pollinators has gone down due to indiscriminate use of pesticides and deterioration in ecosystem. Managed bee pollination is very limited and available bee hives during bloom hardly meet 2-3 per cent of the demand. All these factors have led to poor fruit setting of Delicious. In the Garhwal region of Uttarakhand, total area under fruit cultivation was reported 88384.25 hectares with the production of 427286.98 metric tonnes. Area under fruits orchards was highest in Dehradun (24270 ha), whereas the production was highest in Chamoli (93992 mt).

Table 4.1. Total Area and Production Under Fruits (Ha/MT) 2004-05

District	*Area*	*Production*
Chamoli	10737.00	93992.00
Uttarkashi	5252.11	45688.00
Hardwar	11787.07	103583
Rudraprayag	13999.27	115318
Tehri	18625.01	17860.2
Pauri	3713.79	15845.78
Dehradun	24270.00	35000.00
Total	88384.25	427286.98

Apple cultivation is today widely recognized in the Hindu Kush Himalayan region for the successful diversification of subsistent mountain agriculture into cash crop farming. There are niches in the entire Hindu Kush Himalayan region countries where, due to apple farming, socio-economic conditions of marginal mountain farmers have significantly improved during the last four decades. The future sustainability of apple farming, however, has become a matter of concern due to changing climate, shifting apple production areas, the fall in productivity due to pollination failure, emerging new pest and disease problems and the challenges of trade liberalization.

While analysing the data for entire state it is revealed that the total area under fruits during 2004-05 was reported 176003 hectares and the production during the same year was 667040 metric tonnes with a productivity of 3.8 metric tonnes per hectare. The area was highest in Garhwal region (11.273 hectares), whereas production was highest in the Kumaon region with 353375 metric tonnes. As a result the productivity of fruits in Kumaon region was 5.41 metric tonnes per hectare which was relatively higher than the productivity of fruits in Garhwal region which was 2.84 metric tonnes per hectare.

Table 4.2. Districtwise Area, Production and Productivity in Uttarakhand (2004-05)

Sl. No.	*District*	*Fruits*		
		Area	*Production*	*Productivity*
1.	Nainital	24270.60	80000.00	3.30
2.	Udham Singh Nagar	4101.00	28319.00	6.91
3.	Almora	9419.20	178667.90	18.97
4.	Bageshwar	2986.66	16092.10	5.39
5.	Pithoragarh	14208.00	34100.00	2.40
6.	Champawat	10344.00	16200.00	1.57
	Total Kumaon	65329.46	353379.00	5.41
7.	Dehradun	78771.58	92220.08	1.17
8.	Pauri	3738.46	12519.18	3.35
9.	Tehri	3693.38	9684.98	2.62
10.	Chamoli	5736.85	55036.00	9.59
11.	Rudraprayag	1294.00	3663.00	2.83
12.	Uttarkashi	5252.11	45688.00	8.70
13.	Hardwar	11787.16	94849.76	8.05
	Total Garhwal	110273.54	313661.00	2.84
	Total Uttarakhand	175603.00	667040.00	3.80

Among the various districts in the state of Uttarakhand the productivity was highest in Almora district (18.97 mt/ha) followed by Chamoli (9.59 mt/ha), it is surprising to note that the productivity of fruits was lowest in Dehradun in the entire state.

From the table it is evident that total area under apple crops in the Garhwal region was reported 14221.71 hectares and production was 70290.91 metric tonnes. Among the various districts the coverage under apple orchards was highest in Dehradun (4604 ha) followed by Uttarkashi (4158.78 ha). On the other hand, the production was reported highest in Uttarkashi followed by Chamoli. It may also be noted that the productivity was significantly higher in Uttarkashi and Chamoli districts, which was, computed 10.05 and 8.47 metric tonnes per hectare respectively. In Uttarkashi and Chamoli districts the concentration of apple orchards is mainly in Purola, Mori, Joshimath and Tharali blocks.

However, it is also being produced in Karayanpgayag and Narayanbagad blocks of Chamoli District.

Table 4.3. Districtwise Area, Production and Productivity of Fruits (Apple, Pear and Peach)—2004-05

Name of the District	*Apple*			*Pear*			*Peach*		
	Area	*Produ-ction*	*Produ-ctivity*	*Area*	*Produ-ction*	*Produ-ctivity*	*Area*	*Produ-ction*	*Produ-ctivity*
Chamoli	2155.00	18256.25	8.47	300.00	2625.10	8.75	560.00	4900.00	8.75
Uttarkashi	4158.78	41807.72	10.05	139.38	600.00	4.30	161.70	371.66	2.30
Hardwar	0.00	0.00	0.00	82.62	727.00	8.80	51.20	447.00	8.73
Rudraprayag	86.83	116.50	1.34	91.01	179.50	1.97	108.72	323.00	2.97
Tehri	3003.04	2404.04	0.80	1654.29	1525.34	0.92	619.05	361.41	0.58
Pauri	214.06	539.40	2.52	128.83	558.40	4.33	170.68	334.25	1.96
Dehradun	4604.00	7167.00	1.56	1212.50	2268.00	1.87	1216.00	2655.00	2.18
Total	14221.71	70290.91	4.94	3608.63	8483.34	2.35	2887.35	9392.32	3.25

A pear is a tree of the genus *Pyrus* and the juicy fruit of that tree, edible in some species. The form of the pear and of the apple respectively, although usually characteristic enough, is not by itself sufficient to distinguish them, for there are pears which cannot be distinguished from apples by form alone, and apples which cannot by superficial appearance be recognized from pears. The main distinction is the occurrence in the tissue of the fruit, or beneath the rind, of clusters of cells filled with hard woody deposit in the case of the pear, constituting the "grit," while in the apple no such formation of woody cells takes place. The appearance of the tree—the bark, the foliage, the flowers—is, however, usually quite characteristic in the two species. Cultivated pears, whose number is enormous, are without doubt derived from one or two wild species widely distributed throughout Europe and western Asia, and sometimes forming part of the natural vegetation of the forests.

Earlier, peach (*Prunus persica* Batsch) and pear (*Pyrus* spp.) were considered to be important fruit crops of the temperate world. But the development of low chill cultivars made possible to these crops to grow in the subtropics of the world. Therefore peach and pear cultivation is carried out both in hilly and plain areas of the state. From the Table 4.3 it may be noted that 3608.63 hectares area was reported under cultivation of pear and the production of the same was reported 8483.34

metric tonnes during 2004-5 in the Garhwal region. Among the various districts the coverage of pear was highest in Tehri (1654.29 ha) followed by Dehradun (122.50 ha). In Dehradun the concentration of pear was mainly in Chakrata block whereas in Tehri pear was cultivated in Jaunpur and Pratapnagar blocks. On the other hand the productivity of pear is relatively higher in Chamoli and Hardwar districts of the region.

Table 4.4. Districtwise Area, Production and Productivity of Fruits (Plum, Apricot and Walnuts)—2004-05

Name of the District	*Plum*			*Apricot*			*Walnuts*		
	Area	*Production*	*Productivity*	*Area*	*Production*	*Productivity*	*Area*	*Production*	*Productivity*
Chamoli	215.00	1881.25	8.75	80.00	700.00	8.75	730.00	6562.50	8.99
Uttarkashi	101.49	410.00	4.04	118.26	900.00	7.61	253.60	300.00	1.18
Hardwar	0.00	0.00	0.00	0.00	0.00	0.00	0.00	0.00	0.00
Rudraprayag	75.49	101.80	1.35	34.67	65.40	1.89	175.29	118.00	0.67
Tehri	541.91	2709.55	5.00	1073.63	536.84	0.50	2489.75	1294.93	0.52
Pauri	81.40	282.70	3.47	35.45	102.00	2.88	683.99	320.55	0.47
Dehradun	716.20	1608.00	2.25	806.30	1395.00	1.73	2065.00	1820.00	0.88
Total	1731.49	6993.30	4.04	2148.31	3699.24	1.72	6397.63	10415.98	1.63

The total area under peach orchards was reported 2887.35 hectare, which was highest in Dehradun (1216 ha) followed by Tehri (619.05 ha) and Chamoli (560 ha) respectively. On the other hand the production was highest in Chamoli (4900 mt) followed by Dehradun (2655 mt). In Chamoli the concentration was mainly in Dausoli and Gairsen blocks where as in Dehradun the climatic conditions of Chakrata is more suitable for peach cultivation, whereas in Tehri Garhwal the concentration is more in Kirtinagar, Bhilangana and Chamba blocks.

While looking at the relative acreage of plum orchards in the region, it has been noticed that coverage of the same is highest in Dehradun (716.20 ha) followed by Tehri (541.91 Ha) and Chamoli (215 ha). On the other hand the production was recorded highest in Tehri (2709.25 mt.) followed by Chamoli (1881 mt). Productivity of plum was recorded highest in Chamoli. It may also be noted that the concentration of plum orchards is more in Joshimath, Dausoli, Narayangbagard and Gasirsen blocks of Chamoli as the production and productivity of plum is more in these blocks. In Tehri Garhwal the concentration is more in Chamba, Bhilangana and Narendranagar blocks.

The area under walnuts is reported 10415.98 hectares in the region and about 65 percent of the same was reported in Chamoli. The productivity was also highest in Chamoli which was recorded 8.99 mt/ha. The productivity of walnuts is significantly higher in Chamoli as compared with other districts of Garhwal region. In Chamoli the orchards of walnuts are mainly found in Tharali, Dewal, Joshimath, Narayanbagad and Gairsen blocks.

Similarly the orchards of apricot are mostly found in Tehri, Dehradun, Uttarkashi and Chamoli districts. In Chamoli the orchards are commonly found in Joshimath, Karnproyag and Tharali blocks, whereas in Dehradun the concentration of orchards is mainly Chakrata and Kalsi blocks and in Tehri it was in Chamba, Narendranagar and Pratapnagar blocks. The total area under apricot was reported 2148.31 hectares and the production of the same was 3699.24 metric tonnes during 2004-05.

The lemon tree is one of the oldest cultivated fruit plants originated from India. Today, lemon trees grow in subtropical climates all over the world, especially in Florida and the Mediterranean. Though the fruit and its juice have a sour taste to it, lemon is actually a fantastic buffer in the body and can reduce hyperacidity in the stomach. Lemon juice and peels have an antiseptic effect and the leaves of the tree are used to reduce fever. In addition, lemons are rich in vitamin C which strengthens the immune system and acting as an antioxant, protects cells from radical damage.

Lemon as a therapeutic usage help anti-inflammatory action. It helps the body cleanse itself by promoting perspiration and acting as a natural diuretic. A lemon also stimulates the appetite, aids digestion, strengthen body defense system, relieves cramps and also dilates the blood vessels in the skin. Lemons are known for useful remedies for gout, urine retention, athritis, vitamin C deficiency, inflammation of the mouth and throat, hoarseness, digestive disorders, asthma, nervousness, insomnia, heart pulpitations and helps the system with diseases of the stomach, liver and intestines.

Lemon is another important fruit grown across the state. The important crops under cultivation of lemon includes, *oranges, maltas, kagchi* and *nimbu*. The total area under lemon cultivation was reported 11058 hectares and the production of the same was 65041 metric tonnes during 2004-05. From the table it is evident that the area under lemon orchard was highest in Chamoli Garhwal (6000 ha) followed by Dehradun (2329 ha). The other important districts where lemon orchards are found include Tehri (1440 Ha), Pauri (639) and Rudraprayag (427 ha). Similarly the production of lemon was reported highest in Chamoli (52500 mt) followed by Pauri (5454 mt). The productivity of lemon per hectare was also highest in Chamoli which was reported 8.75 metric tonnes per hectare. It may also be noted that the concentration of orchards in Chamoli was mainly across the district, however it was found more in Dasoli and Pokhari blocks. Similarly in Pauri Garhwal the concentration was more in Bironkhal, Yamkeshwar, and Rikhnikhal Blocks. In Dehradun it was mainly found in Chakrata and Kalsi blcoks.

The mango is naturally adapted to tropical lowlands between 25°N and 25°S of the Equator and up to elevations of 3,000 ft (915 m). It is grown as a dooryard tree at slightly cooler altitudes but is apt to suffer cold damage. The best climate for mango is considered when the rainfall is 30 to 100 in. (75-250 cm) in the four summer months (June to September) followed by 8 months of dry season. The mango tree is not too particular as to soil type, provided it has good drainage. Rich, deep loam certainly contributes to maximum growth, but if the soil is too rich and moist and too well fertilized, the tree will respond vegetative but will be deficient in flowering and fruiting.

Table 4.5. Districtwise Area, Production and Productivity of Fruits (Lemon. Mango and Guava)—2004-05

Name of the District	*Lemon*			*Mango*			*Guawa*		
	Area	*Produ-ction*	*Produ-ctivity*	*Area*	*Produ-ction*	*Produ-ctivity*	*Area*	*Produ-ction*	*Produ-ctivity*
Chamoli	6000.00	52500.00	8.75	250.00	2187.50	8.75	145.00	1268.75	8.75
Uttarkashi	203.59	972.75	4	68.26	100.00	1.46	13.87	40.00	2.88
Hardwar	9.10	79.00	8.68	7835.00	68901.00	8.79	235.00	2067.00	8.80
Rudraprayag	427.31	1800.00	4.21	138.40	254.50	1.84	0.00	0.00	0.00
Tehri	1440.23	1440.23	1.00	3938.29	5630.80	1.43	0.00	0.00	0.00
Pauri	639.01	5454.55	8.54	1044.59	3242.50	3.10	128.51	721.50	5.61
Dehradun	2339.00	2795.00	1.19	5663.00	5802.00	1.02	82.00	218.00	2.66
Total	11058.24	65041.53	5.88	18937.54	86118.30	4.55	604.38	4315.25	7.14

Therefore, mango orchards are mainly concentrated in the valleys and relatively plain districts of the region. The total area under mango orchard was reported 18937 hectares and the production of the same was 86118 metric tonnes with a productivity of 4.55 mt per hectare. Among the various districts the area and production under mango was highest in Hardwar (68901 hectares) followed by Dehradun (5653 hectares). It may also be noted that the productivity was also highest in Hardwar and it was mainly concentrated in Bhadrabad and Bhagwanpur blocks of the district, whereas in Dehradun the concentration was more in Doiwala, Sahaspur, Vikasnagar and Raipur blocks.

While analysing the acreage of guava in the region it was found that the same was reported highest in Hardwar district followed by Dehradun district. However the total area under guava cultivation was 604 hectares and the production of the same was 4315 metric tonnes. In Hardwar the production was mainly in Bhadarabad, Narsan, Bhagwanpur and Lakser blocks. It may also be noted that the guava orchards are mainly found in the plain area of the region. In the hilly districts the suitable areas for cultivation of guava are the areas which are very near to the rivers.

In some of the districts particularly Uttarkashi and Pauri the climate is even suitable for cultivation of almond, however the coverage under almond is very low as it was reported 9.1 hectares in Uttarkashi and 9.45 hectares in Pauri. The data on production of almond in Pauri was not reported. The orchards of almond are mainly found in Bhatwari, Dunda and Chindayalisen blocks. Whereas, in Pauri it is concentrated in Pauri, Kot and Pokhra blocks.

Table 4.6. Districtwise Area, Production and Productivity (Almond, Litchi and Grapes)—2004-05

Name of the District	*Almond*			*Lichi*			*Others*		
	Area	*Produ-ction*	*Produ-ctivity*	*Area*	*Produ-ction*	*Produ-ctivity*	*Area*	*Produ-ction*	*Produ-ctivity*
Chamoli	0.00	0.00	0.00	0.00	0.00	0.00	0.00	282	2511.5
Uttarkashi	8.91	0.60	0.07	0.41	0.30	0.73	0.02	23.46	185.79
Hardwar	0.00	0.00	0.00	271	2382	0.00	0.00	3303.14	29001
Rudraprayag	0.00	0.00	0.00	8.53	3.00	0.00	0.00	147.75	701.3
Tehri	0.00	0.00	0.00	11.46	5.73	0.00	0.00	4188.75	1845.4
Pauri	9.45	0.00	0.00	100.06	346.60	3.46	2.46	566.94	3943.53
Dehradun	0.00	0.00	0.00	3595	5392	1.50	0.00	1937	3791
Total	18.36	0.60	3.60	3986.46	8129.63	1.56	2.48	10449.4	41979.52

Note: Others include grapes, banana, peanut, westnut, kivi, jackfruit, amla, pomegranates.

Litchi (*Litchi chinensis*) a native of China, is grown in India since 18th century. India is probably the second largest producer of litchi. Major litchi producing states in India are Bihar, Jharkhand, Tripura, West Bengal, Uttarakhand, Assam and Punjab with an area of 53600 Ha with a total production of 4.2 lakh tonnes. The most important use of litchi is as table fruit in ripe form. It is also used in processed forms such as squash. The leaves are used for making poultices, the seeds as anodyne for the skin and flowers, bark and roots for making decoctions for throat gargle.

Table 4.7. Statewise Area, Production and Productivity of Litchi (2000-01)

	Area ('000ha)	*Production ('000 t)*	*Productivity (t/ha)*
Assam	4.1	18.4	4.5
Bihar	25.3	303.3	12.0
Jharkhand	0.5	5.0	10.0
Orissa	3.5	8.2	2.3
Punjab	1.2	11.5	9.6
Tripura	1.6	8.9	5.6
Uttarakhand	8.9	8.8	1.0
West Bengal	3.9	42.0	10.00
Others	4.3	5.9	
Total	53.6	412.0	7.7

Source: National Horticulture Board.

Potential States for Litchi Expansion

- Uttarakhand (Dehradun, Pithoragarh, Nainital, Hardwar),
- West Bengal (Murshidabad, 24-Paraganas),
- Bihar (Muzzafarpur, East Champaran Samastipur, Vaisali, Bhagalpur),
- Assam (Kamrup, Sonitpur, Bongaigaon),
- Punjab (Gurdaspur, Ropar, Hoshiarpur),
- Uttar Pradesh (Saharanpur).

Soil and Climatic requirements: Alluvial soil with good drainage is suitable for litchi orchards. It can grow in wide range of soils from light sandy to heavy clay. It cannot withstand water logging for long. Soils taken from the root region of old trees may be added to pits while planting litchi. This practice introduces mycorrhiza that helps growth of litchi.

Litchi requires a moist sub-tropical climate without heavy frost and dry winds. The four essentials for litchi cultivation are freedom from frost, high humidity, rich deep soil and abundant moisture. In litchi growing tracts, the maximum temperature varies from 20°C to 32°C between the flowering time and the fruiting season. Dry atmosphere and cold snaps between 1°C & 4°C in winter are beneficial. Litchi grows successfully on the hills up to an elevation of 1050 m.

Varieties: Statewise commercial varieties are:

Bihar:	Shahi, Rose scented, China, Kasba, Purbi, Early Bedana, Late Bedana.
Uttar Pradesh:	Rose Scented, Dehradun, Calcutta.
Uttarakhand:	Rose Scented, Dehradun, Calcutta.
West Bengal:	Bombay Green, Kalyani Selection.
Punjab:	Muzaffarpur, Dehradun, Seedless, Late Bedana.

The site for raising new orchards of litchi should preferably be in an area where marketing facilities are available. Wind breaks should be provided on the sides from which high winds are expected. Plants suitable for providing wind breaks are seedlings of mango, jamun, eucalyptus, mulberry, shisham etc. Live thorny hedge preferably of 'Karonda' (*Caricas carandas*) or other locally available plant should be provided around the field in order to protect the young trees from animals etc.

Good quality air layered nursery plants purchased from government nurseries or government approved nurseries should be planted. Normally 10 m x 10 m spacing will be provided with a density of 100 plants per ha. *Bombai* and *Muzzafarpur and Dehraduni* varieties, which grow in to huge trees, may also be planted at this density. China and Elachi can be comfortably planted at 124 plants per Ha. High density planting and pruning or thinning of plants is the most modern technology.

Litchi from Dehradun is very famous across the country. There are a large number of litchi orchards spread across Dun valley and tari region. As evident from the table the total area under litchi orchards was reported 3986 hectares and about 90 percent orchards are in Dehradun district. In Dehradun the concentration of orchards is mainly in Raipur, Doiwala, Sahaspur and Vikasnagar blocks. In District Hardwar it is mainly found in Badhrabad and Narsan blocks. Similarly in Pauri the litchi orchards were reported in Dugadda, Yamkeshwar and Rikhnikhal blocks. Litchi from Dehradun is mainly exported across the country.

Grape is one of the important fruit crops and is ranked next to citrus. It is gaining importance in Indian horticulture. Research works have been carried out and researches on both cultivation and processing aspects in various agricultural universities and horticultural research stations mainly in Punjab, Haryana, Rajasthan, Maharashtra, Andhra Pradesh, Karanataka and Tamil Nadu that are located under diversified agro-climatic conditions. In India farmers have taken up the grape cultivation on a large scale. However, the area under grapes has not expanded as much as it should be. Research findings are available in plenty and the various technologies developed on grape cultivation should now reach to the farming community, students of horticulture, research and extension workers so that it can be used for the overall development of the crop. Grapes culture, practices/techniques in India, particularly in South India are different from the other grape growing regions of the world.

Among other important horticulture crops, grapes are mainly cultivated in Pauri, Kot, Khirsu and Pabon blocks of Pauri District, Banana are found in almost all the blocks of district Uttarkashi. Similarly peanut, westnuts and kivi fruits are also reported in Uttarkashi district. On the other hand cultivation of Jackfruits was mainly reported in all the bocks of Hardwar district and Doiwala, Sahaspur, Vikasnagar and Raipur blocks of Dehradun.

Area and Production of Vegetables

India is the second largest producer of vegetables in the world, accounting for about 10 per cent of the world's vegetable production. It is projected that the domestic vegetable requirements will rise from current levels of 83-91 million tonnes to 151-193 million tonnes by the year 2030. In order to achieve this, popularization of scientific and improved methods of vegetable cultivation and their seed production is of utmost importance with reference to specific agro-climatic conditions and unexplored niches in hilly regions of our country, particularly Uttarakhand which permits production of a wide variety of good quality vegetables. Ironically, the farmers in hilly areas are today no longer able to sustain themselves at the level of self-sufficiency. Reduction in the density of forest cover and overgrazing has led to soil erosion of unprecedented proportions. Land and water resources are becoming even scarce.

The only solution to overcome this situation is to popularize scientifically developed methods of vegetable cultivation practices for the improvement of agro-socio-economic conditions of the people. The necessary research and development programmes must be carried out in the hilly region itself, this way the outcome of such work will be best suited to the agro-climatic condition of the region. Greenhouse technology for production of vegetables has been found to be an appropriate intervention in the development of horticulture in these difficult terrains. Even though the present area under greenhouse in our country may be less, there is a large untapped potential in the hilly terrains, which would bring nutritional self-sufficiency besides enhancing the income of people and providing on-farm employment.

While analyzing the area, production and productivity of vegetables for the year 2004-05, it has been noticed that the total area under vegetable cultivation was 50718 hectares and production of the vegetables was in the state was 503254 metric tonnes. The productivity of the same was 9.92 metric tonnes per hectare. Area as well as production under vegetable cultivation was highest in Garhwal region. A marginal change in the productivity of vegetables per hectare was also noticed in the Garhwal region. Among the various districts the productivity of vegetables was highest in Nainital (21.96 metric tonnes per hectares) followed by Uttarkashi district (18.55 mt/ha). On the other hand the productivity was computed lowest in Pauri which was 6.42 metric tonnes per hectare. From the table it can also be noticed that the productivity of vegetables was more than 15 metric tonnes per hectare in Nainital, Udam Singh Nagar, Uttarkashi and Chamoli which indicates that the climatic conditions and soils of these districts are best suited for the cultivation of vegetables.

Potato is a starchy, edible tuber that is cultivated throughout the world and is consumed as a major staple food. This food crop occurs underground, in the stem of the plant on which it is grown. Potato plant comes from the family of Solanaceae and is long lasting in nature. These plants have got white and purple flowers with poisonous fruits and the buds appear on the potato tubers. The potato crop contains high level of nutritive value and ranks 4th among the most important crops of the world. After wheat, rice and maize, potato is the most important food crop in the world. It contributes to almost 50 percent of the total tuber and root crop production. Potato has a good food value as compared to other staple food crops as it is rich in carbohydrates and also contain proteins, minerals like calcium and potassium and vitamins like vitamin C. It is vastly consumed as a vegetable and is also used in various forms such as starch, flour, chips, alcohol, dextrin and livestock fodder.

Table 4.8. Districtwise Area, Production and Productivity of Vegetables (2004-05)

S. No.	*District*	*Vegetables*		
		Area	*Production*	*Productivity*
1.	Nainital	2276.5	50000	21.96
2.	Udham Singh Nagar	3668	58142	15.85
3.	Almora	4984.68	26496.77	5.32
4.	Bageshwar	1056.2	12977.45	12.29
5.	Pithoragarh	4200	42000	10
6.	Champawat	3150	21300	6.76
	Total Kumaon	19335.38	210916.22	10.91
7.	Dehradun	8540	79805	9.34
8.	Pauri	3730.63	23964.35	6.42
9.	Tehri	5595.34	45731.82	8.17
10.	Chamoli	1279.3	22196	17.35
11.	Rudraprayag	607	5549	9.14
12.	Uttarkashi	1893.35	35120.91	18.55
13.	Hardwar	9737	79970.7	8.21
Total Garhwal		31382.62	292337.78	9.32
Total Uttarakhand		50718	503254	9.92

This vegetable is produced worldwide and its production figured at 322 million metric tons in 2005. China leads the production table with approximately 23 percent of share followed by Russian federation and India. The consumption of potato has increased all over the world during the last few years. The continents including Europe, North America, Europe and South America observed a significant rise in the per capita consumption in these continents. However in Africa, per capita consumption remained stable. These trends are likely to maintain in the future according to the various projections done. Potato is a crop that doesn't require complex processes to be cultivated. This crop is a long lasting crop though it is cultivated as an annual crop. It easily grows even on poor quality soils and unfavorable conditions. The best yield is derived when the climatic conditions in which potatoes are grown are cool with a good rainfall and irrigation system. But this crop is not restricted to cooler climates only. It is also grown in the subtropical areas of the world like India, China etc. as a winter crop.

Table 4.8(a). Districtwise Area, Production and Productivity of Vegetables (Potato, Climbers and Others) —2C04-05

Name of the District	*Potato*			*Creepers Legumes (Bailwali)*			*Others*		
	Area	*Produ-ction*	*Produ-ctivity*	*Area*	*Produ-ction*	*Produ-ctivity*	*Area*	*Produ-ction*	*Produ-ctivity*
Chamoli	2100.00	32221.00	15.34	0.00	0.00	0.00	191.00	1839.00	9.63
Uttarkashi	2404.64	38163.40	15.87	296.40	6928.00	23.37	0.00	0.00	0.00
Hardwar	920.00	18400.00	0.00	662.00	9950.00	0.00	320.00	4800.00	0.00
Rudraprayag	514.00	8100.00	15.76	121.25	1079.00	8.90	83.82.00	424.00	5.06
Tehri	3038.00	47272.31	15.56	0.00	0.00	0.00	1010.39	9257.04	9.16
Pauri	1106.50	6458.00	5.84	260.00	2600.00	10.00	908.95	7886.65	9.39
Dehradun	10083.14	150614.71	14.94	0.00	0.00	0.00	4596.96	41400.99	9.01
Total	20166.28	301229.42	14.94	1339.65	20557.00	15.35	7111.12	65607.68	9.23

To grow a potato plant, a potato tuber is sown and not the seed of the plant. In the Indian subcontinent, potato is grown largely as rabi crop. The following three crops are raised per year in the country pertaining to different weather conditions in different areas:

- Summer crop –Planting is done in the months of March and April and harvesting is done in the months of August and September.
- Autumn crop – Planting in the months of August and September and harvesting in December and January.
- Spring crop - Planting in the months of January and February and harvesting in May and June.

Harvesting is done either by hand picking or using the various potato harvester machines. This crop is harvested before the frosty and extreme cold weather begins and the top of the plant starts to wither.

In Uttarakhand potato is grown across the state and the total area under Garhwal region was estimated 20166.28 hectares and the production of the same during 2004-5 was reported 301229.4 metric tonnes and the productivity was about 15 metric tonnes per hectare which is significantly higher. Among the various districts the coverage was highest in Dehradun (10083 Ha) followed by Tehri (3038 hectares). Productivity of potato per hectare was more than 15 metric tonnes in Chamoli, Uttarkashi, Tehri and Rudraprayag Districts. In Chamoli the cultivation was relatively higher in Joshimath, Ghat and Dewal blocks. On the other hand in Uttarkashi district the cultivation and coverage was relatively higher in Naugaon, Purola and Mori blocks. In Rudraprayag it was mainly cultivated in Jakholi and Ukhimath blocks. Whereas in Dehradun the area and production is relatively higher in hilly blocks of Chakrata and Kalsi and in Pauri it was highly concentrated in Dugadda block and in Tehri high concentration was in Jaunpur, Deoprayag and Pratapnagar blocks. However it may be noted that cultivation of potato is done both in hilly and plain areas of the region in a large scale and the demand for hilly potato has always been higher in the market as a result of which farmers are bound to get good prices for their product. However the topographic and climatic conditions some times act as a barrier primarily during monsoon season to transport the potatoes to the market places which force the farmers to incur huge loses.

It is also evident from the table that 1339.65 hectares is under creepers of legumes which includes different types of beans, gourds, pumpkins, bitter gourds etc. The production of the same was recorded 20557 metric tonnes in the Garhwal region. Cultivation of creepers of legumes was mainly reported in Uttarkashi, Rudraprayag, Hardwar and Pauri districts.

Tomato is now grown worldwide for its edible fruits, with thousands of cultivars having been selected with varying fruit types, and for optimum growth in differing growing conditions. The most widely grown commercial tomatoes tend to be in the 5–6 cm diameter range. Most cultivars produce red fruit; but a number of cultivars with yellow, orange, pink, purple, green, or white fruit are also available. Multicolored and striped fruit can also be quite striking. Tomatoes grown for canning are often elongated, 7–9 cm long and 4–5 cm diameter; they are known as plum tomatoes. Tomatoes are one of the most common garden vegetables in the United States and, along with zucchini, have a reputation for outproducing the needs of the grower. As in most sectors of agriculture, there is increasing demand in developed countries for organic tomatoes, as well as heirloom tomatoes, to make up for flavor and texture faults in commercial tomatoes. Quite a few seed merchants and banks provide a large selection of heirloom seeds. Tomato seeds are occasionally organically produced as well, but only a small percentage of organic crop acreage is grown with organic seed.

Table 4.9. Districtwise Area Production and Productivity of Vegetables (Tomato, Radish and Cauliflowers)—2004-05

District	*Tomato*			*Radish*			*Cauliflower*		
	Area	*Production*	*Productivity*	*Area*	*Production*	*Productivity*	*Area*	*Production*	*Productivity*
Chamoli	205.00	2460.00	12.00	260.00	3120.00	12.00	230.00	2760.00	12.00
Uttarkashi	552.53	8561.50	15.50	81.20	1624.00	20.00	78.96	5751.11	72.84
Hardwar	0.00	0.00	0.00	105.00	1575.00	0.00	238.00	3570.00	0.00
Rudraprayag	31.25	375.00	12.00	57.40	697.00	12.14	57.00	797.00	13.98
Tehri	503.37	2576.85	5.12	340.40	1691.77	4.97	429.61	4248.83	9.89
Pauri	290.10	2093.20	7.22	526.50	3711.20	7.05	140.60	614.75	4.37
Dehradun	959.00	14864.00	15.50	211.00	2110.00	10.00	490.00	5390.00	11.00
Total	2541.25	30930.55	12.17	1581.50	14528.97	9.19	1664.17	23131.69	13.90

Tomatoes are now eaten freely throughout the world, and their consumption is believed to benefit the heart among other things. Lycopene, one of nature's most powerful antioxidants, is present in tomatoes, and, especially when tomatoes are cooked, has been found beneficial in preventing prostate cancer. However, other research contradicts this claim. Botanically a fruit, the tomato is nutritionally categorized as a vegetable. Since vegetable is not a botanical term, there is no contradiction in a plant part being a fruit botanically while still being considered a vegetable.

The tomato also has an acidic property that is used to bring out other flavors. This same acidity makes tomatoes especially easy to preserve in home canning as tomato sauce or paste. Tomato juice is often canned and sold as a beverage. Unripe green tomatoes can also be used to make salsa, be breaded and fried, or pickled. Culinary uses of tomatoes include: Tomato paste, Tomato purée, Tomato pie Gazpacho (Andalusian cuisine), Ketchup Pizza and Tomato sauce.

Tomato is widely grown in the state of Uttarakhand. As evident from the Table 4.9, 2541.25 hectares was reported under tomato cultivation and the production of the same was 30930.55 metric tonnes with a productivity of 12.17 metric tonnes per hectares. Among various districts the area under tomato cultivation is highest in Dehradun (959 ha) followed by Uttarkashi (552.53 ha). In Dehradun district the cultivation of tomato was primarily in Vikasnagar and Doiwala blocks, whereas in Uttarkashi the cultivation was focused in Purola and Naugaon blocks. On the other hand area under Radish cultivation was 1581.50 hectares with production of 14528.97 metric tonnes. The productivity of radish in the Garhwal region was computed to 1.19 metric tonnes per hectare. From the table it is pertinent to note that coverage under radish cultivation was highest in Pauri (526.50 ha) followed by Tehri (340.40 ha). However the productivity was highest in Uttarkashi, which was, computed 20 metric tonnes per hectares. It may also be noted that radish cultivation is more popular in Bironkhal and Nainidanda blocks of Pauri while in Tehri it was more concentrated in Deoprayag, Chamba and Jaunpur blocks.

Area under cauliflowers was reported 1664.17 hectares with a production of 23131.69 metric tonnes. The productivity of the same was computed 13.90 metric tonnes per hectare. Among the various districts the highest coverage was reported in Dehradun (490 ha) followed by Tehri with 439.61 hectares. It is surprising to note that the production was highest in Uttarkashi followed by Dehradun. In Uttarkashi it is mainly cultivated in Naugaon whereas in Dehradun it was primarily cultivated in Doiwala, Raipur, Sahaspur and Vikasnagar blocks.

Table 4.10. Districtwise Area, Production and Productivity of Vegetables (Cabbage, Egg Plants and Capsicum)—2004-05

District	*Cabbage*			*Egg Plant (Brinjal)*			*Capsicum*		
	Area	*Production*	*Productivity*	*Area*	*Production*	*Productivity*	*Area*	*Production*	*Productivity*
Chamoli	140.00	1980.00	14.14	165.00	1980.00	12.00	52.00	260.00	5.00
Uttarkashi	18.20	180.20	9.90	49.36	672.94	13.63	28.50	156.75	5.50
Hardwar	239.00	3585.00	0.00	167.00	2505.00	0.00	0.00	0.00	0.00
Rudraprayag	10.73	88.00	8.20	26.95	320.00	11.87	6.30	45.50	7.22
Tehri	41.04	125.17	3.05	71.47	308.92	4.32	176.87	795.93	4.50
Pauri	75.35	220.64	2.93	122.85	898.00	7.31	151.35	428.15	2.83
Dehradun	739.00	15912.00	21.53	334.00	4008.00	12.00	45.00	450.00	10.00
Total	1263.32	22091.01	17.49	936.63	10692.86	11.42	460.02	2136.33	4.64

Area under cabbage was reported 1263.32 hectares with a production of 22091.01 metric tonnes during 2004-05. However the productivity of the same was 17.49 metric tonnes per hectare. The area was highest in Dehradun (729 ha) followed by Hardwar (239 ha). On the other hand the production was also reported highest in Dehradun (15912 metric tonnes), followed by Hardwar (3585 metric tonnes). The productivity was highest again in Dehradun (21.53 metric tonnes per hectares) which is significantly higher than region's average. In Dehradun, it is mainly cultivated in Doiwala, Raipur, Sahaspur and Vikasnagar, whereas in Hardwar the concentration is more in Bhadrabad, Lakshar and Khanpur blocks.

Egg plants are widely cultivated across the state of Uttarkhand and area under the same was reported 936.63 hectares with a production of 10692.86 metric tonnes and the productivity was 11.42 metric tonnes per hectare during 2004-05. Among the various districts the coverage was highest in Dehradun (334 ha) followed by Hardwar (167 ha). The coverage of capsicum was reported significantly higher in Tehri with an area of 176.87 hectares and production of 795.93 metric tonnes. In Dehradun the coverage was mainly in Doiwala, Raipur, Sahaspur and Vikasnagar blocks, whereas in Hardwar it was in Narsan and Bhadrabad blocks. On the other hand, total area under capsicum was reported 460.02 hectares with a production of 2136.33 metric tonnes. The productivity of capsicum was reported, 4. 64 metric tonnes per hectares. Besides, Tehri and Pauri the cultivation of capsicum in other districts of the region is relatively low as a result the production was also reported low. Howevcer, it was noticed that the productivity of Capsicum was highest in Dehradun district.

Table 4.11. Districtwise Area, Production and Productivity of Peas, Beans and Lady's Finger (2004-05)

Name of the District	*Pea*			*Beans*			*Lady's finger*		
	Area	*Production*	*Productivity*	*Area*	*Production*	*Productivity*	*Area*	*Production*	*Productivity*
Chamoli	260.00	2080.00	8.00	190.00	1140.00	6.00	105.00	630.00	6.00
Uttarkashi	453.50	9070.00	20.00	334.20	0.00	0.00	0.00	0.00	0.00
Hardwar	314.00	4710.00	0.00	0.00	0.00	0.00	132.00	1980.00	0.00
Rudraprayag	86.00	447.00	5.20	51.25	439.00	8.57	43.65	249.00	5.70
Tehri	1611.16	14500.26	9.00	454.36	3657.59	8.05	231.04	1152.89	4.99
Pauri	480.43	998.50	2.08	369.70	2047.50	5.54	298.00	832.50	2.79
Dehradun	1461.00	5844.00	4.00	873.00	5229.00	5.99	644.00	4344.00	6.75
Total	4666.09	37649.76	8.07	2272.51	12513.09	5.51	1453.69	9188.39	6.32

Total coverage under cultivation of pea was reported 4666.09 hectares with a production of 37649.76 metric tonnes and the productivity of the same for the entire region was computed 8.07 metric tonnes per hectares during 2004-5. As is evident from the table the coverage was highest in Tehri (1611.16 ha) followed by Dehradun (1461 ha). The production was also highest in Tehri where it is mainly cultivated in Jaunpur, Thaldhar and Jakhindhar blocks. Whereas in Dehradun it was mainly reported in Vikasnagar, Sahaspur, Raipur and Doiwala blocks. On the other hand, the total area under beans cultivation was reported 2272.51 hectares with a production of 12513.09 metric tonnes and the productivity of the same was 5.51 metric tonnes per hectare. Among the various districts the coverage was highest in Dehradun (873.00 hectares) followed by Tehri (454.36 ha) similar trend was noticd for production also. The production was also highest in Dehradun and Tehri. In Dehradun the coverage was highest in Doiwala followed by Chakrata block. The beans from the hilly blocks of Chakrata and Kalsi are very famous across the country. On the other hand, the coverage under cultivation of lady's finger was reported 1453.69 hectares with a production of 9188 metric tonnes. The coverage was highest in Dehradun (644 ha) district followed by Pauri (298 ha). However, the productivity of Chamoli was 6 metric tonnes per hectare which was relatively higher considering the coverage of 105 hectares only. In Dehradun cultivation is mainly focused in Doiwala, Sahaspur, Raipur and Vikasnagar blocks, whereas in Chamoli the cultivation is more or less same across the district.

Area and Production of Spices

Spice industry has been witnessing phenomenal growth both in the international and domestic sector. The growth in this sector can be attributed to the change in the lifestyle patterns of the consumers all over the world. The shift in the consumption trend toward natural products has also contributed to the increased global demand of spices and culinary herbs. Spice and derivatives market is booming because these products find applications in a number of industries including pharmaceutical, medicine, beverages, food processing, personal hygiene products to name a few. Developing countries especially in the Asian continent are the major producers of variety of spices. A large percentage of international and domestic trade takes place in the dried form. India, Indonesia, China are few of the prime producers of a variety of high quality spices and also significant contributors to the global spice trade. The international trade in various forms of spices has grown tremendously in the last decade. According to an estimate, 85 percent of the international trade in spices is dried and is used after cleaning but without further processing. Pepper is one of the most valuable spice in the global trade. Countries including China, India, Madagascar, Indonesia are emerging as the leading spice traders.

The culinary herb market is also expanding though the production areas are widely distributed. India is one of the prime producers and suppliers of raw herbs to USA and the EU. This is a labour intensive industry, therefore producers must have a sound knowledge of the methods and processes involved in the production of herbs and spices. Spice is a strongly flavored and aromatic part of a plant used in small quantities as either a preservative or flavoring agent in cooking. It is generally the dried part of the plant, i.e. the bark, root, stem of a plant are used as spice. Indian spices have their essence in the hard parts of a plant.

Types of Spices

- *Whole Spices:* These spices are used in their original form after being thoroughly cleaned. These spices are used both for garnishing as well as flavoring. e.g. Cloves, Cinnamon, Black Pepper.
- *Ground Spices:* Grinded spices are used as they deliver flavor quickly and also they blend easily into a product; this is so, because grinding a spice breaks down the protective cell structure.

Table 4.12. Parts of a Plant Used as a Spice

Part	*Spice*
Barks	Cinnamon
Berries	Black pepper, Chilli
Buds	Cloves
Bulbs	Garlic, Leek
Pistil (female part of flower)	Saffron
Kernel	Nutmeg
Leaf	Basil, Bay Leaf, Mint, Marjoram, Sage, Curry Leaf
Rhizome/Roots	Ginger, Turmeric
Roots	Ajowan, Aniseed, Celery
Seeds	Seed

Parts of a Plant Used as a Spice

Spice is a strongly flavored and aromatic part of a plant used in small quantities as either a preservative or flavoring in cooking. It is generally the dried part of the plant, i.e. the bark, root, or stem of a plant which is used for various purposes. Indian spices have their essence in the hard parts of a plant.

Spices Extraction Methods

A number of extraction methods' of spices are there being used depending on the technology and also the kind of spice being extracted. Some of the popular extraction methods are:

- Steam distillation
- Hydrocarbon extraction
- Chlorinated Solvent Extraction
- Enzymatic Treatment and Fermentation
- Carbondioxide Extraction

Application of Spices

Spices are used mainly for food flavoring and preservation. However, spices have medicinal and aromatic properties that also make them useful in a number of industries including:

- Perfumes
- Cosmetics
- Medicine
- Beverages.

In Uttarakhand important spices grown are chilli, ginger, turmeric, coriander, fenugreek and garlic. Total area under spices in Uttarakhand was 5495 hectares in 2001 which has gone to 5905 hectare in 2003. Similarly production has increased from 23635 metric tonnes to 33431 metric tonnes. However during 2004-05 the area and production under spices was reported 6067 hectare and 45365 metric tonnes respectively. It has also been noticed that among the various crops the coverage under chilly was significantly higher.

Table 4.13. Spice Production in Uttarakhand

Spices	*2000-01*		*2001-02*		*2002-03(P)*	
	Area	*Production*	*Area*	*Production*	*Area*	*Production*
Chilli	2356	3925	2406	4062	2406	4082
Ginger	1095	11084	1270	15815	1270	16015
Turmeric	437	3062	467	3469	483	3469
Coriander	515	623	539	2007	535	2000
Fenugreek	183	243	261	396	261	396
Garlic	909	4688	950	7468	950	7468
State Total	5495	23625	5893	33217	5905	33431

Ginger (*Zingiber officinale*), is one of the most traded spice globally. The spice is used extensively for culinary and medicinal application. Though often thought of as the root of the plant, but actually ginger is the rhizome of the *Zingiber officinale* plant. The spice was initially found in China, but later the production extended to other Asian countries including India. In Uttarakhand it is commonly known as *adrak* and it is used in fresh forms and also in dried forms. Ground ginger and ginger oil is also used.

Dried form of ginger is the mostly traded in European countries. Ginger oil and Oleoresins are also widely traded for its flavoring and medicinal properties. India, China, Nigeria, Indonesia, Bangladesh, Thailand, Philippines, Jamaica are the major production centres of ginger. India is the largest producer of dried ginger and contributes approximately 35 percent to the total world production. United Kingdom, United States and Saudi Arabia are major ginger importing countries.

It is evident from the above table that total area under spices cover was reported 6067 hectares with a production of 45365 metric tonnes. The productivity of spices was 6.65 metric tonnes per hectares. Area under spices was marginally higher in Garhwal region whereas the production was higher Kumaon as a result the productivity of Kumaon was 8.31 metric tonnes per hectares which was higher than the state average of 7.48 metric tonnes per hectare. Among the various districts the productivity was highest in Nainital District (11.34 ha/mt) followed by Hardwar (6.65 metric tonnes per hectare). It may by noted that productivity of spices in all the districts of Kumaon was above the state average, except Bageshwar which was equal to state average.

Table 4.14. Districtwise Area, Production and Productivity of Spices in Uttarakhand (2004-05)

S. No.	*Districts*	*Spices*		
		Area	*Production*	*Productivity*
1.	Nainital	358.00	4060.00	11.34
2.	Udham Singh Nagar	721.95	5907.96	8.18
3.	Almora	854.60	6477.86	7.58
4.	Bageshwar	297.25	2223.43	7.48
5.	Pithoragarh	293.00	2540.00	8.67
6.	Champawat	491.10	3854.80	7.85
	Total Kumaon	3015.90	25064.05	8.31
7.	Dehradun	563.30	3665.20	6.51
8.	Pauri	446.00	2697.82	6.05
9.	Tehri	525.80	2213.89	4.21
10.	Chamoli	406.80	2605.22	6.40
11.	Rudraprayag	378.58	2777.37	7.34
12.	Uttarkashi	371.42	2986.92	8.04
13.	Hardwar	359.20	3354.53	9.34
	Total Garhwal	3051.10	20300.95	6.65
	Total Uttarakhand	6067.00	45365.00	7.48

India is one of the major ginger producing country. Indian Ginger is known for its high quality and strong flavor. It is the largest producer of dry ginger and caters to the European and US market. Large scale mechanized operations take place in a few Indian states. There are numerous cultivators in India growing a variety of ginger with varying properties. The exports of Indian Ginger has been on the rise because of competitive pricing and high quality. Ginger is a versatile spice popularly known for its medicinal properties and benefits. It is used for treating cough and cold and is a major ingredient in quite a few cough syrups. It is also used as a cure for gastro-intestinal and carminative problems. Ginger is said to have analgesic, sedative, antipyretic, antibacterial properties. Dried ginger is extensively used for as a condiment and for food flavoring including pies, puddings, cookies and biscuits. It is also used for beverage flavoring including tea, ginger ale and ginger beer.

Area under ginger production was 857.27 hectares in the Garhwal region during 2004-5 and the total production was 7261.79 metric tonnes with a productivity of 8.47 metric tonnes per hectare. The coverage was highest in Tehri (294.17 ha) followed by Dehradun (289.00 ha) on the other hand the productivity was computed highest in Uttarkashi district (13.20 metric tonnes per hectare). In Dehradun the coverage and production is relatively higher in Kalsi, Chakrata, Vikasnagar and Raipur Blocks. On the other hand, in Tehri the coverage and production is relatively more in Narendra Nagar and Kirtinagar.

Turmeric (*Curcuma longa*) belonging to the ginger family is a perennial plant found in the tropical regions of Southern Asia including India. Turmeric is mostly traded in the whole form, and then processed into powder, oil or oleoresin by the industrial sector. The Indian name of turmeric is *haldi.* It is used in the form of turmeric powder and fluid extract. The global trade in turmeric has been increasing in the last few years owing to the increasing awareness of the numerous benefits of turmeric in a number of products and industries. India is the largest producer and exporter of turmeric powder. Bangladesh, Pakistan, Taiwan, Srilanka, Myanmar are other significant producers of turmeric powder. US is the largest exporter of turmeric and India provides 90 percent of the US demand. India is one of the major producers of turmeric and most of the production is used for domestic consumption. The city of Sangli, in Maharashtra is one of the largest trading centres in the world. The export figures from India has doubled in the last decade, with a major rise in turmeric oils and oleoresin exports.

Table 4.15. Area, Production and Productivity of Spices (Ginger, Turmeric, Coriander) (2004-05)

District	*Ginger*			*Turmeric*			*Coriander (Dhania)*		
	Area	*Produ-ction*	*Produ-ctivity*	*Area*	*Produ-ction*	*Produ-ctivity*	*Area*	*Produ-ction*	*Produ-ctivity*
Chamoli	90.00	900.00	10.00	60.00	600.00	10.00	40.00	106.00	2.65
Uttarkashi	21.45	283.13	13.20	6.27	61.40	9.79	49.90	38.27	0.77
Hardwar	30.90	295.00	9.55	29.90	275.00	9.20	34.00	295.00	8.68
Rudraprayag	30.75	191.50	6.23	20.45	181.00	8.85	20.00	33.00	1.65
Tehri	294.17	2206.27	7.50	35.80	213.80	5.97	4.24	1.29	0.30
Pauri	101.00	621.89	6.16	32.40	134.38	4.15	644.50	51.36	0.08
Dehradun	289.00	2764.00	9.56	51.00	141.00	2.76	44.00	65.00	1.48
Total	857.27	7261.79	8.47	235.82	1606.58	6.81	836.64	589.92	0.71

Turmeric has been traditionally used for curing a number of diseases. It is known to prevent various sexual transmitted diseases, has anti-tumoral effects and is considered to be a possible treatment for cancer etc. Coded as E100, turmeric is a widely used food additive for products that are specially packaged to protect from sunlight. It is also used in mustard, pickles for compensating fading colour. Used in a number of products including bakery products, dairy products, cereals, sauces and ketchups, biscuits, cakes etc. Turmeric is used to manufacture various sunscreen, fairness creams and lotions. The anti-oxidant properties helps lighten the skin and also used for treating skin inflammations.

Total area under turmeric in the state was reported 235.82 hectares with a production of 1606.58 metric tonnes. The productivity of turmeric was computed 6.81 metric tonnes per hectare. Table (4.15) also shows that the coverage was highest in Chamoli (60ha) followed by Dehradun (51 ha). Whereas the production was highest in Chamoli (600 mt) followed by Hardwar (275 mt). In Chamoli the coverage and production was relatively more in Karnaprayag block, whereas in Dehradun the main blocks of cultivation were Doiwala and Raipur.

Coriander (*Coriandrum sativum*) is an annual herb popularly grown and prized for its culinary and medicinal use. It is native to North Africa and Southwest Asia. Coriander is always used fresh, as its leaves lose the flavor and aroma on drying. Coriander is never cooked as it also diminishes its flavor. It is used in the end for flavoring the dish. Coriander seeds are also used in whole or powdered form for food seasoning and flavoring. Canada, Morocco, India, Pakistan, Bulgaria and Romania are the major coriander producing countries in the world. Russia is the prime producer of coriander oil used in liquor, pharmaceutical and chemical industry. India is a major coriander powder producing country. Production is done in a number of states on a commercial basis. Gujarat, Rajasthan, Andhra Pradesh, Tamil Nadu and Madhya Pradesh are major Indian production areas. It is also produced in Uttarakhand. A significant percentage of the total coriander produced is used for domestic consumption and the rest is exported. All parts of the herb are edible and widely used in a number of cuisine for flavoring and aroma. Coriander Powder is also used for garnishing.

- Dhania Seeds is known to possess antibacterial properties and has been used in traditional medicine to relieve anxiety and insomnia. Dhania powder also helps to clear the body of lead, mercury and aluminum.

- Pharmaceutical: Dhania powder is used as a flavoring agent in a number of pharmaceutical preparations, especially the digestive medicines.

Total area under coriander was reported 836.64 hectares with the production of 598.92 metric tonnes and the productivity of the same was 0.71 metric tonnes per hectares in the Garhwal region during 2004-05. The area was highest in Pauri with 644.50 hectares followed by Uttarkashi (49.50 hectares). On the other hand in Tehri area under coriander was lowest (4.24 ha). A wide variation has been noticed in the coverage of coriander among the various districts of the state. The important blocks where concentration of coriander in Pauri was reported in Pabaun, Kot and Khirsu and in Uttarkashi the concentration was mainly in Chindiyalisain block.

Chilli (*Capsicum annum* L., *Capsicum frutescens* L.) is one of the largest traded spice in the international market. It is also known as Capsicum, Red pepper, Paprika depending on the species and variety. This spice is extensively used for food flavoring and coloring and also for certain medicinal properties. Chillies are available in a number of varieties, colors and fragrances. Fruit of chilly is used and important countries of chill production are India, China, Spain, Mexico, Pakistan, Morocco and Turkey. India is the largest producer and consumer of Red chilli. Till recently India had a considerable market share, but now the exports of chillies has declined owing to high domestic consumption. Trade in chillies accounts for 16 percent of the global spice trade. China has also emerged as one of the top most exporters of chillies. Japan is known for producing special kinds of chillies including Santaka, Hontaka etc. India is the largest producer of a variety of chillies. Countries including USA, Sri Lanka, Nepal, Bangladesh are the major importers of various forms of chillies. The high domestic consumption of the spice limits the export potential to a certain extent. India faces tough competition in terms of product pricing from Pakistan and China. Chilliies are used for following purposes:

- Dry and powdered chillies are widely used for coloring and flavoring in different cuisines and dishes. It is also used as a major ingredient in various seasonings, pepper and tabasco sauce.

- Chilli powder is also used for natural food coloring.
- Chillies are used to control rheumatic disorders. It is also a good source of vitamin C.

Chilli is also produced in the entire Uttarakhand region. The area under Chilli in Garhwal region during 2004-05 was reported 567.35 hectares with a production of 997.12 metric tonnes. The productivity of chilli was 1.76 metric tonnes per hectare. Among the various districts the coverage was highest in Pauri (141.96 ha) followed by Tehri (100.24 ha). However, the production was highest in Rudraprayag district which was recorded 217 metric tonnes. On the other hand the productivity was highest in Hardwar which was computed 9.32 metric tonnes per hectare. Though cultivation of chilli is practiced across the state, however in Rudraprayag district it is more concentrated in Augustmuni and Jakholi blocks while in Pauri, it is mainly produced in Nainidanda, Khirsu, Yamkeshwar and Kot blocks.

Table 4.16. Area, Production and Productivity of Spices (Chilli, Garlic, Bari Ilaichi)

District	*Chilli*			*Garlic*			*Bari Ilaichi*		
	Area	*Production*	*Productivity*	*Area*	*Production*	*Productivity*	*Area*	*Production*	*Productivity*
Chamoli	82.00	123.55	1.51	105.00	735.00	7.00	10.00	1.00	0.10
Uttarkashi	84.30	36.16	0.43	35.80	64.07	1.79	0.55	1.95	3.54
Hardwar	13.20	123.00	9.32	55.00	506.00	9.20	0.00	0.00	0.00
Rudraprayag	62.65	217.00	3.46	30.00	132.00	4.40	5.63	5.57	0.99
Tehri	100.24	185.12	1.85	91.04	318.63	3.50	0.81	3.89	4.80
Pauri	141.96	192.29	1.35	78.10	333.25	4.27	0.56	0.36	0.64
Dehradun	83.00	120.00	1.45	64.00	535.00	8.36	3.00	3.00	1.00
Total	567.35	997.12	1.76	458.94	2623.95	5.72	20.55	15.77	0.77

Cardamom (*Elettaria cardamonum*) finds extensive use in Scandinavian and Indian cuisine. It is found in Asian countries and also Australia depending on the type. It is one of the most expensive spice after saffron and vanilla. The important varieties of cardamom are given below:

- Green Cardamom (*Eletarria*), also known as True or Small

Cardamom is found in east Asian countries including India and Malaysia.

- Black Cardamom (*Amomum*), also known as Java or Siamese Cardamom is found in Australia and Asia.
- Madagascar Cardamom (*Aframomum*) is found in Africa and Madagascar.

Large cardamom farming is suitable for the people of hill state. As it grows well under the shade in humid environments, it can be cultivated under nitrogen-fixing tree species in moist wastelands— with annual rainfall between 150 mm to 2,500 mm — along water channels, field *bunds* and terraces. Large cardamom plantations may extensively use the nitrogen-fixing *Alnus nepalensis* as its shade tree. However, extreme cold or frost and waterlogged conditions adversely affect plant growth. Cardamom grows best in a slightly acidic, sandy loam soil. Plants can be raised from seeds and fruits after about five years, but vegetative propagation from slips is preferred as they fruit within three years from planting. Composting is very important. It is also valued for its medicinal properties, this high-priced spice crop may become a boon for the people of Uttarakhand. It doesn't require much external input, is low-volume, non-perishable and less labour-intensive. It also gives high economic returns, with a market price of Rs 100 per kilogram.

Thus, large cardamom gives impoverished farmers a comparative advantage. Despite being a cash crop, it's still a sustainable option that keeps the forest intact, using shade trees that protect the landscape from soil erosion and nutrient loss. With the rate of forest depletion in our mountains, large cardamom offers a strong forestry component that meets the basic requirements of fuel, fodder and timber. It is both an ecological and economically viable resource.

Guatemala, India, Sri Lanka, Indo-China and Tanzania are the major producers. Both black and green cardamom are extensively grown for exports. Guatemala supplies nearly two-thirds of the total world production. Saudi Arabia is the largest consumer of this spice, followed by Kuwait. The use of cardamom oil and oleoresins is also on the rise in the international market. It is cultivated and grown in the forests of the western ghats in Southern India, where it grows wild. Indian Cardamom is more aromatic and hence in huge demand. The southern states of Kerala, Karnataka, and Tamil Nadu are the major growing areas in India. Kerala accounts for nearly 70 percent of the total production. India consumed almost 90 percent of the spice production and the remaining 10 percent is exported to countries including Saudi Arabia, Japan etc. The uses of Cardamom are given below:

- It is used as a stimulant, for indigestion and flatulence. It is also sometimes considered to be an aphrodisiac in traditional systems of medicine.
- It is widely used in flavoring drinks like milk shakes and tea.
- The spice is also used for aroma and flavoring of a variety of food products including biscuits, ice cream and milk shake powders, cakes, confectionery, candies etc.

In Uttarakhand cardamom is mainly grown in the hilly districts of Chamoli, Pauri, Uttarkashi and Rudraprayag and also in the hilly blocks of district Dehradun. Total area under this crops was only 20 hectares with a production of 15.77 metric tonnes. It is mainly grown in Ghat and Karnaprayag blocks of Chamoli, Augastmuni and Jakholi blocks of Rudraprayag district, Bhatwari and Chindiyalsain of Uttarkashi district, Kirtinagar and Pratapnagar of Tehri district, Pauri and Kot of Pauri District and Kalsi of Dehradun District.

Garlic is an important medicinal herb that is readily available everywhere. It is one of the safest herbs, and as such can be taken often. Garlic does indeed have scientifically-proven medicinal properties. It contains a substance called Allicin, which has anti-bacterial properties that are equivalent to a weak penicillin. It appears that cooked garlic weakens the anti-bacterial effects considerably, however, so don't count on cooked garlic with meals for much in the way of a curative. Garlic appears to have anti-bacterial and anti-viral properties. The list is long when it comes to its uses as a remedy. This list includes wounds, ulcers, skin infections, flu, athlete's foot, some viruses, strep, worms, respiratory ailments, high blood pressure, blood thinning, cancer of the stomach, colic, colds, kidney problems, bladder problems, and ear aches, to name a few. It is believed to cure worms in both people and animals - try giving the dog a clove of garlic daily (but he's not gonna like it). For most internal problems, eating garlic raw is probably the most potent way to take it. However, due to the obvious lingering odors associated with this, a tincture can be made by soaking 1/4 pound of peeled and separated garlic cloves in 1/2 quart of brandy.

Seal tightly and shake every day. Strain and bottle after two weeks of this, and take in drops - 25-30 a day, if desired.

Garlic, common name for several strongly scented herbs of the lily family, and for the bulbs of these plants, which are used as a flavoring. Garlic, like the related onion, has small, six-part, whitish flowers borne on umbels. The fruit is a capsule containing black, kidney-shaped seeds. Common garlic has been cultivated since ancient times. The bulb, which has a strong characteristic odor and taste, is covered with a papery skin and may be broken into constituent bulblets, called cloves. Garlic is used as a flavoring agent in cooking and pickling, sometimes in the form of whole or grated cloves and sometimes in the form of a cooked extract, as in sauces and dressings. In medicine, garlic is used as a digestive stimulant, diuretic, and antispasmodic.

On the other hand, garlic is grown across the region and total area under garlic was reported 458.94 hectares with a production 2623. 95 metric tonnes. The productivity of garlic was computed 5.72 metric tonnes per hectare. The area and production under garlic was highest in Chamoli where it is mainly found in Gairsain, Ghat Karanprayag and Narayanbagad blocks.

Table 4.17 . Area, Production and Productivity of Spices (Onion and Others)

District	*Onion*			*Other*			*Total*		
	Area	*Production*	*Productivity*	*Area*	*Production*	*Productivity*	*Area*	*Production*	*Productivity*
Chamoli	0.00	0.00	0.00	20.00	140.00	7.00	407.00	2605.00	6.40
Uttarkashi	73.14	501.95	6.86	0.0	0.00	0.00	271.41	1026.92	3.78
Hardwar	171.00	1629.00	9.53	25.00	232.00	9.28	359.00	3355.00	9.35
Rudraprayag	0.00	0.00	0.00	9.10	17.30	1.90	178.58	777.37	4.35
Tehri	0.00	0.00	0.00	0.00	0.00	0.00	515.44	2930.01	5.68
Pauri	180.00	1800.00	10.00	0.00	0.00	0.00	1178.06	3201.28	2.72
Dehradun	0.00	0.00	0.00	29.00	37.00	1.28	563.00	3665.00	6.51
Total	424.14	3930.95	9.27	583.1	324.30	7.20	3472.49	17560.58	5.06

Onion, common name for any of a genus of biennial herbs, of the lily family, native to Asia but cultivated in temperate and subtropical regions for thousands of years. The true onion is a bulb-bearing plant. Its long, hollow leaves with thickened bases make up most of the bulb. The white or pink flowers, which are borne in umbels, have six sepals, six petals, six stamens, and a solitary pistil. In the varieties known as top onions, the flowers are supplanted by bulblets, which may be grown to obtain new plants. The plant contains sulfurous, volatile oils that give it a characteristic pungent taste; one component readily dissolves in water to produce sulphuric acid, which may be produced in the eyes and induce tears. Onions are one of the most versatile vegetables. They are eaten raw in salads, are cooked or pickled in a variety of ways, and are used as a flavoring or seasoning. Dehydrated onion products provide popular flavorings for soups and stews.

Onions raised in warm areas are planted as winter crops and are milder in taste and odor than onions planted during the summer in cooler regions. Yellow Bermuda and white Spanish onions are among the mildest cultivated onions. Onions are easily grown from seed that may be either field-grown directly or planted in beds to produce small bulbs, or sets. These are commonly dried and shipped to gardeners and commercial growers. Onions are adaptable to temperature and can be planted year-round as long as the soil is rich and moist. They are sown four to six weeks before the last frost in the spring or are planted in late summer for a fall crop. The crop is allowed to ripen in the field until tops begin to bend and break. The bulbs are then pulled up and spread or hung in a dry area to cure. Once dry, they are normally stored and shipped in slotted or open-mesh bags to keep them dry enough to prevent sprouting. United States' commercial production of onions at the beginning of the 21st century exceeded 3,000,000 metric tons. Other onions in the genus include the nodding wild onion, the shallot, the chive, and the green onion, or common leek. Both the shallot and the green onion, which have small bulbs, are also known as scallions.

Total area under onion was 424.14 hectares with a production of 3930 metric tonnes. The productivity of onion was commuted 9.27 metric tonnes per hectare. Among the various districts it was reported in three districts only and area under onion cultivation was highest in Pauri (180.00 ha) followed by Hardwar (171 hectares). In Pauri the concentration was mainly in Yamkeshwar, Dwarikhal, Jahrikhal and Dugadda blocks, and in Hardwar the area under onion cultivation was mainly reported in Bhadarabad and Lakshar blocks.

Infrastructure Available for Horticulture Development

The exploit the potential of horticulture in Uttarakhand hills and state government has developed infrastructure under the department of horticulture and food processing. The detailed infrastructural facilities is given in Table 4.18.

Table 4.18. Available Infrastructure for Horticulture Development

S.N.	*Infrastructure*	*Number*
1.	Horticulture Experiment and Research Centres and Sub-centers	12
2.	Horticulture Training Center	1
3.	Food science Training Centre	2
4.	Fruit Preservation Centre	45
5.	Horticultre Mobile Teams	186
6.	Compost Pasteurization Plant and Spawan Production Centre	2
7.	Govt. Cold Storage (under construction)	2
8.	Bee Keeping Centre	2
9.	Govt. Nurseries	75
10.	Private Sector Nurseries	57
11.	Progeny Orchards	20
12.	Govt. Gardens	9
13.	Potato Seed Multiplication Farm	10
14.	Vegetable Seed Production Farm	7
15.	Elite Garden	5

The main horticultural Experiment and Training Centres each for valley areas and temperate areas are located at Srinagar (Pauri dist.) and Chaubatia (Almora dist.). The subcentres are located at Dunda (Uttarkashi), Chakarata and Dakrani (Dehradun), Kothialsain (Chamoli), Rudrapur (US Nagar), Matela (Almora), Jeolikot (Nainital) and Pithoragarh. Horticulture Experiment and Training Centres and subcentres are engaged in experiments and trials on various aspects of horticultural crops. These centres also provide technical guidance and training to growers and enthusiasts. At these centres various germplasms of fruit and vegetables are also being maintained for future use. The Horticlture Training Centre located at Chaubatia (Ranikhet) is engaged in training local youth for various horticultural practices and encourage them to adopt horticulture as a profession. Food Science Training Centers located at Nainital and Kotdwara run one-year training course in three subjects—(i) Fruit Preservation, (ii) Cookery and (iii) Baking and

Confectionary. In order to increase home scale about 14000 personnel and housewives are being trained and about 5 lakh kgs of fruit and vegetable products are being prepared at 45 fruit preservation centres annually.

Problems of Fruit Production in Uttarakhand

In the hills of Uttarakhand fruit production is still low both in quality and quantity. The returns to the farmers are also comparatively lower in this region. The important geographical, ecological, cultural, social and marketing factors which are mainly responsible for this are being discussed here.

Acute Hill Slopes: In comparison to the neighboring hill state Himachal Pradesh, the hill of Uttaralhand are mostly steep so much so that some tracts are entirely unfit for growing of any crop. Steeper slopes accelerate soil erosion reducing their organic matter content and leaching-out important minerals from the soil leading to reduced fertility.

Poor Soils: In this region at many places soils are invariably infertile, acidic and shallow resulting into low water retention capacity. The soils have varying percentage of stones and pebbles and are thus susceptible to severe drought.

Small and Scattered Holdings: The land holdings of farmers are small and scattered. The per capita land holding of the farmers in this region is 0.14 ha. Besides, the holdings are scattered at different sites making their management very difficult. Moreover, fruit growing is a long term venture and farmers are not in a position to ensure their safety at many sites. In such a institution, high investment in land development is not possible.

Frequent Hailstorms: The entire hill region of Uttarakhand hills is prone to hailstorms whereas in H.P. & J.&K. only some pockets are hail prone. Hence, almost every year the fruit crops are damaged making the fruit growing a gamble. High intensity of hail not only damage the fruits but also harm to foliage, permanent nature.

Unavailability of Irrigation: In the Uttranchal hills the annual rainfall is low and unevenly distributed. The rainy season commencing from the second week of June last till the middle of September. The average rainfall is 1525 mm raining from 1016 to 2360 mm. Nearly 80 percent rain occurs in monsoon while only 11 percent in winter season.

The summer season is a drought period in which fruits grow on the trees and thereby their development is adversely affected. The fruits are mainly cultivated under rainfed conditions as irrigation facilities are not available. Due to the lack of water, the fruit size and quality become poor.

Plantation of Obsolete Varieties: All over the world, the varieties of delicious group of apples are being cultivated mainly. In Himachal Pradesh the percentage of area under the delicious group is 94 and in Jammu and Kashmir is 50, while in Uttranchal hills it is only 30 percent. Many of the apple varieties grown are obsolete, fetching less income to the orchardists.

Inadequate Cultural Practices: In Uttrakhand the orchardists do not pay sufficient attention on the cultural practices as substantial number of them are absentee landlords. Even the survival of plants after plantation is very poor. Likewise, manuring, trimming and pruning, intercultural operations and control of pests and diseases are neglected.

Improper Grading and Packing: Proper grading and packing systems are not followed in Uttaranchal hills, resulting in low rate of produce in the market. In fact, many a time growers pack diseased and damaged fruits which spoil good fruits during transit. Sometime apples are packed and transported in gunny bags. The packing materials still in use are pine niddles, grasses.

Defective Marketing System: Most of the orcards in Uttranchal are sold preharvest to contractors. This system deprives farmers from his due income as contractors pay very low rate. In such a situation, the functioning of coooperative marketing is also not possible.

Difficult Transportation: Fruit orchards are usually planted at remote sites, away from the road heads making transportation of fruits to the road heads very costly and cumbersome.

Inadequate Research and Extension Support: Fruit culture is a highly technical enterprise whereas farmers are accustomed to traditional agriculture. Due to lack of technical knowledge they do not venture to take up fruit growing. The research support on various aspects of cultivation in different agro-climatic conditions is not available. Although extension infrastructure of the department is available, yet it is not adequate and well trained.

ANNEXURE 4.1

Fruit Crops, Varieties, Months of Availability and Important Localities of Cultivation

Name of fruit crop with important varieties	*Month of availability*	*Districtwise important localities of cultivation*
Apple: Fanny, Benoni, Early Shanburry, Chaubattia Princess, Red Delicious, Starking Delicious, Golden Delicious, Buckingom, Rymer, etc.	June to October	Almora: Lamgarha, Saharfatak, Garurabanj, Tarikhet Nainital: Ramgarh, Dhari, Paharpani. Tehri: Chamba, Dhanulty, Kanatal. Uttarkashi: Naugaon, Barkot, Purola. Chamoli: Joshimath, Gwaldam. Dehradun: Chakarata.
Pear: Gola, Victoria, Thumbear, Baurre, Hardy, Jargonelle, Doyenne, Du comice,	July to October	Almora: Lamgarha, Tarikhet Nainital: Ramgarh, Dhari, Bhimtal Tehri: Chamba Belt. Uttarkashi: Naugaon, Purola.
Peach: Crowford, Early, Early elbarta, Parigriene Alexender, Sunred, Nectrine	July to August	Nainital: Ramgarh, Dhari, Bhimtal Almora: Lamgarha, Tarikhet Tehri: Pratapnagar Uttarkashi: Purola.
Plum: First plum, New plum, Santarosa, Mariposa, Maynard	May to July	Almora: Lamgarha, Tarikhet Nainital: Ramgarh, Bhimtal Pithoragarh: Didihat, Champawat Pauri: Khirsu, Pauri.
Apricot: Charmagha, Turky, Kaisa, Chaubattina Madhu, Moorpark, Newlarge Early Royal	May to June	Almora: Lamgarha, Tarikhet Nainital: Ramgarh, Bhimtal Pithoragarh: Didihat, Champawat Pauri: Khirsu, Pauri.
Walnut: Tutle, Xinea Hartley, Japan, Walnut, Eueka, Lake English	November to June	Almora: Lamgarha, Tarikhet Nainital: Ramgarh, Bhimtal Pithoragarh: Didihat, Champawat Pauri: Khirsu, Pauri.

ANNEXURE 4.2

Varieties of Different Fruits Recommended for Different Zones in Uttarakhand

Zones	*Name of Fruit*	*Varieties*
1. Tarai Bhabar area and Dehradun Valley	Mango	Bomabay Green, Bombay yellow, Langra, Chausa, Dashehri,
	Citrus	Eureka Lemon, Kagzi, Kalan
	Litchi	Early large Red, Calcuttia, Rose scented Dehradun local late seedless
	Guava	Lucknow-49, Safeda Local
	Jackfruit	Local
	Papaya	Ranchi, Dwarf, Pusa Nanha, Coorg honeydew
2. Humid Valleys and Hills of outer Hima-laya upto 1500 masl.	Mango	Same as in first
	Citurus	Sweet orange, (Malta common), Hill lemon,
	Pear	Eurika lemon
	Walnut	Gola
	Peach	Grafted plants on terraces and seedlings in Ravines
	Plum	Florida sun, Crow ford Early, Early Alberta
	Apricot	SantarosaKisa, Shipleys Early
3. Hot and Dry valleys and low hills upto 1500 masl.	Peach	Same as in 2
	Pear	Same as in 2
	Citrus	Sweet orange (Malta common), Mandarin (Srinagar and Kinnu) hill lemon and Kagzi lime
	Mango	Same as in 1
	Almond	California paper shell, Brigs hard shell, Ne plus altra and drake
	Walnut	Same as in 2
	Apricot	Same as in 2
	Main Areas of Cultivation	
	Almora	Chaukhutia valley to Dwarahat, Gagas valley, Someshwar Manan valley, Garur Valley, Kuj garh valley, Sylde block, Bhikiyasen and Salt block
Pithoragarh	Askote, Dharchulla Valley	
Dehradun	Tons valley in Teoni area	
Pauri	Panar valley, Alaknanda valley from Srinagar to Rudraprayag, Pokhra block	
Tehri	Bhagirathi valley from Tehri to Dharasu, Bhilangana valley	
Uttarkashi	Bhagirathy valley from Dharasu to Uttarkashi, Yamuna valley from Damta to Gangnani, Mori to Naitwar in Tons valley, Purola area	

Chamoli	Alaknanda valley from Rudraprayag to Pipalkoti, Mandal, Simli-Adi Badri, Pindar valley from Karnprayag to Narayanbagar, Rudraprayag, Guptkashi to Mandakini valley	
	Main Areas of Cultivation	
Almora	Mohan to Machhor, Bhikiasen valley, Bageshwar valley	
Nanital	Most of the Bhimtal Block, Talla Ramgarh, Betalghat, Garampani, Kotabag block	
Pithorgarh	Tanakpur to Ghat	
Dehradun	Kalsi to Damta, Kalsi to Sayha	
Pauri	Dugadda block, Alaknanda valley from Muni ki Reti to Devprayag	
4. (ii) Above 2000 to 2500 masl.	Apple	Royal Delicious, Golden Delicious, McIntosh and Spartan
	Hazelnut	Same as in 4
	Walnut	Same as in 2
	Main Areas of Cultivation	
Almora,	Takula, Gacanath, Bhainsoli, Sama, Binsar, Lamgarha, Sitlakhet, Saharphatak, Bargaon, Jalana, Dol, Dunagiri, Dadholi, Manila, Seoni, Kunelakhet, Garurbanj and Doram	
Nainital	Natchuwa-Richi, Ramgarh, Gagar, Satbunga, Khan, Dhari, Padampuri, Gunalekh, Mukteshwar, Hartola	
Pithoragarh	Kanalichhina, Minarigaon, Champawat, Gansari, Lohaghat, Tomik, Bhaka, Sirkha, Jarapani, Pokhri, Kali-dhek, Baugaon and Gangnause	
Pauri	Pauri, Buwakhal, Khandusain, Khirsu, Chobatta, Thalisain, Gumkhal, Chellusain, Dumakote, Berunkhal, Pokhra and Yamkeshwar	
Dehradun	Chakarata, Chausal, Barotha, Naugaon, Mussoorie	
Tehri	Jaunpur, Magra, Thadur, Majaf, Pratapnagar, Lambgaon, Chamba, Gaja, Jaripani, Narendranagar, Fakote, Ranichauri, Thauldhar, Saklana	
Chamoli	Bachher, Dasholi, Ghat, Mailchauri, Gwaldum, Talwari, Joshimath, Badgaon, Rabigram, Parsari	
Uttarkashi	Bhatwari, Harsil, Raithal, Maneri, Dwari, Brahamkhal, Seori, Badkot, Gangnani, Purola, Jarmola, Ringali, Thadiyar, Valcha	
5. High hills above 2500 m to 3000 masl.	Walnut Hazelnut	Seedlings Same as in 4

	Areas of Cultivation
Almora	Kapkote and Bhatkote
Pithoragarh	Munsyari, Balanti
Chamoli	Parsari, Auli
Uttarkashi	Balcha, Harsil, Gangotri and Yamnotri area

Source: Department of Horticulture & Food Processing, Uttarakhand.

5

Horticulture in Survey Region: Emerging Issues

In the Himalayan region sustainable management of the marginal holdings is getting increasing priority with the increasing population pressure, poverty, soil erosion and degradation, and loss of natural resources for food security, improved livelihood and environmental protection. Diversification of farm activities into high value commercial crops, and processing of agricultural and other natural resource based materials, while adequately maintaining soil, forest and other natural resources, are most logical steps to improving livelihood of mountain people. Mountains provide an excellent avenue of diverse agro-environments, thereby scope for horticulture, floriculture, spices and medicinal plants. Poverty, small holding size and food security are the critical challenges in the mountain areas and call for a holistic approach to address them for improvement and sustainability.

The economy of Uttarakhand is primarily subsistence in nature and mainly dependent on the agriculture produce, which cater to day to day requirements of the households. Due to small landholdings surplus in the form of foodgrain is rarely produced, particularly in the hilly districts. However the hilly districts are climatically best suited for diversification of agriculture crops. This will not only contribute substantially to enhance the cash income of the households but also address the issues of livelihood to a great extent. Further the sector may provide ample opportunities of employment to the local people not only on the farm related activities but also in the secondary and tertiary sectors in the form of processing, transportation and marketing of produce. Nevertheless, designing of proper policies at the government level is very vital for the over-all growth and development of this sector. Therefore the role of state machinery cannot be ignored totally.

Therefore, in the present chapter an attempt is being made to elucidate various issues related to horticulture development in the state of Uttarakhand. The analysis is based on the survey carried out during 2002 in the six blocks of three districts in Garhwal region of the state. The criteria followed for selection of districts, blocks and thereby villages have already been discussed.

Profile of Sample Villages

Distribution of Sample Villages: While selecting the sample villages attempt has been made to consider accessibility to motarable road as an important criteria. This criteria is significant primarily because of difficult hilly terrain, which itself is a major bottleneck for the development of any sector in the hilly region. Since the horticulture produce in terms of fruits and vegetable are perishable items, therefore this factor itself is of paramount interest. As evident from the table the selection of the villages from the road side, within 1 –3 km. from the road and more than 3 km from the road is proportionally distributed. Nevertheless, number of villages selected from the roadside are marginally higher (35.63 percent). Among the serveyed blocks the proportion of villages selected from the roadside is higher in Joshimath block and proportion of villages selected beyond 3 km from roadside was lowest in Purola

Table 5.1. Distribution of Sample Village According to Distance by Road

Blocks	*Villages at road side*	*Villages 1-3 km. from road head side*	*Village more than 3 km. from road side*	*Total*
Joshimath	4 (40.00)	3 (30.00)	3 (30.00)	10 (100.00)
Pokhri	9 (36.00)	8 (32.00)	8 (32.00)	25 (100.00)
Chamba	8 (34.78)	8 (34.78)	7 (30.44)	23 (100.00)
Pratapnagar	4 (33.33)	4 (33.33)	4 (33.33)	12 (100.00)
Purola	3 (37.50)	3 (37.50)	2 (25.00)	8 (100.00)
Bhatwari	3 (33.33)	3 (33.33)	3 (33.33)	9 (100.00)
Total	31 (35.63)	29 (33.33)	27 (31.04)	87 (100.00)

block. On the whole the villages were proportionally distributed among the selected blocks under the criteria chosen for this purpose.

Age Distribution of Selected Orchard Owner: While analyzing the age wise distribution of selected orchard owner it is revealed that majority of them falls in the age group 36-59 followed by age group 60 and above. The proportion of orchard owners reporting their age 15-35 were 14.95 percent only. Similar trend has been noticed among the surveyed blocks, however the proportion of orchard owners having age in the range of 35-69 years was reported highest in Partapnagar block (76.66 percent).

Table 5.2. Age Wise Distribution of Selected Orchard Owner

Blocks/Age Group	*15-35*	*36-59*	*More than 59*	*Total*
Joshimath	4 (8.00)	31 (62.00)	15 (30.00)	50 (100.00)
Pokhri	23 (20.00)	60 (52.18)	32 (27.82)	115 (100.00)
Chamba	18 (14.40)	68 (54.40)	39 (31.28)	125 (100.00)
Pratapnagar	4 (6.67)	46 (76.66)	10 (16.67)	60 (100.00)
Purola	7 (17.50)	23 (57.50)	10 (25.00)	40 (100.00)
Bhatwari	9 (20.00)	25 (55.55)	11 (24.45)	45 (100.00)
Total	65 (14.94)	253 (58.16)	117 (26.90)	435 (100.00)

Educational Level of Orchards Owners: On the analysis of Table 5.4, it is revealed that among the surveyed orchard owners 41.14 percent have attained education upto 5th standard followed by 25.74 percent upto 8th standard. The percentage of illiterate owners was reported 17.70, which is also significantly higher. On the other hand the proportion of orchard owners having education level 12th and above is considerably low as only 2.75 such owners have attained education level 12th and above. Among the surveyed blocks the proportion of orchard owners having attained education level upto 8th was recorded highest (46.66 percent) in Barkot block. It may also be noted that in Pokhari, Pratapnagar, Purola and Barkot block even a signle farmer has not attained educational level upto 12th standard. In general it can be concluded that in the study area the average educational level of orchardists is primary level.

Table 5.3. Family Size of the Selected Orchardists

Block / Persons	*0-4*	*4-6*	*6-8*	*More than 8*	*Total*
Joshimath	9 (18.00)	13 (26.00)	22 (44.00)	6 (12.00)	50 (100.00)
Pokhri	13 (10.40)	62 (49.60)	37 (29.60)	13 (10.40)	125 (100.00)
Chamba	23 (20.00)	56 (48.70)	26 (22.60)	10 (8.70)	115 (100.00)
Pratapnagar	7 (11.66)	38 (63.34)	12 (20.00)	3 (5.00)	60 (100.00)
Purola	4 (10.00)	17 (42.50)	12 (30.00)	7 (17.00)	40 (100.00)
Barkot	2 (10.00)	22 (48.98)	17 (37.78)	4 (8.89)	45 (100.00)
Total	58 (13.33)	208 (47.82)	126 (28.96)	43 (9.89)	435 (100.00)

Table 5.4. Education Level-wise Distribution of Orchardists

Block	*Illiterate*	*Up to 5th*	*Up to 8th*	*Up to 10th*	*Up to 12th*	*Total*
Joshimath	4 (8.00)	24 (48.00)	12 (24.00)	7 (14.00)	3 (6.00)	50 (100.00)
Pokhri	26 (20.80)	48 (38.40)	32 (25.60)	19 (15.00)	—	125 (100.00)
Chamba	12 (10.4)	57 (49.56)	23 (20.00)	14 (12.18)	9 (7.82)	115 (100.00)
Pratapnagar	14 (23.34)	21 (35.00)	17 (28.4)	8 (13.33)	—	60 (100.00)
Purola	12(30.00)	17 (42.5)	7 (17.50)	4 (10.00)	—	40 (100.00)
Barkot	9 (20.00)	12 (26.66)	21 (46.66)	3 (6.67)	—	45 (100.00)
Total	77 (17.70)	179 (41.14)	112 (25.74)	55 (12.64)	12 (2.75)	435 (100.00)

Main Occupation of the Orchard Owners

Attempt has also been made to understand the occupation of the orchard owners in the study area. It is surprising to note that only 14.53 percent households have reported horticulture as the main occupation.

Whereas the proportion of households reported agriculture and horticulture as main occupation was significantly higher as it constitutes ¾ of the total households covered in the survey. This also indicate that the farmers of the region have crop diversification, which is perhaps the best suited strategy for the over-all development of the region. In the hilly region owners have to think in terms of alternative as the incidence of seasonal unemployment immensely affects the economic conditions of the farmers. The physiographic conditions and transport and communication network badly affect overall activities of the region, particularly during the rainy seasons, which also prompt the growers to think in terms of subsistence. This has always been primary cause of concern to farmers of the hilly terrain.

The seasonal rhythm of agricultural operations is a peculiar characteristic of the sector. It is peculiar because certain agriculture operations are to be completed before beginning or end of the particular season. This rash nature of agricultural activities draws many non-farm workers in the field during peak season, while during slack seasons even the regular farm workers have to sit idle. This idleness or seasonal unemployment is enforced and inevitable feature of vacation arises mainly because of the inelastic time pattern of the primary sector and horticulture is also adversely affected by this.

Table 5.5. Main Occupation of the Selected Orchardists

Blocks	*Horticulture Only*	*Horti. & Agriculture*	*Industry*	*Service*	*Total*
Joshimath	9 (18.00)	36 (72.00)	1 (12.00)	4 (18.00)	50 (100.00)
Pokhri	6 (4.83)	96 (77.42)	8 (6.45)	14 (11.30)	124 (100.00)
Chamba	19 (16.52)	72 (62.60)	4 (3.44)	20 (17.39)	115 (100.00)
Pratapnagar	4 (6.60)	47 (78.33)	3 (5.00)	6 (10.00)	60 (100.00)
Purola	12 (30.00)	24 (60.00)	1 (2.00)	3 (7.50)	40 (100.00)
Barkot	9 (19.56)	28 (60.86)	2 (4.34)	7 (15.21)	46 (100.00)
Total	59 (14.53)	303 (67.24)	19 (4.67)	54 (13.54)	435 (100.00)

In the study region, the majority of the household operate mix-farming system. Over the years many changes have been taking place in terms of land resource allocation, production, and productivity of cereal foodgrain crops, horticultural crops, livestock structure and composition generally influenced by forest and other natural resources, input supplies, marketing and other socio-economic infrastructures. The important conditions characterising mountain agriculture are inaccessibility, fragility, marginality, diversity and niche. The critical challenges in mountain agriculture are crop land security, soil erosion and declining soil fertility, increasing poverty and farming on marginal farms (Sah, 2001). The studies have indicated numerous indicators of unsustainable mountain agriculture in the HKH (Jodha and Shrestha, 1994).

Land Holding

Mountain farmers in their desperate bid to maintain their livelihoods under these complex challenges, have adopted multiple strategies to cope with the problems. These include, among others, extending cultivation to steep slopes and increasing male migration to plains and urban areas. The net result has been the accentuation of environmental degradation, abandonment of land, increased drudgery of women, and ultimately immiserisation, impoverishment and endemic poverty.

The state of affairs of mountains agriculture described above poses difficult questions and paints a grim picture for time to come as:

- Where we go from here?
- How to ensure livelihood and food security?
- What are hopes and options?
- How we preserve environment and rich biodiversity of mountains?

The availability of vast amount of marginal land including waste land, grazing land, range land, shrub land and unclassed forest etc in the HKH can provide a ray of hope to mountain farmers to provide support to farming and livelihood in the hills and mountains (Pratap 2001). This requires identification and promotion of suitable technologies with necessary logistic supports to bring about impacts and economic transformation.

Usually marginal lands are defined as low potential, resource poor, fragile, vulnerable or degraded lands. However, in real sense a land could be marginal or highly productive depending upon its use, other biophysical/institutional and socio-economic factors. For example, a tract of sloping land is marginal for crop production, but highly potential for grazing, fruit farming or for important herbs. The nature, composition and interaction of the factors, can also differ widely. Also, there are number of factors that may shift such land from one category to another. The shift could be upward through application of appropriate technologies, or downwards as a result of land degradation and/or lack of necessary institutional support to promote a particular enterprise. Hence, marginality is a dynamic process—a land unsuitable for rice due to topography, lack of irrigation, could be highly productive for fruit farming or livestock farming.

The forest and grazing lands are the foundations upon which sustainability of hill farming system is based and thereby food security and livelihood of the mountain people. The crop-livestock-forest relationship has begun to weaken in the areas where forest resources are scarce, and where strong influence of market forces on farming exists. In many countries, the marginal land has been over-exploited for crop production even on steep slopes and gravel soils that have further aggravated the environment and natural resources in the mountains.

Table 5.6. Land Holdings of the Selected Orchardists

(Area in Nali)

Blocks	*0 - 20*	*20 - 40*	*40 - 60*	*60 - 80*	*80 - 100*	*> 100*	*Total*
Joshimath	3 (6.00)	5 (10.00)	14 (28.00)	10 (20.00)	12 (24.00)	6 (12.00)	50 (100.00)
Pokhri	12 (9.60)	38 (30.40)	27 (21.6)	33 (26.40)	11 (8.80)	4 (3.20)	125 (100.00)
Chamba	17 (14.78)	16 (13.92)	19 (16.52)	29 (25.22)	21 (18.26)	13 (11.30)	115 (100.00)
Pratapnagar	7 (11.67)	9 (15.00)	19 (31.67)	15 (25.00)	7 (11.66)	3 (5.00)	60 (100.00)
Purola	2 (5.00)	5 (12.50)	5 (12.50)	13 (32.50)	10 (25.00)	5 (12.50)	40 (100.00)
Badkot	2 (4.44)	7 (15.56)	4 (8.88)	10 (22.23)	12 (26.66)	10 (22.23)	45 (100.00)
Total	43 (9.89)	80 (18.39)	88 (20.23)	110 (25.28)	73 (16.79)	41 (9.42)	435 (100.00)

Note: Nali is a vernacular name of local measurement unit of area still prevalent in Garhwal Himalaya, one nali= 196 sq meters, or 51 nali = 1 hectare).

The forest do play an important ecological role for maintaining the hydrology and soil movement from the sloping land.

The above Table clearly indicates that out of the 435 households covered in the study 43 are having land upto 20 nali only which is significantly low. The number of households having land upto 20-40 and 40-60 nali was reported 80 and 88 respectively. It may also be noted that highest number of households (110) were having land between 60-80 nali. On the other hand only 41 households were having land beyond 100 nali. A significant variation has been noticed in distribution of land among the surveyed blocks. As evident from the table in Joshimath and Pratapnagar blocks highest number of households are reported having 40-60 nali of land. On the other hand in Pokhari block highest number of households were having land between 20-40 nali.

The vast amount of marginal sloppy lands available in the region provide a big hope for future. Marginal lands have been over-exploited and misused leading to increased poverty, soil degradation and loss of natural resources. Suitable agriculture/forestry enterprise and their technologies need to be developed and implemented for increased income, employment and sustainability. It is equally important that necessary infrastructure, logistics inputs and marketing system are in place to bring about desired impacts.

Table 5.7. Classification of Orchdists According to the Area of Orchards

Blocks	*< 50*	*50-100 Nalis*	*100-150 Nalis*	*150-200 Nalis*	*> 200 Nalis*	*Total*
Joshimath	—	—	5 (10.00)	36 (72.00)	9 (18.00)	50 (100.00)
Pokhri	12 (9.60)	27 (21.60)	40 (32.00)	31 (24.80)	15 (12.00)	125 (100.00)
Chamba	4 (3.48)	7 (6.08)	46 (40.00)	30 (26.09)	28 (24.39)	115 (100.00)
Pratapnagar	8 (13.34)	12 (20.00)	29 (48.33)	7 (11.66)	4 (6.67)	60 (100.00)
Purola	—	5 (12.50)	7 (17.50)	10 (25.00)	18 (45.00)	40 (100.00)
Badkot	8 (17.78)	12 (26.66)	5 (11.11)	8 (17.78)	12 (26.67)	45 (100.00)

Attempt has also been made to classify the orchards with regard to the size of land. As noticed in the Table 5.7 in Joshimath block relatively higher proportion of orchards are having land in a range of 150-200 nali whereas in Pokhri block the proportion is relatively higher in 100-150 nali. On the other hand in Chamba and Pratapnagar the majority of orchards are having land in a range of 100-150 nali. In all the blocks 32 orchards are having land in a range of 50 nali only. It can be concluded that the size of orchards in the region is relatively small and the same can be attributed to the prevalence of low land holdings.

Land Utilization and Agricultural Production of Selected Orchards

Blockwise land use pattern of selected orchards is given in the Table 5.8. From the table it is noticed that in Joshimath Block 48 percent of the reported land is under orchards, whereas in Pokhari block the proportion of land under orchards is significantly low compared to Joshimath block and distribution of land is proportionate. Similar pattern has been noticed in Chamba and Pratapnagar blocks of Tehri Garhwal. On the other hand, the proportion of land under orchards in two blocks of Uttarkashi district (Purola and Pratapnagar) was reported relatively higher. On the other hand the area under irrigation ranges from 7.14 per cent Badkot block to 23.81 percent in Chamba block . Similarly Unirrigated area was reported 21.40 percent in Barkot block and 30.00 percent in Partapnagar Block.

Table 5.8. Blockwise Land Use of Selected Orchadists Per Orchardist Land Use

(Area in Nali)

Block	*Irrigated land*	*Unirrigated land*	*Under orchards*	*Fallow land*	*Others*	*Total*
Joshimath	20 (16.00)	30 (24.00)	60 (48.00)	10 (8.00)	5 (4.00)	125 (100.00)
Pokhri	10 (18.87)	15 (28.30)	20 (37.73)	5 (9.43)	3 (5.67)	53 (100.00)
Chamba	25 (23.81)	25 (23.81)	40 (38.10)	10 (9.52)	5 (4.76)	105 (100.00)
Pratapnagar	15 (15.00)	30 (30.00)	40 (40.00)	10 (10.00)	5 (5.00)	100 (100.00)
Purola	20 (11.12)	50 (27.77)	100 (55.55)	5 (2.78)	5 (2.78)	180 (100.00)
Badkot	10 (7.14)	30 (21.43)	90 (64.29)	5 (3.57)	5 (3.57)	140 (100.00)

Table 5.9. Blockwise Production of Food Crops

Blocks	*Paddy*	*Wheat (Qtl.)*	*Madua (Qtl.)*	*Sanwa (Qtl.)*	*Pulses (Qtl.)*	*Oil*	*Choulai Seeds*	*Pota-toes*	*Vege-tables*
Joshimath	0.75	2.5	4.1	2.1	5.50	.50	3.50	40.00	50.00
Pokhri	2.10	2.60	3.50	3.00	.30	.20	1.50	15.00	10.00
Chamba	2.15	2.90	3.10	2.90	4.50	.40	2.10	12.00	40.00
Pratapnagar	1.80	3.60	3.50	3.10	.40	.30	2.10	10.00	8.00
Purola	1.10	2.80	1.20	2.10	15.50	.60	5.00	30.00	40.00
Badkot	1.30	2.60	1.10	1.50	14.50	.40	2.00	12.00	40.00

While analyzing the agriculture production of the various crops in selected orchards in the surveyed area it is revealed that in Joshimath Block the average production of paddy is .75 quintal per orchard owner whereas same was reported relatively higher in other blocks of the area. The average production of paddy was reported highest in Chamba block, where it was reported 2.15 quintal per orchard owners. Similarly the average production of wheat per orchard owner was reported highest in Joshimath block and lowest in Badkot Block. It is evident that the average production of foodgrains is relatively low. Similar pattern has been noticed for other cereals and pulses. On the other hand the average production of potatoes and other vegetables was reported 40 and 50 kg per orchard owner in Joshimath blocks and significant variation has been noticed among the various blocks. It may be pointed out that the problem of food security is persistent in the study area.

Availability of Foodgrains

Starvation and paucity are the two intimidating development challenges confronting the world today. Of the world population of around 6 billion in 1996, about 1.3 billion people in the developing countries live on an inadequate income of less than US$ 1/day (WDR 1996). About 800 million people are foods insecure and about 500 million are persistently emaciated. It is not the production, but the distribution and access to food for healthy and active life is the critical challenge (IFAD, 1993). The lack of food and deficiency situation is more alarming in the developing world including mountain region. Food security is linked to food intake at the individual level, and food accessibility at a higher level. Food security will be achieved when poor and susceptible households living in the marginal areas, have physical and economic access to food, and will be achieved when they have sustainable livelihood. The FAO indicator for subsistence level is 2250 calories/day/cap (0.8 gm/kg body wt. protein and other essential fats and vitamins) food requirement.

Food security is greatly influenced by physical, economic, natural resources, sociocultural, gender and ethnic factors; and could be chronic or transitory. This has direct and indirect effect on health and behaviour of the people. Sustainable livelihood therefore, focus not only on assets but capabilities (including social resources) and activities for a means of living that can cope with and recuperate from stresses and shocks.

Table 5.10. Availability of Foodgrains by Selected Orchardists

No of Cultivators	*Block*	*3-6 months*	*6-9 months*	*9-12 months*	*Total*
15	Joshimath	2 (4.00)	29 (58.00)	19 (38.00)	50 (100.00)
12	Pokhri	17 (13.60)	82 (65.60)	26 (20.80)	125 (100.00)
30	Chamba	37 (32.17)	42 (36.53)	36 (31.30)	115 (100.00)
14	Pratapnagar	12 (20.00)	30 (50.00)	18 (30.00)	60 (100.00)
12	Purola	4 (10.00)	22 (55.00)	14 (35.00)	40 (100.00)
13	Badkot	7 (15.55)	18 (40.00)	20 (44.45)	45 (100.00)
86	Total	79 (18.16)	223 (51.27)	133 (30.57)	435 (100.00)

A similar attempt in the study area reveals that only 30.57 per cent households are having access to food for 9-12 months. Looking at the block picture, the situation in Pokhari block where only 20.80 percent orchard owners are having accessibility to food for 9-12 months is very depressing. On the other hand 18.16 percent orchard owners are having accessibility to food for 3-6 months and the situation of Chamba block is very harsh as 32.17 percent orchard owners were reported having availability of food for 3-6 months. The issues of food security needs careful attention at the policy level. The development of any region cannot be addressed and ensured unless the basic issues like hunger is not paid due attention. The analysis of the data clearly indicate that policy interventions and further investigation by identifying the months of greatest vulnerability may highlight the gravity of the problem. Therefore serious efforts are required to sort out the problem of food security in the region.

Table 5.11. Per Cultivator Marketable Foodgrains (KG)

Blocks	*Pulses*	*Madua*	*Chaulai*	*Potato*	*Vegetable*
Joshimath	5.50	2.50	5.50	38.00	50.00
Pokhri	—	2.00	1.50	12.00	10.00
Chamba	4.50	2.00	2.00	31.00	40.00
Pratapnagar	—	—	2.10	10.00	8.00
Purola	1.50	—	5.00	30.00	40.00
Badkot	1.40	—	2.00	12.00	40.00

Table 5.11 gives the picture of per cultivator marketable food-grains in the study area. As evident from the table there is no surplus wheat and paddy and the situation of surplus for pluses, madua and chaulai is also very discouraging. However, the position of surplus for potato and vegetable is satisfactory in some blocks. In Joshimath block 38 kg of potato and 50 kg vegetable per cultivator is reported as surplus and can be marketed. The surplus position for potato and

Table 5.12. Per Orchard Employment

Block	*Family members*			*Wage Labour*			*Total*
	Male	*Female*	*Total*	*Male*	*Female*	*Total*	
Joshimath	1	2	3 (60.00)	1	1	2 (40.00)	5 (100.00)
Pokhri	2	2	4 (100.00)	-	-	-	4 (100.00)
Chamba	2	2	4 (57.15)	2	1	3 (42.85)	7 (100.00)
Pratapnagar	2	2	4 (66.16)	1	1	2 (33.34)	6 (100.00)
Purola	2	2	4 (44.44)	3	2	5 (55.56)	9 (100.00)
Badkot	1	2	3 (42.85)	2	2	4 (57.14)	7 (100.00)
Total			22 (57.90)			16 (42.10)	38 (100.00)

vegetables in Chamba and Purola blocks is relatively better than the other blocks of the region. On the whole per cultivator surplus is significantly low in all the blocks of the study area.

Position of Employment

Attempt has also been made to assess the situation of employment in the study area. It is noticed that primarily the horticulture activities in the region is carried out by the members of the households themselves. However, as and when additional labour is required same is hired from the local area. In Joshimath on an average 5 persons engaged per orchard basis out of which three were own family members and two hired wage labour. Whereas in Purola per orchard average employment is 9 persons (four family members and 5 hired labour). The average wage paid ranges from Rs.70 to Rs 100 per day and the labour is easily available.

Production of Fruits

Rapid economic transformation has taken place on marginal farms in Himachal Pradesh (India) through apple farming. Majority of the farmers (80%) have small farms 90.5 - 2.0 ha) of sloping land, produce a net return of US$ 2700/ha/yr (Sharma 1996). The farming system has changed from subsistence crop-base to fruit farming including livestock component, has increased food security and living standard. The adoption of the niche friendly production system on large areas of marginal farms in the temperate region made huge economic and environmental impacts. This resulted in a net increase of domestic product in Himachal two hundred times and net per capita income twenty six times between 1971 and 1991. There is hard evidence to show that fruit farming on marginal lands is a superior production option both economically and ecologically (Sharma 1996; Pratap 1995).

- Similarly, fruit farming has brought economic transformation in Pakistan (Gilgit) supported by Aga Khan Rusal Support Project (App 1995).
- In China, west-Sichuwan, the biophysical condition suitable for apple and pear farming, had very limited programme due to lack of transport and R and D programmes. With priority programmes and support from the Government, the state has now commercial production system and has transformed their livelihood.

Examples of such niche success stories for orange, mango, temperate fruits and others do exist in the HKH, and need dissemination. Cardamom and ginger farming on the forest floors of Sikkim and Eastern hills of Nepal present an example of technical feasibility of developing economically productive and ecologically sound and stable production system on the marginal and sloping areas (Sharma 1998).

Off-season vegetable production has brought economic transformation in many mountain areas of HKH region. Necessary technological breakthrough, transportation and marketing systems were vital to bring impacts for their commercialization and impact on economy. In Sichuan Basin of China, off-season vegetables have covered an area of 3933 ha with a production of 94,000 tons valuing 8.48 million US$. Similar examples are available in India and Nepal where utilizing the mountain niches, off-season vegetable production is getting highly remunerative in recent years, to improve livelihood and economy of mountain farmers through direct and indirect effects in income and employment. In certain mountain niches of Nepal (Dhading, Panchkhal, Pakhribas, Lumle RCA-Dhanubase and Yampaphant) off-season vegetable production has gone on commercial scale and transformed their livelihood. A good crop of tomato or cucumber can bring upto US$ 5000/ha net return in 120 days (Sah 2001).

Mountain agro-environments provide an excellent avenue for quality vegetable seed production. Several national and international/multi-national companies had attracted to seed production in the mountains including India. Vegetable seed production has become a very attractive enterprise, but due to lack of suitable varieties, production, processing and marketing system, farmers have faced several constraints.

Tea, coffee, citrus, dry-fruits, honey, cikate mushrooms could be other potential enterprises. Also, identification of suitable livestock enterprises for milk, meat, skin and fibre could be potential alternatives that suit well in the system without environment and natural resource degradation.

In the survey of six blocks in Tehri, Chamoli and Uttarkashi districts the major fruit crops grown were reported apple, citrus, walnut, peach and pear. From the table it appears that apple is dominating crops in the region. And the total production of apple of 435 households was reported 1392.85 quintals. On the other hand the production of citrus was reported 838 quintals. Among the various blocks Joshimath, Purola, Chamba and Barkot the production of apple is relatively higher. On the other hand in Pokhari block the dominant crop is citrus.

Table 5.13. Blockwise Production of Fruits by the Selected Orchardists

(in Quintal)

Surveyed Orchardists	*Block*	*Apple*	*Citrus*	*Walnut*	*Peach/Pear and other*	*Total*
50	Joshimath	300.50	120.00	20.15	20.00	460.65
125	Pokhri	130.25	250.00	15.00	25.00	420.25
115	Chamba	345.10	160.00	11.50	60.00	574.60
60	Pratapnagar	120.40	90.00	00.90	12.00	223.30
40	Purola	260.40	80.00	6.00	16.00	362.40
45	Badkot	236.20	138.00	46.00	12.00	432.20
435	Total	1392.85	838.00	99.55	145.00	2475.40

Indicative Measures for Horticulture Development

In order to increase the production and productivity of horticultural crops in the state of Uttarakhand suitable measures are required to be adopted. The important issues need immediate attention are given below:

- Rejuvenation of old orchards.
- High density plantation of fruit trees at 2m x 2m and 3 x 3m for higher yields.
- Special thrust to grow/cultivate improved/imported varieties of fruit plants like apple, peach, pear, plum, apricot etc.
- Diversification of horticultural crops by increasing area under horticultural crops
- Special thrust to cultivate precious horticultural crops like (i) Kiwi, (ii) Saffron, (iii) Spices like turmeric, ginger, cardamom etc. (iv) Olive, (v) Mushroom, (vi) Ornamental flowers, (vii) Horticulture-based vocations like bee-keeping.
- Improvement in the quality of planting material, seeds etc. to be supplied to fruits and vegetable growers; technological improvement of existing nurseries and to encourage private nurseries for speedy production of plant material; subsidy for

fruit nursery plants, vegetable seeds and seedling, plant protection measures; long term horticultural loans to promote horticultural development in hill region of Uttarakhand

- Development of citrus (malta, kinnu, sweat lemon) species in Rudraparyag and Chamoli district and induction of price support to channelise the sale of horticultural produce.
- To create and develop the post-harvest infrastructure and establishment of processing units and market federation(s) or Uttarakhand Hill Development Board for speedy improvement in processing and marketing of horticultural produce.
- Transfer of advanced technology to growers regarding fruit preservation and fruit processing technique; research and modern technology backup and transfer of modern management practice to fruit and vegetable growers for the improvement in quality and yield of horticultural crops.
- Construction of cold storages/cool houses/warehouses in fruit belts of hill region to facilitate the storage of horticulture produce.
- Intensive off-season vegetable cultivation in different tribal areas under T.S.P; development of vegetable belts for off-season vegetables to boost up the vegetable production, area and productivity.
- Special campaign to control/combat the serious pests and diseases of horticultural crops.
- Since water is a scarce commodity, it is almost important to utilise the water in most productive and commercial way. Drip irrigation system in mid and high hilly area and sprinkler system in low hills and valley area will help to maximize the production per unit of water used.
- Construction of net houses, poly houses and mist chambers to facilitate the speedy production of planting materials, seeds, seedling etc. of horticultural crops.
- In poor accessible hilly areas where there is a great problem of packaging and heavy transportation cost, the adoption of 'low volume high cost' crops like spices or mushrooms, nut crops like walnuts, almonds, hazelnuts etc.

State Interventions

With a view to streamline the intensive development of horticulture during the Plan period, it was proposed to strengthen infrastructure facilities for speedy production of planting material of improved/imported varieties of fruits, vegetable seeds, potato, flowers etc. and to improve fruit preservation services, transfer of technology from lab to land, development of departmental units as plant revival and multiplication of planting material. Model orchards and Govt. Nurseries under irrigated horticultural development project with the World Bank assistance are also established. It is also proposed to establish bee-keeping centres, mushroom seed (spawn) production centre, poly green houses, drip irrigation and mist chambers at experimental stations, strengthening of horticultural experiments in training centres, establishment of medicinal plant research and medicinal plants and production facilities at Chaubatiya (Almora) with assistance of Central Institute of Medicinal and Aromatic Plants (CIMAP), Lucknow were also taken up.

Besides, for the speedy production of the mushroom in Uttarakhand hills, bulk pasteurization plant has been established at Jeolikot (Nainital) with the assistance of Dutch Govt. The Indo-Dutch Mushroom Project not only imparts training in mushroom production technique, but also supplies pasteurized compost and spawn (seed) to the enthusiastic growers. One more pasturisation plant has been established at Shankarpur, Dehradun.

With a view to explore the possibility of cultivation of Olive and other exotic varieties of fruits, a fruit development project was started in the year 1984 in the state. The programme is mainly operating at Govt. demonstration farms, Dhakrani (Dehradun), Jeolikot (Nainital). The demonstration plots at different Govt. and private farm have been established in order to study the performance of different imported varieties in different micro climatic zones, so that large scale plantations could be taken up with selected varieties.

It is well established that on harvesting at proper maturity, the fruits not only maintain good quality but their storage life is also improved. Soon after harvest, the fruits are graded and packed in appropriate containers and their disposal to terminal markets is essential as early as possible. The grading standard of hill region of Uttarakhand is different from those in H.P. and J & K. and roughly 60 per cent produce is sold by mid August before H.P. apple start picking up to avoid the competition and consequent lowering prices. This also fetch less price for the growers of Uttarakhand. The issue needs careful attention as it is primarily associated with the fruits and vegetables economy of the region.

To avoid vicious circle of pre-harvest contractors and commission agents engaged in sale system, the Directorate has proposed following interventions:

- Bulk purchases of fruits by the government.
- Replacement of wooden packing cases and induction of corrugated cartons.
- Installation of rope -way/construction of link road to facilitate the speedy transshipments of horticultural produce.
- Training to orchardist/fruit growers regarding the harvesting, grading and packing techniques.
- Establishment of grading-cum-packing centre in intensive fruit producing areas of Uttarakhand hills.
- Construction of warehouses/cold storage to store the horticultural produce.
- Establishment of transshipment centres at road head/ railhead terminals.
- Establishment of processing factories to utilise the bulk of fruits and canning and preserving the excess horticultural produce.

During the Eighth Five Year Plan period main emphasis was laid down on increasing the area and production of fruits, vegetable and potato crops. However the main objective of Ninth Plan are to boost the production of different horticulture crops, expansion of area, increase productivity through transfer of technology, control of pests and disease and diversification of horticultural crops. In order to achieve objectives, major thrust was on the following aspects.

Major Thrust

- Introduction of improved varieties of different horticultural crops and modern cultivation/cultural practices.
- Concentrated development of individual horticultural crops in best suited to agro climatic area only, where minor millets are usually grown.

- Technological improvement of existing nurseries and to encourage private nurseries, multiplication of planting materials through tissue culture technique
- Diversification of horticulture by increasing area under low volume high value crops (e.g. nuts, olive, mushroom, bee-keeping and tea).
- To create post-harvest infrastructure in order to save the losses of horticultural produce.
- Transfer of technology for human resource development.
- Proposed Programmes included :
  - Fruit development.
  - Vegetable and spice development.
  - Development of Floriculture and ornamental grading.
  - Mushroom development.
  - Bee-keeping.
  - Special component and Tribal sub-plan.
  - Food processing and marketing.
  - Herbal medicinal and aromatic plants.
  - Tea plantation.

Future Strategies

***Preparation of Horticultural Maps*:** At present, the orchardists do not know about the various fruits which can be grown in their locality. The department is preparing horticultural maps from block to state level which will depict the fruit can be grown in block. Thus instead of planting apple everywhere the most suitable fruits for the locality will be planted.

- Some horticultural crops have very specific agro-climatic and soil requirements. Cultivation is, therefore, limited to certain areas only; the Hindu Kush-Himalayan Region has features that are favorable for the development of certain horticultural crops. There are other crops which have greater adaptability and can be grown in various locations, provided the basic requirements are met wholly for partially, either naturally or artificially.

- Temperate fruits have a monopoly in the Region because they can only be grown under temperate conditions and therefore do not compete with the kinds of fruit grown on the plains. Sub-tropical and tropical fruits have the additional advantage of maturing later because of the lower temperatures and, therefore, given better economic return to the farmer because they can be marketed. It is also observed that hill fruits have a better colour and taste. Therefore preparation of horticulture map will help the farmers opt for the crops which can yield better result for them.

Demarcations of Zones: The Garhwal region is divided into four zones and important fruit crops which are more friendly for a particular zone has been identified and indicated below: For the overall development of horticulture in the region each zone should have different stragegy.

Altitudinal Fruit Zones

Below - 750 meters	Guava, Mango, Litchi and Papaya.
750 - 1500 meters	Strawberries, Peaches, Plums and Apricot.
750 - 1800 meters	Persimmons,
900 - 1500 metres	Pears.
1350 - 2400 meters	Quinces, Apples, Cherries

***Diversification of Fruit Growing*:** After identifying the locality suitable for various fruits the efforts will be made to grow more than one fruit in a locality so that the farmer will be able to utilize his resources in better way. In the past main emphasis has been laid on apple while other fruits have been neglected. Now diversification programme includes the cultivation of pear, peach, apricot, plum, cherrey at higher altitude and mango, guava, papaya, citrus fruits at lower altitude and valleys. Plantation of low volume and high value such as almond, walnut, hazelnut, pista, chest nut will be encouraged. Interestingly, green almond cultivation has got the fancy.

There are opportunities for the development of ancillary horticultural crops in the region can be promoted because of the suitable agro climatic conditions. In Uttarakhand floriculture and mushroom cultivation have been given some priority and, in certain areas, they have become popular, although the cultivation of these crops has still to gain impetus in the entire region. However, the cultivation of spices and medicinal plants and the practice of apiculture are carried out all over the region with varying degrees of success. There is need to develop technologies on different aspects of these undertakings before they can be launched commercially.

***Planting of new varieties*:** In each temperate fruit renewed commercial varieties which are high yielding and of high fruit quality is to be supplied to growers for planting. A list of such varieties for each temperate fruit has been prepared by the horticulture department and performance of these varieties will be observed in regional trials after introduction. For instance in apple, the spur varieties, i.e. red chief, Oregon spur, Starkrimson, and red Fuji and royal gola are already under observation. An early variety, Chaubatia princes, is also being distributed for cultivation. In pear red type can be introduced.

***Introduction of new fruits*:** Among new fruits kiwi, olive, pista, hazelnut and macadamia are very promising. The kiwi fruit has already been planted and is destined be a great success. The locations for growing of olive, pista and hazelnuts have been identified. The planting material is to be introduced now. The package of practices for olive cultivation is under preparation.

***Raising of good planting material*:** The yield per unit area is very low in comparison to international standards. The main reason for this is that the strains, or the varieties, earlier introduced did not have yield capacity or resistance to pests and disease as found in new varieties. Furthermore, there was no research back-up programmes and various problems have arisen such as scab disease in apples, brown rot in potatoes, and die-back in citrus fruits. With the introduction of research programmes, it is expected that the serious problems will be resolved. In the mean time, the industry can import modern technology if proper quarantine measures are adhered to. Without good planting material, the establishment of a sound fruit industry can not be imagined. Efforts are being made to raise healthy nursery plants by adopting latest propagation techniques viz., mist propagation and tissue culture. Planting materials is being raised both in Government and private nurseries. The scion wood will be taken for the elite mother plants.

***Adoption of latest cultural techniques*:** Research result have shown that the production per unit area of the existing plantations can be doubled if orchard management is improved. The important cultural practices which need to be properly applied a training and pruning, fertilizer application, spraying against pest and disease and grading and packing. The latest cultural techniques such as high density planting, drip irrigation, tissue analysis, use of plant regulators and integrated pest and disease management practices is to be introduced.

Training: Both extension workers and orchardists require training to keep them aware of the latest technical development in fruit growing. Though, the training arrangements exist at departmental stations but these are to be updated by providing more audio-visual aids. Highly qualified scientist and professors from the central institutes and state agricultural universities are being involved. In Uttarakhand hills mostly women attend the orchard operation, hence, special courses for their training have to be organized for them.

Marketing arrangements: With the increase in production of horticultural crops, especially fruits, vegetables, and potatoes marketing has become a serious problem in the Himalayan mountains. The markets are far away from the production areas and the produce has to pass through different types of climates before reaching the market. Marketing of horticultural produce includes not only the commercial transactions of buying and selling but also physical distribution. This physical distribution includes all the handling and forwarding activities such as harvesting, collecting, grading, packing, storing and subsequent dispersal through the markets to the consumers. In addition, there are various other auxiliary functions of marketing such as pre-harvest information, market finance and administration, marketing intermediaries market training, and extension and research. Creation of a Uttarakhand horticultural marketing corporation is under consideration of the state government which will take care of marketing aspect of temperate fruits. All aspects of marketing, collection, grading, packing, transportation, storage, processing and sale will be looked after by this corporation. A project with the assistance of French Government is also under preparation for marketing of temperate fruits. The cultivation of off-season vegetables has increased near the townships in the mountains and in areas from where they can be distributed easily to the plains when temperate vegetables are not available. The mountain sites are also suitable for raising the seeds of vegetables that do not set in the plains because they require a temperate climate. Remote areas that are suitable for vegetables, but are inaccessible, can cultivate seeds, which have high value and low volume. Such areas are ideal for raising hybrid seeds because cross-pollination with other varieties or species can be avoided in the new areas by suitable combinations of crops which are not compatible with each other. There is a specific distance for each crop to eliminate cross-pollination, the hybridization programme.

Encouragement of processing and caning: As per an estimate, about 30-40 percent fruits are wasted in Uttarakhand hills since these do not reach market. Such culled, deformed fruits can be processed or canned in processing and canning units established by the department all over the state.

Reorientation of research to tackle practical problems: The research on temperate fruits are going on in big way in advanced countries. However, their research results will be tried and tested under our conditions before adoption. Therefore, a reorientation will be given to research activities.

Institutional Credit: Large numbers of farmers, in particular small and marginal farmers, are discouraged from growing horticultural crops because of the initial heavy investment required and long crop gestation periods. The amount of investment required to produce apples, oranges, vegetables, potatoes and ginger clearly indicates that, without institutional credit assistance, small and marginal farmers will not be able to establish and maintain cultivation. In certain regions, along with other facilities, horticultural loans are made available on easy terms at subsidized interest rates and this has encouraged horticultural development. The success experienced by farmers in such regions will, it is hoped, be repeated elsewhere. Nevertheless, land holdings in the mountains are small, and farmers find it difficult to find alternative sources of income during the long gestation periods.

DIVERSIFICATION OF HORTICULTURE THROUGH ANCILLARY HORTICULTURAL PROGRAMMES

Mushrooms

Cultivated mushrooms are becoming popular and in certain areas they area cultivated under employment programmes with technical facilities and institutional finance provided. The mushrooms thus cultivated are *Volvariell* sp. (tropical paddy straw mushroom), *Lentinus edudis* (shistake), and *Agricus bisporus* (button, a white, European temperate mushroom). *Agricus bisporus* is commercially cultivated in India. Under these programmes young entrepreneurs are given loans, spawn, and pasteurized compost. They are also trained in different aspects of development. This has created employment opportunities. However, mushroom cultivation could give a new dimension to economic development in the mountains.

Flowers are another well-known resource of the Himalayas. Commercial cultivation has not been established significantly because of lack of proper packing and cultivation practices, scarcity of genuine plant material, and lack of technology for packing and storage. Flowers such as gladioli, roses, carnations and orchids have export possibilities and their cultivation should be developed.

The agro-climatic conditions in the region, especially in the valley areas, are suitable for growing spices such as ginger, turmeric, onions, garlic, chillies, and saffron. Some of these crops, depending on their marketing potential, have been commercially cultivated. However, some of the spices are also successfully grown in the plains. To be commercially viable, therefore, mountain products have to compete with those of the plains. The cost of cultivation is lower in the plains than in the hills. This is main reason why spice cultivation in the mountains is not gaining momentum in spite of the emphasis given to these crops. In dry regions, saffron provides a steady source of income.

The mountain region contains a large number of medicinal plants. Many plants are used, in both fresh and dried forms, as curatives and preventives for various diseases and ailments. Their importance has, however, increased because of the commercialization of extraction and purification methods. The latter methods are essential for the active ingredients to exert the desired effects. Due to increasing demands for plants that are exploited too drastically without concomitant measures for their regeneration, and because of the depletion of natural resources, the present demands of the pharmaceutical industry, efforts are made to preserve plant materials and to cultivate them where facilities are available. In Tibet, the wide use of medicinal plants has encouraged their development and conservation.

Horticulture sector in the surevey region is facing daunting problems associated with promotion, extension, storage and marketing. Due to initiatives of some of enterprising farmers the activities have flourished on some patches of the region. The issues of marginal holding also needs to be addressed as the increasing demands of growing population, limited crop land and degradation of natural resources have contributed to poverty and unstainable mountain agriculture. Marginal lands provide future hope to mountain people - the challenge is to conserve the natural resources, maintain and use the valuable agro-biodiversity, and generate and promote niche specific technologies for greater economic and ecological returns. Comparative advantages of niches potentials should be exploited for high value cash crop and enterprises as seen successful in other mountain regions around the world. The use of bio-technical tools, organic farming, nitrogen-fixation activities should be promoted to improve quality of mountain products and protect environment and natural resources. Development of necessary infrastructures, input supplies, industries and marketing system and other logistic supports are vital to bring sustainable impacts. Strong national, regional and global commitments are vital with priority research and development programmes for improving food security and livelihood of mountain people through a collective participatory approach. The horticulture sector will automatically developed it the issues raised are tackled effectively and successfully.

ANNEXURE–5.1

Block-wise Area and Production of Fruits (2004-05)

(Hectares / Metric Tonnes)

District/ Block	Apple		Pear		Peach		Plum		Apricot	
	Area	Production	Area	Production	Area	Production	Area	Production	Area	Production
Chamoli										
Joshi Math	1440.00	12600.00	19.00	166.25	20.00	175.00	27.00	236.25	18.00	157.50
Dasholi	85.00	143.75	27.00	236.25	152.00	1330.00	52.00	455.00	3.00	26.25
Ghat	80.00	700.00	18.00	157.50	35.00	306.25	14.00	122.50	3.00	26.25
Karnpryag	55.00	481.25	36.00	315.10	67.00	586.25	26.00	227.50	12.00	105.00
Pokhri	45.00	393.75	18.00	157.50	42.00	367.50	6.00	52.50	7.00	61.25
Gairsen	70.00	612.50	75.00	656.25	82.00	717.50	31.00	271.25	8.00	70.00
Narainbagad	65.00	568.75	23.00	201.25	43.00	376.25	16.00	140.00	6.00	52.50
Tharali	230.00	2012.50	56.00	490.00	54.00	472.50	29.00	253.75	15.00	131.25
Devaal	85.00	743.75	28.00	245.00	65.00	568.75	14.00	122.50	8.00	70.00
Total	2155.00	18256.25	300.00	2625.10	560.00	4900.00	215.00	1881.25	80.00	700.00
Uttarkashi										
Bhatwari	267.17	1880.30	10.05	11.52	2.10	11.65	1.91	10.73	1.27	21.00
Dunda	100.90	114.66	20.51	100.00	31.73	61.20	12.45	67.23	13.81	230.00
Chinyalisad	169.54	1274.00	3.23	1.13	32.77	167.00	7.06	42.62	22.11	275.00
Naugaon	1360.17	26943.76	63.29	400.00	40.05	102.31	39.47	243.72	45.87	300.00
Parola	353.00	1000.00	6.00	21.00	14.05	8.50	3.60	15.00	5.20	20
Mori	1908.00	10595.00	36.30	66.35	41.00	21.00	37.00	30.70	30.00	54
Total	4158.78	41807.72	139.38	600.00	161.70	371.66	101.49	410.00	118.26	900.00
Hardwar										
Narsan	0.00	0.00	69.40	610.00	12.20	107.00	0.00	0.00	0.00	0.00
Bhagwanpur	0.00	0.00	5.80	51.00	3.00	26.00	0.00	0.00	0.00	0.00
Roorkee	0.00	0.00	5.02	44.00	13.00	114.00	0.00	0.00	0.00	0.00
Bahadrabad	0.00	0.00	1.20	11.00	18.00	158.00	0.00	0.00	0.00	0.00
Laksar	0.00	0.00	0.80	7.00	3.00	26.00	0.00	0.00	0.00	0.00
Khanpur	0.00	0.00	0.40	4.00	2.00	16.00	0.00	0.00	0.00	0.00
Total	0.00	0.00	82.62	727.00	51.20	447.00	0.00	0.00	0.00	0.00
Rudraprayag										
Agustmuni	25.70	25.00	41.39	52.50	65.37	170.50	36.48	30.50	18.73	30.50
Ukhimath	33.04	50.50	28.34	85.50	22.37	74.50	22.42	44.50	12.16	27.40
Jakholi	28.09	41.00	21.28	41.50	20.98	78.00	16.59	26.80	3.78	7.50
Total	86.83	116.50	91.01	179.50	108.72	323.00	75.49	101.80	34.67	65.40

District/ Block	*Apple*		*Pear*		*Peach*		*Plum*		*Apricot*	
	Area	*Prod-uction*	*Area*	*Prod-uction*	*Area*	*Prod-uction*	*Area*	*Prod-uction*	*Area*	*Prod-uction*
Tehri										
Chamba	645.00	516.00	187.16	169.16	100.20	50.10	109.80	549.00	180.15	90.08
Narendranagar	20.50	16.40	58.25	52.43	40.20	24.12	46.50	232.50	104.80	52.40
Bhilangana	156.00	126.40	162.50	146.25	125.79	75.47	70.26	351.30	99.90	49.95
Thauldhar	633.20	506.56	242.4	254.16	70.26	42.16	35.78	178.90	101.98	50.99
Jaunpur	662.50	530.00	330.25	297.23	17.69	10.61	42.56	212.80	121.20	60.60
Jakhnidhar	190.46	152.37	115.37	103.59	23.56	14.14	28.99	144.95	66.89	33.45
Kirtinagar	91.52	73.22	102.80	92.52	134.55	80.73	76.26	381.30	110.23	55.12
Pratapnagar	565.30	452.24	329.56	296.60	52.20	31.32	76.26	381.30	172.23	86.12
Devprayag	38.56	30.85	126.00	113.40	54.60	32.76	55.50	277.50	116.25	58.13
Total	3003.04	2404.04	1654.29	1525.34	619.05	361.41	541.91	2709.55	1073.63	536.84
Pauri										
Pauri	21.30	39.10	5.38	28.40	3.40	9.50	2.85	11.50	2.60	5.00
Kot	21.46	38.15	5.30	30.00	10.15	16.10	5.20	6.10	1.75	3.50
Kaljikhal	6.20	3.50	1.40	29.00	3.00	2.00	0.95	1.90	1.20	4.50
Khirsu	29.70	22.10	3.50	20.10	21.25	26.50	10.73	41.10	2.40	12.75
Pabaon	7.35	13.25	1.00		4.25	14.50	5.05	8.75	0.70	3.15
Thalisen	36.80	9.50	12.90	42.15	7.85	9.60	5.12	5.85	2.90	3.10
Ekeshwar	9.40	5.95	1.50	13.10	8.03	2.15	6.05	2.00	0.45	2.15
Pokhra	8.85	4.85	10.85	25.65	4.75	3.90	2.45	5.50	4.45	7.85
Birokhal	27.00	145.00	25.00	105.00	22.00	40.00	13.00	22.00	10.00	32.00
Nainidanda	30.00	211.00	8.00	36.00	7.00	10.00	9.00	14.00	3.00	10.00
Rikhnikhal	7.00	15.00	15.00	64.00	24.00	66.00	3.00	6.00	2.00	6.00
Yamkeshwar	5.00	0.00	12.00	50.00	28.00	65.00	4.00	6.00	0.00	0.00
Jaiharikhal	4.00	30.00	17.00	70.00	12.00	65.00	12.00	140.00	3.00	10.00
Dwarikhal	0.00	2.00	2.00	10.00	5.00	2.00	2.00	12.00	1.00	2.00
Dugadda	0.00	0.00	8.00	35.00	10.00	2.00	0.00	0.00	0.00	0.00
Total	214.06	539.40	128.83	558.40	170.68	334.25	81.40	282.70	35.45	102.00
Dehradun										
Doiwala	0.00	0.00	0.00	0.00	5.00	0.00	2.00	5.00	0.00	0.00
Raipur	30.00	46.00	23.00	43.00	30.00	65.00	17.00	38.00	22.00	23.00
Sahaspur	61.00	95.00	17.00	32.00	12.50	27.00	5.20	12.00	7.30	12.00
Vikasnagar	0.00	0.00	0.00	0.00	13.50	30.00	3.00	7.00		
Kalsi	264.00	409.00	55.00	103.00	40.00	87.00	44.00	95.00	41.00	72.00
Chakrata	4249.00	6617.00	1117.50	2090.00	1115.00	2446.00	645.00	1451.00	736.00	1288.00
Total	4604.00	7167.00	1212.50	2268.00	1216.00	2655.00	716.20	1608.00	806.30	1395.00
Grand Total	14221.71	70290.91	3608.63	8483.34	2887.35	9392.32	1731.49	6993.30	2148.31	3699.24

District/ Block	Walnut		Lemon		Mango		Guava		Almond	
	Area	Prod-uction	Area	Prod-uction	Area	Prod-uction	Area	Prod-uction	Area	Prod-uction
Chamoli										
Joshi Math	65.00	743.75	226.00	1977.50	0.00	0.00	0.00	0.00	0.00	0.00
Dasholi	67.00	586.25	1275.00	11156.25	45.00	393.75	52.00	455.00	0.00	0.00
Ghat	28.00	245.00	570.00	4987.50	5.00	43.75	8.00	70.00	0.00	0.00
Karnpryag	65.00	568.75	820.00	7175.00	56.00	490.00	26.00	227.50	0.00	0.00
Pokhri	42.00	367.50	615.00	5381.25	38.00	332.50	14.00	122.50	0.00	0.00
Gairsen	152.00	1330.00	836.00	7315.00	38.00	332.50	8.00	70.00	0.00	0.00
Narainbagad	82.00	717.50	695.00	6081.25	36.00	315.00	15.00	131.25	0.00	0.00
Tharali	110.00	962.50	611.00	5346.25	14.00	122.50	6.00	52.50	0.00	0.00
Devaal	119.00	1041.25	352.00	3080.00	18.00	157.50	16.00	140.00	0.00	0.00
Total	730.00	6562.50	6000.00	52500.00	250.00	2187.50	145.00	1268.75	0.00	0.00
Uttarkashi										
Bhatwari	35.12	50.00	10.76	51.10	0.08	0.50	0.87	5.10	1.95	0.20
Dunda	95.54	116.00	51.43	280.00	21.40	20.50	6.92	20.00	3.08	0.20
Chinyalisad	18.80	30.00	67.80	292.65	27.17	78.50	5.00	13.30	1.18	0.10
Naugaon	89.19	100.00	56.20	331.00	19.61	0.50	0.08	0.60	0.00	0.00
Parola	7.00	2.00	5.40	3.00	0.00	0.00	1.00	1.00	1.20	0.00
Mori	7.95	2.00	12.00	15.00	0.00	0.00			1.50	0.10
Total	253.60	300.00	203.59	972.75	68.26	100.00	13.87	40.00	8.91	0.60
Hardwar										
Narsan	0.00	0.00	2.10	19.00	1240.00	10900.00	50.00	440.00	30.00	263.00
Bhagwanpur	0.00	0.00	1.20	10.00	2600.00	22854.00	30.00	264.00	12.00	105.00
Roorkee	0.00	0.00	3.10	27.00	830.00	7295.00	10.00	88.00	20.00	176.00
Bahadrabad	0.00	0.00	1.00	8.00	2710.00	23848.00	108.00	950.00	195.00	1714.00
Laksar	0.00	0.00	1.20	10.00	360.00	3168.00	16.00	140.00	9.00	80.00
Khanpur	0.00	0.00	0.50	5.00	95.00	836.00	21 00	185.00	5.00	44.00
Total	0.00	0.00	9.10	79.00	7835.00	68901.00	235.00	2067.00	271.00	2382.00
Rudraprayag										
Agustmuni	65.85	39.70	231.03	606.00	101.99	178.00	0.00	0.00	7.53	3.00
Ukhimath	68.42	49.50	101.54	851.00	5.44	18.00	0.00	0.00		
Jakholi	41.02	28.80	94.74	343.00	30.97	58.50	0.00	0.00	1.00	
Total	175.29	118.00	427.31	1800.00	138.40	254.50	0.00	0.00	8.53	3.00

District/ Block	*Walnut*		*Lemon*		*Mango*		*Guava*		*Almond*	
	Area	*Prod-uction*	*Area*	*Prod-uction*	*Area*	*Prod-uction*	*Area*	*Prod-uction*	*Area*	*Prod-uction*
Tehri										
Chamba	285.20	142.60	102.20	102.20	188.20	259.72	0.00	0.00	1.25	0.63
Narendranagar	298.25	149.13	145.20	145.20	365.56	504.47	0.00	0.00	2.75	1.38
Bhilangana	285.53	142.77	196.20	196.20	193.19	166.60	0.00	0.00	0.00	0.00
Thauldhar	198.90	149.45	128.89	128.89	669.99	952.18	0.00	0.00	1.11	0.56
Jaunpur	298.80	149.40	120.56	120.56	698.89	964.47	0.00	0.00	0.00	0.00
Jakhnidhar	262.20	131.10	135.44	135.44	470.89	649.83	0.00	0.00	1.99	1.00
Kirtinagar	305.56	152.78	414.23	414.23	532.55	734.92	0.00	0.00	2.25	1.13
Pratapnagar	338.81	169.45	112.29	112.29	287.69	397.01	0.00	0.00	0.00	0.00
Devprayag	216.50	108.25	85.22	85.22	531.33	1001.60	0.00	0.00	2.11	1.03
Total	2489.75	1294.93	1440.23	1440.23	3938.29	5630.80	0.00	0.00	11.46	5.73
Pauri										
Pauri	31.25	30.10	36.07	23.65	31.40	60.00	2.15	3.50	1.50	0.00
Kot	69.30	10.50	62.93	65.35	20.15	15.65	13.27	4.60	0.60	0.00
Kaljikhal	36.75	5.60	22.58	60.10	10.53	6.15	4.44	3.10	1.30	0.00
Khirsu	39.97	8.75	54.17	90.15	84.01	14.15	15.10	2.25		0.00
Pabaon	29.50	6.25	54.95	56.45	20.00	29.50	0.60	0.00	1.20	0.00
Thalisen	74.57	2.50	42.06	35.40	0.00		1.00	0.00	3.00	0.00
Ekeshwar	105.75	3.75	20.20	16.10	15.80	13.55	1.00	4.50		0.00
Pokhra	34.90	1.10	29.05	7.35	12.70	3.50	2.95	5.55	1.85	0.00
Birokhal	90.00	85.00	44.00	1600.00	23.00	80.00	0.00	0.00	0.00	0.00
Nainidanda	35.00	30.00	31.00	390.00	27.00	90.00	6.00	45.00	0.00	0.00
Rikhnikhal	52.00	60.00	36.00	460.00	73.00	260.00	20.00	160.00	0.00	0.00
Yamkeshwar	15.00	12.00	75.00	980.00	215.00	700.00	5.00	40.00	0.00	0.00
Jaiharikhal	28.00	25.00	65.00	800.00	57.00	200.00	27.00	210.00	0.00	0.00
Dwarikhal	15.00	13.00	30.00	400.00	35.00	120.00	4.00	32.00	0.00	0.00
Dugadda	27.00	27.00	36.00	470.00	420.00	1650.00	26.00	211.00	0.00	0.00
Total	683.99	320.55	639.01	5454.55	1044.59	3242.50	128.51	721.50	9.45	0.00
Dehradun										
Doiwala			153.00	182.00	1315.00	1341.00	17.00	40.00	0.00	0.00
Raipur	5.00	6.00	167.00	199.00	750.00	765.00	15.00	38.00	0.00	0.00
Sahaspur	15.00	19.00	655.00	779.00	1498.00	1528.00	25.00	70.00	0.00	0.00
Vikasnagar			813.00	968.00	1149.00	1172.00	25.00	70.00	0.00	0.00
Kalsi	155.00	191.00	401.00	478.00	937.00	956.00	0.00	0.00	0.00	0.00
Chakrata	1890.00	1604.00	150.00	189.00	14.00	40.00	0.00	0.00	0.00	0.00
Total	2065.00	1820.00	2339.00	2795.00	5663.00	5802.00	82.00	218.00	0.00	0.00
Grand Total	6397.63	10415.98	11058.24	65041.53	18937.54	86118.30	604.38	4315.25	309.35	2391.33

Banana *Block*	*Peanut*		*West nut*							
	Area	*Prod-uction*	*Area*	*Prod-uction*	*Area*	*Prod-uction*	*Area*	*Prod-uction*	*Area*	*Prod-uction*
Chamoli										
Joshi Math	0.00	0.00	0.00	0.00	0.00	0.00	0.00	0.00	0.00	0.00
Dasholi	0.00	0.00	0.00	0.00	0.00	0.00	0.00	0.00	0.00	0.00
Ghat	0.00	0.00	0.00	0.00	0.00	0.00	0.00	0.00	0.00	0.00
Karnpryag	0.00	0.00	0.00	0.00	0.00	0.00	0.00	0.00	0.00	0.00
Pokhri	0.00	0.00	0.00	0.00	0.00	0.00	0.00	0.00	0.00	0.00
Gairsen	0.00	0.00	0.00	0.00	0.00	0.00	0.00	0.00	0.00	0.00
Narainbagad	0.00	0.00	0.00	0.00	0.00	0.00	0.00	0.00	0.00	0.00
Tharali	0.00	0.00	0.00	0.00	0.00	0.00	0.00	0.00	0.00	0.00
Devaal	0.00	0.00	0.00	0.00	0.00	0.00	0.00	0.00	0.00	0.00
Total	0.00	0.00	0.00	0.00	0.00	0.00	0.00	0.00	0.00	0.00
Pauri										
Bhatwari	0.00	0.00	0.02	0.02	1.00	5.31	0.10	0.01	0.03	0.10
Dunda	0.41	0.30	0.00	0.00	11.94	100.00	1.17	0.10		
Chinyalisad	G.00	0.00	0.00	0.00	4.00	40.00	0.00	0.00	0.00	0.00
Naugaon	0.00	0.00	0.00	0.00	2.00	20.00	0.00	0.00	0.00	0.00
Parola	0.00	0.00	0.00	0.00	1.00	10.00	0.00	0.00	0.00	0.00
Mori	0.00	0.00	0.00	0.00	1.00	10.00	0.00	0.00	0.00	0.00
Total	0.41	0.30	0.02	0.02	20.94	185.31	1.27	0.11	0.03	0.10
Hardwar										
Narsan	0.00	0.00	0.00	0.00	0.00	0.00	0.00	0.00	0.00	0.00
Bhagwanpur	0.00	0.00	0.00	0.00	0.00	0.00	0.00	0.00	0.00	0.00
Roorkee	0.00	0.00	0.00	0.00	0.00	0.00	0.00	0.00	0.00	0.00
Bahadrabad	0.00	0.00	0.00	0.00	0.00	0.00	0.00	0.00	0.00	0.00
Laksar	0.00	0.00	0.00	0.00	0.00	0.00	0.00	0.00	0.00	0.00
Khanpur	0.00	0.00	0.00	0.00	0.00	0.00	0.00	0.00	0.00	0.00
Total	0.00	0.00	0.00	0.00	0.00	0.00	0.00	0.00	0.00	0.00
Rudraprayag										
Agustmuni	0.00	0.00	0.00	0.00	0.00	0.00	0.00	0.00	0.00	0.00
Ukhimath	0.00	0.00	0.00	0.00	0.00	0.00	0.00	0.00	0.00	0.00
Jakholi	0.00	0.00	0.00	0.00	0.00	0.00	0.00	0.00	0.00	0.00
Total	0.00	0.00	0.00	0.00	0.00	0.00	0.00	0.00	0.00	0.00

District/ Block	Leechi		Grapes		Banana		Peanut		West nut	
	Area	Production	Area	Production	Area	Production	Area	Production	Area	Production
Tehri										
Chamba	0.00	0.00	0.00	0.00	0.00	0.00	0.00	0.00	0.00	0.00
Narendranagar	0.00	0.00	0.00	0.00	0.00	0.00	0.00	0.00	0.00	0.00
Bhilangana	0.00	0.00	0.00	0.00	0.00	0.00	0.00	0.00	0.00	0.00
Thauldhar	0.00	0.00	0.00	0.00	0.00	0.00	0.00	0.00	0.00	0.00
Jaunpur	0.00	0.00	0.00	0.00	0.00	0.00	0.00	0.00	0.00	0.00
Jakhnidhar	0.00	0.00	0.00	0.00	0.00	0.00	0.00	0.00	0.00	0.00
Kirtinagar	0.00	0.00	0.00	0.00	0.00	0.00	0.00	0.00	0.00	0.00
Pratapnagar	0.00	0.00	0.00.	0.00	0.00	0.00	0.00	0.00	0.00	0.00
Devprayag	0.00	0.00	0.00	0.00	0.00	0.00	0.00	0.00	0.00	0.00
Total	0.00	0.00	0.00	0.00	0.00	0.00	0.00	0.00	0.00	0.00
Pauri										
Pauri	3.78	1.10	1.14	0.02	0.00	0.00	0.00	0.00	0.00	0.00
Kot	0.28		0.04	0.01	0.00	0.00	0.00	0.00	0.00	0.00
Kaljikhal	0.80	0.65	0.05	0.03	0.00	0.00	0.00	0.00	0.00	0.00
Khirsu	7.35	1.75		0.00	0.00	0.00	0.00	0.00	0.00	0.00
Pabaon	0.00	0.00	0.08	0.10	0.00	0.00	0.00	0.00	0.00	0.00
Thalisen	0.00	0.00	0.03	0.05	0.00	0.00	0.00	0.00	0.00	0.00
Ekeshwar	8.40	3.10	0.00	0.00	0.00	0.00	0.00	0.00	0.00	0.00
Pokhra	0.45	0.00	1.30	2.10	0.00	0.00	0.00	0.00	0.00	0.00
Birokhal	0.00	0.00	0.00	0.00	0.00	0.00	0.00	0.00	0.00	0.00
Nainidanda	2.00	8.00	0.00	0.00	0.00	0.00	0.00	0.00	0.00	0.00
Rikhnikhal	10.00	50.00	0.00	0.00	0.00	0.00	0.00	0.00	0.00	0.00
Yamkeshwar	12.00	48.00	0.00	0.00	0.00	0.00	0.00	0.00	0.00	0.00
Jaiharikhal	5.00	20.00	0.00	0.00	0.00	0.00	0.00	0.00	0.00	0.00
Dwarikhal	5.00	18.00	0.00	0.00	0.00	0.00	0.00	0.00	0.00	0.00
Dugadda	45.00	196.00	0.00	0.00	0.00	0.00	0.00	0.00	0.00	0.00
Total	100.06	346.60	2.64	2.31	0.00	0.00	0.00	0.00	0.00	0.00
Dehradun										
Doiwala	208.00	312.00	0.00	0.00	0.00	0.00	0.00	0.00	0.00	0.00
Raipur	1237.00	1855.00	0.00	0.00	0.00	0.00	0.00	0.00	0.00	0.00
Sahaspur	600.00	900.00	0.00	0.00	0.00	0.00	0.00	0.00	0.00	0.00
Vikasnagar	1003.00	1505.00	0.00	0.00	0.00	0.00	0.00	0.00	0.00	0.00
Kalsi	0.00	0.00	0.00	0.00	0.00	0.00	0.00	0.00	0.00	0.00
Chakrata	0.00	0.00	0.00	0.00	0.00	0.00	0.00	0.00	0.00	0.00
Total	3048.00	4572.00	0.00	0.00	0.00	0.00	0.00	0.00	0.00	0.00
Grand Total	3148.47	4918.90	2.66	2.33	20.94	185.31	1.27	0.11	0.03	0.10

Source: Directorate of Horticulture, Ranikhet Uttarakhand

ANNEXURE–5.2

Block-wise Area and Production of Vegetables (2004-05)

(Hectares/ Metric Tonnes)

District/ Block	Tomato		Radish		Cauliflower		Cabbage		Egg Plant	
	Area	Production	Area	Production	Area	Production	Area	Production	Area	Production
Chamoli										
Joshi Math	10.00	120.00	45.00	540.00	55.00	660.00	30.00	660.00	5.00	60.00
Dasholi	50.00	600.00	35.00	420.00	30.00	360.00	15.00	180.00	27.00	324.00
Ghat	25.00	300.00	30.00	360.00	40.00	480.00	15.00	180.00	10.00	120.00
Karnpryag	30.00	360.00	25.00	300.00	20.00	240.00	12.00	144.00	30.00	360.00
Pokhri	25.00	300.00	30.00	360.00	20.00	240.00	12.00	144.00	25.00	300.00
Gairsen	25.00	300.00	35.00	420.00	25.00	300.00	20.00	240.00	23.00	276.00
Narainbagad	15.00	180.00	15.00	180.00	10.00	120.00	12.00	144.00	15.00	180.00
Tharali	10.00	120.00	20.00	240.00	15.00	180.00	12.00	144.00	15.00	180.00
Devaal	15.00	180.00	25.00	300.00	15.00	180.00	12.00	144.00	15.00	180.00
Total	205.00	2460.00	260.00	3120.00	230.00	2760.00	140.00	1980.00	165.00	1980.00
Uttarkashi										
Bhatwari	6.00	60.00	7.00	140.00	18.53	409.51	0.20	0.20	3.86	39.79
Dunda	27.17	271.70	13.20	264.00	8.20	181.22	0.50	5.00	11.80	135.70
Chinyalisad	48.34	483.40	6.00	120.00	4.23	99.48	3.00	30.00	15.50	188.25
Naugaon	138.53	1421.50	40.00	800.00	29.00	861.9	0.00	0.00	6.20	71.20
Parola	303.76	6037.60	4.50	90.00	5.50	1215.50	4.50	45.00	8.50	97.75
Mori	28.73	287.30	10.50	210.00	13.50	2983.50	10.00	100.00	3.50	140.25
Total	552.53	8561.50	81.20	1624.00	78.96	5751.11	18.20	180.20	49.36	672.94
Hardwar										
Narsan	0.00	0.00	36.00	540.00	24.00	360.00	24.00	360.00	45.00	675.00
Bhagwanpur	0.00	0.00	19.00	285.00	51.00	765.00	34.00	510.00	24.00	360.00
Roorkee	0.00	0.00	11.00	165.00	19.00	285.00	27.00	405.00	22.00	330.00
Bahadrabad	0.00	0.00	13.00	195.00	75.00	1125.00	67.00	1005.00	40.00	600.00
Laksar	0.00	0.00	9.00	135.00	39.00	585.00	49.00	735.00	19.00	285.00
Khanpur	0.00	0.00	17.00	255.00	30.00	450.00	38.00	570.00	17.00	255.00
Total	0.00	0.00	105.00	1575.00	238.00	3570.00	239.00	3585.00	167.00	2505.00
Rudraprayag										
Agustmuni	18.15	197.00	34.85	389.00	25.00	347.00	5.11	37.00	14.60	178.00
Ukhimath	4.10	67.00	10.95	173.00	16.00	270.00	3.89	34.00	3.35	48.00
Jakholi	9.00	111.00	11.60	135.00	16.00	180.00	1.73	17.00	9.00	94.00
Total	31.25	375.00	57.40	697.00	57.00	797.00	10.73	88.00	26.95	320.00

District/ Block	Tomato		Radish		Cauliflower		Cabbage		Egg Plant	
	Area	Production	Area	Production	Area	Production	Area	Production	Area	Production
Tehri										
Chamba	70.23	351.15	65.56	325.83	65.26	645.42	7.26	22.14	4.56	19.84
Narendranagar	43.36	216.80	26.69	132.65	20.29	200.67	3.52	10.74	14.56	63.34
Bhilangana	27.56	137.80	23.25	115.55	23.60	233.40	0.56	1.71	7.59	33.02
Thauldhar	22.26	111.30	32.22	160.13	79.99	791.10	6.25	19.06	2.56	11.14
Jaunpur	103.36	576.80	40.26	200.09	90.69	896.92	8.22	25.07	0.59	2.57
Jakhnidhar	60.36	301.80	22.22	110.43	17.89	176.93	2.55	7.78	14.56	63.34
Kirtinagar	87.89	439.45	26.69	132.65	56.23	556.11	4.56	13.91	13.56	56.99
Pratapnagar	46.99	234.95	31.25	155.31	32.30	319.45	3.23	9.85	1.23	5.35
Devprayag	41.36	206.80	72.26	359.13	43.36	428.83	4.89	14.91	12.26	53.33
Total	503.37	2576.85	340.40	1691.77	429.61	4248.83	41.04	125.17	71.47	308.92
Pauri										
Pauri	14.00	155.00	22.00	50.70	12.40	45.00	11.75	2.28	5.30	85.00
Kot	24.50	176.00	23.00	61.00	12.75	41.00	2.65	1.96	5.45	73.00
Kaljikhal	21.75	162.00	26.50	77.50	11.10	36.15	0.35	0.70	2.30	25.00
Khirsu	22.25	155.00	25.70	81.50	15.75	49.10	5.10	1.78	7.35	81.00
Pabaon	26.75	181.50	26.10	82.00	8.10	31.20	2.50	1.19	2.40	14.00
Thalisen	23.50	152.10	27.30	85.00	3.75	15.20	2.75	1.27	4.30	60.00
Ekeshwar	12.60	145.50	25.90	80.00	5.65	20.10	0.35	0.46	5.35	51.00
Pokhra	14.75	101.10	23.00	61.50	6.10	17.00	1.90	1.00	5.40	24.00
Birokhal	14.00	85.00	80.00	800.00	10.00	65.00	6.00	24.00	10.00	55.00
Nainidanda	17.00	107.00	80.00	800.00	11.00	60.00	12.00	50.00	10.00	55.00
Rikhnikhal	14.00	90.00	30.00	350.00	10.00	55.00	14.00	55.00	15.00	85.00
Yamkeshwar	15.00	95.00	30.00	300.00	5.00	30.00	4.00	15.00	10.00	55.00
Jaiharikhal	22.00	135.00	40.00	350.00	5.00	25.00	2.00	8.00	15.00	80.00
Dwarikhal	11.00	67.00	30.00	150.00	6.00	25.00	2.00	9.00	10.00	55.00
Dugadda	37.00	286.00	37.00	382.00	18.00	100.00	8.00	49.00	15.00	100.00
Total	290.10	2093.20	526.50	3711.20	140.60	614.75	75.35	220.64	122.85	898.00
Dehradun										
Doiwala	193.00	2914.00	43.00	430.00	102.00	1122.00	164.00	3526.00	92.00	1104.00
Raipur	168.00	2604.00	37.00	370.00	107.00	1177.00	197.00	4236.00	67.00	804.00
Sahaspur	165.00	2557.00	36.00	360.00	97.00	1067.00	161.00	3461.00	59.00	708.00
Vikasnagar	184.00	2852.00	33.00	330.00	92.00	1012.00	120.00	2580.00	57.00	684.00
Kalsi	128.00	1984.00	33.00	330.00	63.00	693.00	70.00	1505.00	39.00	468.00
Chakrata	121.00	1953.00	29.00	290.00	29.00	319.00	27.00	604.00	20.00	240.00
Total	959.00	14864.00	211.00	2110.00	490.00	5390.00	739.00	15912.00	334.00	4008.00
Grand Total	2541.25	30930.55	1581.50	14528.97	1664.17	23131.69	1263.32	22091.01	936.63	10692.86

District/ Block	*Capsicum*		*Pea*		*Bean*		*Lady's finger*		*Onion*	
	Area	*Prod-uction*	*Area*	*Prod-uction*	*Area*	*Prod-uction*	*Area*	*Prod-uction*	*Area*	*Prod-uction*
Chamoli										
Joshi Math	4.00	20.00	60.00	480.00	15.00	90.00	5.00	30.00	10.00	80.00
Dasholi	8.00	40.00	25.00	200.00	30.00	180.00	20.00	120.00	40.00	320.00
Ghat	5.00	25.00	30.00	240.00	25.00	150.00	8.00	48.00	35.00	280.00
Karnpryag	8.00	40.00	30.00	240.00	30.00	180.00	18.00	108.00	45.00	360.00
Pokhri	5.00	25.00	30.00	240.00	23.00	138.00	12.00	72.00	35.00	280.00
Gairsen	8.00	40.00	35.00	280.00	22.00	132.00	12.00	72.00	45.00	360.00
Narainbagad	5.00	25.00	20.00	160.00	15.00	90.00	12.00	72.00	30.00	240.00
Tharali	5.00	25.00	20.00	160.00	18.00	108.00	10.00	60.00	25.00	200.00
Devaal	4.00	20.00	10.00	80.00	12.00	72.00	8.00	48.00	20.00	160.00
Total	52.00	260.00	260.00	2080.00	190.00	1140.00	105.00	630.00	285.00	2280.00
Uttarkashi										
Bhatwari	2.50	4.25	85.00	1700.00	63.00	0.00	0.00	0.00	0.00	0.00
Dunda	5.00	47.50	93.01	1860.20	48.43	0.00	0.00	0.00	0.00	0.00
Chinyalisad	2.00	10.00	63.69	1273.80	67.77	0.00	0.00	0.00	0.00	0.00
Naugaon	6.50	32.50	87.20	1744.00	65.00	0.00	0.00	0.00	0.00	0.00
Parola	7.00	35.00	34.10	682.00	45.00	0.00	0.00	0.00	0.00	0.00
Mori	5.50	27.50	90.50	1810.00	45.00	0.00	0.00	0.00	0.00	0.00
Total	28.50	156.75	453.50	9070.00	334.20	0.00	0.00	0.00	0.00	0.00
Hardwar										
Narsan	0.00	0.00	66.00	990.00	0.00	0.00	56.00	840.00	0.00	0.00
Bhagwanpur	0.00	0.00	45.00	675.00	0.00	0.00	25.00	375.00	0.00	0.00
Roorkee	0.00	0.00	21.00	315.00	0.00	0.00	19.00	285.00	0.00	0.00
Bahadrabad	0.00	0.00	55.00	825.00	0.00	0.00	16.00	240.00	0.00	0.00
Laksar	0.00	0.00	71.00	1065.00	0.00	0.00	9.00	135.00	0.00	0.00
Khanpur	0.00	0.00	56.00	840.00	0.00	0.00	7.00	105.00	0.00	0.00
Total	0.00	0.00	314.00	4710.00	0.00	0.00	132.00	1980.00	0.00	0.00
Rudraprayag										
Agustmuni	4.05	31.50	38.00	198.00	23.50	211.00	23.75	138.00	22.30	294.00
Ukhimath	1.15	7.00	24.00	123.00	12.75	93.00	9.35	51.00	8.85	136.50
Jakholi	1.10	7.00	24.00	126.00	15.00	135.00	10.55	60.00	11.25	157.00
Total	6.30	45.50	86.00	447.00	51.25	439.00	43.65	249.00	42.40	587.50

District/ Block	Tomato		Radish		Cauliflower		Cabbage		Egg Plant	
	Area	Production	Area	Production	Area	Production	Area	Production	Area	Production
Tehri										
Chamba	16.98	76.41	240.56	2165.04	67.89	546.51	10.36	51.70	56.56	513.56
Narendranagar	10.56	47.52	45.56	410.04	22.20	178.71	16.69	83.28	80.29	729.00
Bhilangana	7.66	34.47	68.28	614.52	25.24	203.18	34.26	170.96	36.45	330.97
Thauldhar	20.33	91.49	222.25	2000.25	49.96	402.18	23.36	116.57	310.50	2819.34
Jaunpur	69.98	314.91	522.25	4700.07	82.26	662.19	22.26	111.08	37.51	340.59
Jakhnidhar	15.24	68.58	180.88	1627.92	31.23	251.40	14.26	71.16	35.56	322.88
Kirtinagar	16.69	75.11	122.26	1100.34	54.26	436.79	34.60	172.65	56.59	513.84
Pratapnagar	9.56	43.02	103.23	929.07	51.02	410.71	24.56	122.55	46.21	419.59
Devprayag	9.87	44.42	105.89	953.01	70.30	565.92	50.69	252.94	65.65	596.01
Total	176.87	795.93	1611.16	14500.26	454.36	3657.59	231.04	1152.89	725.32	6585.78
Pauri										
Pauri	12.50	11.00	42.10	43.25	26.50	115.00	21.00	66.00	41.10	200.00
Kot	11.30	9.50	26.53	31.20	40.50	251.00	26.00	76.50	50.50	226.00
Kaljikhal	15.50	12.50	30.10	46.35	35.70	201.00	30.50	81.00	22.70	96.00
Khirsu	11.00	9.30	30.60	44.10	40.50	256.00	39.00	86.00	36.10	210.00
Pabaon	15.70	11.50	31.10	42.50	35.50	200.50	30.50	81.00	23.00	91.00
Thalisen	16.10	9.75	32.00	46.00	35.70	211.00	32.00	91.00	41.00	200.00
Ekeshwar	13.15	10.50	25.50	31.10	31.20	205.00	31.00	101.00	35.50	201.00
Pokhra	11.10	12.10	23.50	29.00	24.10	195.00	28.00	40.00	35.70	111.00
Birokhal	4.00	25.00	20.00	55.00	15.00	60.00	8.00	27.00	15.00	150.00
Nainidanda	10.00	77.00	42.00	120.00	10.00	40.00	7.00	25.00	25.00	250.00
Rikhnikhal	6.00	45.00	40.00	115.00	15.00	60.00	5.00	18.00	12.00	120.00
Yamkeshwar	5.00	40.00	20.00	45.00	10.00	43.00	10.00	35.00	40.00	400.00
Jaiharikhal	7.00	55.00	55.00	135.00	10.00	40.00	10.00	35.00	20.00	190.00
Dwarikhal	3.00	25.00	20.00	55.00	10.00	40.00	5.00	15.00	20.00	210.00
Dugadda	10.00	75.00	42.00	160.00	30.00	130.00	15.00	55.00	48.00	480.00
Total	151.35	428.15	480.43	998.50	369.70	2047.50	298.00	832.50	465.60	3135.00
Dehradun										
Doiwala	9.00	90.00	283.00	1132.00	184.00	1104.00	200.00	1200.00	60.00	720.00
Raipur	10.00	100.00	266.00	1064.00	159.00	954.00	101.00	1086.00	58.00	696.00
Sahaspur	8.00	80.00	215.00	860.00	128.00	768.00	111.00	666.00	51.00	612.00
Vikasnagar	7.00	70.00	185.00	740.00	109.00	654.00	100.00	600.00	45.00	540.00
Kalsi	5.00	50.00	234.00	936.00	133.00	789.00	126.00	756.00	50.00	600.00
Chakrata	6.00	60.00	278.00	1112.00	160.00	960.00	6.00	36.00	86.00	1032.00
Total	45.00	450.00	1461.00	5844.00	873.00	5229.00	644.00	4344.00	350.00	4200.00
Grand Total	460.02	2136.33	4666.09	37649.76	2272.51	12513.09	1453.69	9188.39	1868.32	16788.28

District/ Block	*Creeper Legumes (Bailwali sabji)*		*Rai*		*Other*		*Potato*		*Total*	
	Area	*Prod-uction*	*Area*	*Prod-uction*	*Area*	*Prod-uction*	*Area*	*Prod-uction*	*Area*	*Prod-uction*
Chamoli										
Joshi Math	0.00	0.00	0.00	0.00	28.00	252.00	970.00	14889.00	1237.00	17881.00
Dasholi	0.00	0.00	0.00	0.00	22.00	198.00	125.00	1917.00	427.00	4859.00
Ghat	0.00	0.00	0.00	0.00	24.00	216.00	285.00	4372.00	532.00	6771.00
Karnpryag	0.00	0.00	0.00	0.00	22.00	198.00	80.00	1227.00	350.00	3757.00
Pokhri	0.00	0.00	0.00	0.00	18.00	162.00	80.00	1227.00	315.00	3488.00
Gairsen	0.00	0.00	0.00	0.00	22.00	198.00	160.00	2454.00	432.00	5072.00
Narainbagad	0.00	0.00	0.00	0.00	17.00	153.00	60.00	920.00	226.00	2464.00
Tharali	0.00	0.00	0.00	0.00	18.00	162.00	80.00	1227.00	248.00	2806.00
Devaal	0.00	0.00	0.00	0.00	20.00	300.00	260.00	3988.00	416.00	5652.00
Total	0.00	0.00	0.00	0.00	191.00	1839.00	2100.00	32221.00	4183.00	52750.00
Uttarkashi										
Bhatwari	20.00	400.00	0.00	0.00	0.00	0.00	394.85	6802.20	600.94	9555.95
Dunda	36.40	728.00	0.00	0.00	0.00	0.00	201.56	1831.10	445.27	5324.42
Chinyalisad	76.00	1520.00	0.00	0.00	0.00	0.00	199.23	1113.80	485.76	4838.73
Naugaon	74.00	1480.00	0.00	0.00	0.00	0.00	654.00	9265.30	1100.43	15676.40
Parola	59.50	1190.00	0.00	0.00	0.00	0.00	460.00	9251.00	932.36	18643.85
Mori	30.50	1610.00	0.00	0.00	0.00	0.00	495.00	9900.00	732.73	17068.55
Total	296.40	6928.00	0.00	0.00	0.00	0.00	2404.64	38163.40	4297.49	71107.90
Hardwar										
Narsan	96.00	1440.00	0.00	0.00	50.00	750.00	178.00	3560.00	575.00	9515.00
Bhagwanpur	54.00	810.00	0.00	0.00	37.00	555.00	190.00	3800.00	479.00	8135.00
Roorkee	42.00	630.00	0.00	0.00	28.00	420.00	158.00	3160.00	347.00	5995.00
Bahadrabad	122.00	1830.00	0.00	0.00	51.00	765.00	210.00	4200.00	649.00	10785.00
Laksar	209.00	3155.00	0.00	0.00	99.00	1485.00	96.00	1920.00	600.00	9500.00
Khanpur	139.00	2085.00	0.00	0.00	55.00	825.00	88.00	1760.00	447.00	7145.00
Total	662.00	9950.00	0.00	0.00	320.00	4800.00	920.00	18400.00	3097.00	51075.00
Rudraprayag										
Agustmuni	39.50	409.00	0.00	0.00	36.87	195.00	124.00	1790.00	409.68	4414.50
Ukhimath	33.25	245.00	0.00	0.00	23.95	116.00	170.00	2790.00	321.59	4153.50
Jakholi	48.50	425.00	0.00	0.00	23.00	113.00	220.00	3520.00	400.73	5080.00
Total	121.25	1079.00	0.00	0.00	83.82	424.00	514.00	8100.00	1132.00	13648.00

District/ Block	*Creeper Legumes (Bailwali sabji)*		*Rai*		*Other*		*Potato*		*Total*	
	Area	*Production*	*Area*	*Production*	*Area*	*Production*	*Area*	*Production*	*Area*	*Production*
Tehri										
Chamba	0.00	0.00	0.00	0.00	154.09	1564.45	60.26	1272.00	819.57	7554.05
Narendranagar	0.00	0.00	0.00	0.00	109.58	120.86	62.56	1321.27	455.86	3514.88
Bhilangana	0.00	0.00	0.00	0.00	81.36	825.71	230.32	4864.36	566.13	7565.65
Thauldhar	0.00	0.00	0.00	0.00	97.86	991.37	370.89	7833.20	1238.43	15347.13
Jaunpur	0.00	0.00	0.00	0.00	82.48	829.27	580.40	12258.05	1640.26	20917.61
Jakhnidhar	0.00	0.00	0.00	0.00	87.13	879.84	55.56	1179.87	537.44	5061.93
Kirtinagar	0.00	0.00	0.00	0.00	106.46	1079.05	289.20	6107.90	868.99	10684.79
Pratapnagar	0.00	0.00	0.00	0.00	181.22	1847.23	499.12	10541.41	1029.92	15038.49
Devprayag					110.21	1119.26	889.69	1894.25	1476.43	6488.81
Total	0.00	0.00	0.00	0.00	1010.39	9257.04	3038.00	47272.31	8633.03	92173.34
Pauri										
Pauri	0.00	0.00	11.00	4.50	26.00	196.50	96.00	480.00	341.65	1454.23
Kot	0.00	0.00	16.50	5.10	28.75	142.75	45.00	285.00	313.43	1380.01
Kaljikhal	0.00	0.00	9.60	3.00	21.50	217.00	82.00	421.00	309.60	1379.20
Khirsu	0.00	0.00	5.50	2.50	77.00	465.00	122.00	600.00	437.85	2041.28
Pabaon	0.00	0.00	9.30	3.00	22.00	332.20	63.50	302.00	296.45	1373.59
Thalisen	0.00	0.00	7.10	3.70	44.00	280.80	95.00	421.00	364.50	1576.82
Ekeshwar	0.00	0.00	5.80	2.90	47.00	295.50	75.00	374.00	314.00	1518.06
Pokhra	0.00	0.00	7.40	4.00	43.50	267.20	71.00	350.00	295.45	1212.90
Birokhal	35.00	350.00	0.00	0.00	50.00	531.00	68.00	480.00	335.00	2707.00
Nainidanda	30.00	300.00	0.00	0.00	80.00	850.00	97.00	735.00	431.00	3469.00
Rikhnikhal	30.00	300.00	0.00	0.00	85.00	780.00	40.00	300.00	316.00	2373.00
Yamkeshwar	25.00	250.00	0.00	0.00	60.00	740.00	52.00	350.00	286.00	2398.00
Jaiharikhal	40.00	380.00	0.00	0.00	57.00	640.00	45.00	310.00	328.00	2383.00
Dwarikhal	35.00	360.00	0.00	0.00	45.00	490.00	50.00	340.00	247.00	1841.00
Dugadda	65.00	660.00	0.00	0.00	150.00	1630.00	105.00	710.00	580.00	4817.00
Total	260.00	2600.00	72.20	28.70	836.75	7857.95	1106.50	6458.00	5195.93	31924.09
Dehradun										
Doiwala	0.00	0.00	0.00	0.00	395.00	3160.00	0.00	0.00	1725.00	16502.00
Raipur	0.00	0.00	0.00	0.00	348.00	2784.00	0.00	0.00	1518.00	15875.00
Sahaspur	0.00	0.00	0.00	0.00	357.00	2856.00	0.00	0.00	1388.00	13995.00
Vikasnagar	0.00	0.00	0.00	0.00	289.00	2315.00	0.00	0.00	1221.00	12377.00
Kalsi	0.00	0.00	0.00	0.00	397.00	3176.00	0.00	0.00	1278.00	11287.00
Chakrata	0.00	0.00	0.00	0.00	369.00	2932.00	0.00	0.00	1131.00	9538.00
Total	0.00	0.00	0.00	0.00	2155.00	17223.00	0.00	0.00	8261.00	79574.00
Grand Total	1339.65	20557.00	72.20	28.70	4596.96	41400.99	10083.14	150614.71	34799.45	392252.33

Source: Directorate of Horticulture, Ranikhet (Uttarakhand).

ANNEXURE–5.3

Block-wise Area and Production of Spices (2004-05)

(Hectares/ Metric Tonnes)

District/ Block	*Ginger*		*Turmeric*		*Coriander*		*Chilli*		*Garlic*	
	Area	*Production*	*Area*	*Production*	*Area*	*Production*	*Area*	*Production*	*Area*	*Production*
Chamoli										
Joshi Math	8.00	80.00	5.00	50.00	4.00	10.00	10.00	15.00	8.00	56.00
Dasholi	15.00	150.00	8.00	80.00	5.00	12.50	14.00	21.00	15.00	105.00
Ghat	10.00	100.00	7.00	70.00	5.00	12.50	12.00	18.00	12.00	84.00
Karnpryag	12.00	120.00	10.00	100.00	5.00	12.00	9.00	13.05	12.00	84.00
Pokhri	14.00	140.00	8.00	80.00	4.00	12.00	10.00	15.00	10.00	98.00
Gairsen	8.00	80.00	7.00	70.00	4.00	12.50	10.00	15.00	24.00	140.00
Narainbagad	7.00	70.00	6.00	60.00	4.00	12.00	6.00	10.00	9.00	63.00
Tharali	6.00	60.00	5.00	50.00	4.50	11.25	7.00	10.50	8.00	56.00
Devaal	10.00	100.00	4.00	40.00	4.50	11.25	4.00	6.00	7.00	49.00
Total	90.00	900.00	60.00	600.00	40.00	106.00	82.00	123.55	105.00	735.00
Uttarkashi										
Bhatwari	1.00	25.00	0.70	0.50	4.50	4.06	3.60	4.00	3.80	6.00
Dunda	5.00	13.53	0.30	0.60	7.90	8.07	13.20	8.55	10.50	15.02
Chinyalisad	10.95	161.05	2.15	28.00	32.00	14.59	50.00	12.10	17.00	35.70
Naugaon	2.50	45.05	0.72	18.20	1.50	3.15	0.50	4.65	1.00	2.10
Parola	0.50	12.50	0.70	0.60	2.00	4.20	12.00	5.65	1.00	2.1
Mori	1.50	26.00	1.70	13.50	2.00	4.20	5.00	1.21	2.50	3.15
Total	21.45	283.13	6.27	61.40	49.90	38.27	84.30	36.16	35.80	64.07
Hardwar										
Narsan	1.50	14.00	3.00	28.00	2.00	19.00	2.50	22.00	3.00	28.00
Bhagwanpur	2.40	23.00	1.40	14.00	3.00	28.00	1.20	12.00	5.00	47.00
Roorkee	7.00	65.00	3.50	30.00	7.00	63.00	7.00	28.00	7.00	63.00
Bahadrabad	14.00	136.00	7.00	64.00	7.00	64.00	2.00	37.00	17.00	155.00
Laksar	5.00	47.00	9.00	83.00	8.00	57.00	0.50	19.00	12.00	110.00
Khanpur	1.00	10.00	6.00	56.00	7.00	64.00		5.00	11.00	103.00
Total	30.90	295.00	29.90	275.00	34.00	295.00	13.20	123.00	55.00	506.00
Rudraprayag										
Agustmuni	15.00	98.00	12.25	123.00	11.50	19.00	30.15	106.50	15.00	63.00
Ukhimath	6.75	50.50	4.25	33.00	3.1	6.00	12.60	51.50	11.30	49.00
Jakholi	9.00	43.00	3.95	25.00	5.40	8.00	19.90	59.00	3.70	20.00
Total	30.75	191.50	20.45	181.00	20.00	33.00	62.65	217.00	30.00	132.00

District/ Block	Ginger		Turmeric		Coriander		Chilli		Garlic	
	Area	Production	Area	Production	Area	Production	Area	Production	Area	Production
Tehri										
Chamba	0.16	1.20	0.11	0.66	0.50	0.15	0.24	0.47	0.08	0.28
Narendranagar	98.14	736.05	13.46	80.76	0.45	0.14	10.62	20.00	12.10	42.35
Bhilangana	25.00	187.50			0.56	0.17	12.00	23.40	10.00	35.00
Thauldhar	20.00	150.00	1.08	6.48			3.60	7.02	2.16	7.56
Jaunpur	31.22	234.15	4.04	24.24	0.55	0.17	28.97	56.50	31.39	109.86
Jakhnidhar	8.60	64.50	0.3	1.80	0.45	0.14	7.57	14.17	1.18	4.13
Kirtinagar	90.33	677.47	13.31	78.86	0.53	0.16	20.08	30.10	9.15	32.02
Pratapnagar	5.32	39.90	0.2	1.20	0.60	0.18	1.16	2.26	11.48	40.18
Devprayag	15.40	115.50	3.3	19.80	0.60	0.18	16.00	31.20	13.50	47.25
Total	294.17	2206.27	35.80	213.80	4.24	1.29	100.24	185.12	91.04	318.63
Pauri										
Pauri	0.50	5.00			21.00	1.65	2.60	10.30	1.00	5.20
Kot	3.50	30.36	1.00	1.80	120.50	1.50	19.00	21.85	7.50	8.60
Kaljikhal	1.00	40.00			20.00	1.61	2.00	0.11	0.50	0.03
Khirsu	3.50	40.10	2.10	3.60	150.00	3.40	21.50	12.17	7.50	37.10
Pabaon	3.10	40.50	3.50	4.01	186.00	3.60	4.70	1.39	1.10	0.42
Thalisen	1.00	20.00			34.00	3.50	0.55	0.06	5.50	38.30
Ekeshwar	1.15	21.51	0.30	0.05	11.00	1.50	3.00	10.00	1.00	17.10
Pokhra	1.25	21.42	1.50	1.92	80.00	4.60	5.61	11.41	3.00	16.50
Birokhal	1.00	5.00	1.00	5.00	1.00	1.00	16.00	24.00	2.00	8.00
Nainidanda	20.00	100.00	5.00	25.00	5.00	6.00	25.00	37.00	10.00	40.00
Rikhnikhal	2.00	10.00	2.00	10.00	1.00	2.00	3.00	5.00	2.00	8.00
Yamkeshwar	30.00	150.00	1.00	5.00	1.00	1.00	20.00	30.00	10.00	40.00
Jaiharikhal	7.00	35.00	8.00	40.00	8.00	9.00	10.00	15.00	11.00	45.00
Dwarikhal	6.00	24.00	1.00	5.00	2.00	3.00	1.00	2.00	3.00	12.00
Dugadda	20.00	79.00	6.00	33.00	4.00	8.00	8.00	12.00	13.00	57.00
Total	101.00	621.89	32.40	134.38	644.50	51.36	141.96	192.29	78.10	333.25
Dehradun										
Doiwala	31.00	297.00	12.00	33.00	14.00	20.00	18.00	26.00	14.00	117.00
Raipur	35.00	335.00	19.00	52.00	8.00	12.00	11.00	16.00	15.00	125.00
Sahaspur	25.00	239.00	9.00	25.00	8.00	12.00	18.00	26.00	8.00	67.00
Vikasnagar	59.00	565.00	6.00	17.00	6.00	9.00	18.00	26.00	8.00	67.00
Kalsi	106.00	1014.00	3.00	8.00	4.00	6.00	9.00	13.00	11.00	92.00
Chakrata	33.00	314.00	2.00	6.00	4.00	6.00	9.00	13.00	8.00	67.00
Total	289.00	2764.00	51.00	141.00	44.00	65.00	83.00	120.00	64.00	535.00
Grand Total	857.27	7261.79	235.82	1606.58	836.64	589.92	567.35	997.12	458.94	2623.95

District/ Block	Cardamom (Bari Ilaichi)		Methi		Onion		Other		Total	
	Area	Production	Area	Production	Area	Production	Area	Production	Area	Production
Chamoli										
Joshi Math	0.00	0.00	0.00	0.00	0.00	0.00	2.00	14.00	37.00	225.00
Dasholi	5.00	0.50	0.00	0.00	0.00	0.00	3.00	21.00	65.00	389.00
Ghat	5.00	0.20	0.00	0.00	0.00	0.00	3.00	21.00	51.00	305.70
Karnpryag	2.00	0.10	0.00	0.00	0.00	0.00	2.00	14.00	51.00	343.60
Pokhri	1.00	0.10	0.00	0.00	0.00	0.00	2.00	14.00	54.00	359.10
Gairsen	1.00	0.10	0.00	0.00	0.00	0.00	2.00	14.00	52.00	331.60
Narainbagad	0.00	0.00	0.00	0.00	0.00	0.00	2.00	14.00	34.00	229.00
Tharali	0.00	0.00	0.00	0.00	0.00	0.00	2.00	14.00	32.00	201.75
Devaal	0.00	0.00	0.00	0.00	0.00	0.00	2.00	14.00	31.00	220.25
Total	15.00	1.00	0.00	0.00	0.00	0.00	20.00	140.00	407.00	2605.00
Uttarkashi										
Bhatwari	0.20	1.28	0.00	0.00	0.14	3.00	0.00	0.00	13.94	83.84
Dunda	0.15	0.54	0.00	0.00	1.00	32.00	0.00	0.00	38.05	78.31
Chinyalisad	0.05	0.01	0.00	0.00	70.00	403.55	0.00	0.00	182.15	654.99
Naugaon		0.12	0.00	0.00	0.50	15.40	0.00	0.00	6.72	88.55
Parola	0.15	0.00	0.00	0.00	1.00	32.00	0.00	0.00	17.35	57.17
Mori	0.00	0.00	0.00	0.00	0.50	16.00	0.00	0.00	13.20	64.06
Total	0.55	1.95	0.00	0.00	73.14	501.95	0.00	0.00	271.41	1026.92
Hardwar										
Narsan	0.00	0.00	0.00	0.00	7.00	64.00	4.00	37.00	23.00	212.00
Bhagwanpur	0.00	0.00	0.00	0.00	2.00	18.00	5.00	46.00	20.00	188.00
Roorkee	0.00	0.00	0.00	0.00	5.00	52.00	3.00	28.00	35.50	329.00
Bahadrabad	0.00	0.00	0.00	0.00	61.00	585.00	6.00	56.00	116.00	1097.00
Laksar	0.00	0.00	0.00	0.00	65.00	605.00	4.00	37.00	105.00	958.00
Khanpur	0.00	0.00	0.00	0.00	31.00	305.00	3.00	28.00	59.50	571.00
Total	0.00	0.00	0.00	0.00	171.00	1629.00	25.00	232.00	359.00	3355.00
Rudraprayag										
Agustmuni	1.18	1.32	0.00	0.00	0.00	0.00	3.15	7.30	88.23	418.12
Ukhimath	4.25	4.00	0.00	0.00	0.00	0.00	4.95	7.50	47.20	201.50
Jakholi	0.20	0.25	0.00	0.00	0.00	0.00	1.00	2.50	43.15	157.75
Total	5.63	5.57	0.00	0.00	0.00	0.00	9.10	17.30	178.58	777.37

District/ Block	*Cardamom (Bari Ilaichi)*		*Methi*		*Onion*		*Other*		*Total*	
	Area	*Production*	*Area*	*Production*	*Area*	*Production*	*Area*	*Production*	*Area*	*Production*
Tehri										
Chamba	0.00	0.00	0.00	0.00	0.00	0.00	0.00	0.00	1.09	2.76
Narendranagar	0.00	0.00	0.00	0.00	0.00	0.00	0.00	0.00	134.77	879.30
Bhilangana	0.00	0.00	0.00	0.00	0.00	0.00	0.00	0.00	37.00	246.07
Thauldhar	0.00	0.00	0.00	0.00	0.00	0.00	0.00	0.00	26.84	171.06
Jaunpur	0.00	0.00	0.00	0.00	0.00	0.00	0.00	0.00	96.17	424.92
Jakhnidhar	0.30	1.38	0.00	0.00	0.00	0.00	0.00	0.00	18.1	86.12
Kirtinagar	0.51	2.51	0.00	0.00	0.00	0.00	0.00	0.00	133.91	822.13
Pratapnagar	0.00	0.00	0.00	0.00	0.00	0.00	0.00	0.00	18.76	83.72
Devprayag	0.00	0.00	0.00	0.00	0.00	0.00	0.00	0.00	48.8	213.93
Total	0.81	3.89	0.00	0.00	0.00	0.00	0.00	0.00	515.44	2930.01
Pauri										
Pauri	0.20	0.12	0.00	0.00	0.00	0.00	0.00	0.00	24.30	24.97
Kot	0.36	0.24	0.00	0.00	0.00	0.00	0.00	0.00	152.36	64.35
Kaljikhal	0.00	0.00	0.00	0.00	0.00	0.00	0.00	0.00	23.50	106.10
Khirsu	0.00	0.00	0.00	0.00	0.00	0.00	0.00	0.00	184.60	97.37
Pabaon	0.00	0.00	0.00	0.00	0.00	0.00	0.00	0.00	198.44	49.92
Thalisen	0.00	0.00	0.00	0.00	0.00	0.00	0.00	0.00	41.05	61.86
Ekeshwar	0.00	0.00	0.00	0.00	0.00	0.00	0.00	0.00	16.45	50.16
Pokhra	0.00	0.00	0.00	0.00	0.00	0.00	0.00	0.00	91.36	55.55
Birokhal	0.00	0.00	0.00	0.00	15.00	150.00	0.00	0.00	36.00	193.00
Nainidanda	0.00	0.00	0.00	0.00	25.00	250.00	0.00	0.00	90.00	458.00
Rikhnikhal	0.00	0.00	0.00	0.00	12.00	120.00	0.00	0.00	22.00	155.00
Yamkeshwar	0.00	0.00	0.00	0.00	40.00	400.00	0.00	0.00	102.00	626.00
Jaiharikhal	0.00	0.00	0.00	0.00	20.00	200.00	0.00	0.00	64.00	334.00
Dwarikhal	0.00	0.00	0.00	0.00	20.00	200.00	0.00	0.00	33.00	256.00
Dugadda	0.00	0.00	0.00	0.00	48.00	480.00	0.00	0.00	99.00	669.00
Total	0.56	0.36	0.00	0.00	180.00	1800.00	0.00	0.00	1178.06	3201.28
Dehradun										
Doiwala	0.00	0.00	9.00	11.00	0.00	0.00	0.00	0.00	98.00	504.00
Raipur	0.00	0.00	6.00	8.00	0.00	0.00	0.00	0.00	94.00	548.00
Sahaspur	0.00	0.00	5.00	6.00	0.00	0.00	0.00	0.00	73.00	375.00
Vikasnagar	0.00	0.00	5.00	6.00	0.00	0.00	0.00	0.00	102.00	690.00
Kalsi	3.00	3.00	2.00	3.00	0.00	0.00	0.00	0.00	138.00	1139.00
Chakrata	0.00	0.00	2.00	3.00	0.00	0.00	0.00	0.00	58.00	409.00
Total	3.00	3.00	29.00	37.00	0.00	0.00	0.00	0.00	563.00	3665.00
Grand Total	25.55	15.77	29.00	37.00	424.14	3930.95	54.10	389.30	3472.49	17560.58

Source: Directorate of Horticulture, Ranikhet (Uttarakhand).

ANNEXURE–5.4

Block-wise Area and Production of Cut Flowers (2004-05)

(Hectares/ Metric Tonnes)

District/ Block	*Marigold*		*Gladiolus*		*Dahlia*		*Rose*		*Halihack*	
	Area	*Prod-uction*	*Area*	*Prod-uction*	*Area*	*Prod-uction*	*Area*	*Prod-uction*	*Area*	*Prod-uction*
Chamoli										
Joshi Math	1.20	1.24	0.80	0.82	0.80	0.82	0.40	0.41	0.00	0.00
Dasholi	1.50	1.54	0.60	0.62	0.70	0.72	0.50	0.52	0.00	0.00
Ghat	0.80	0.82	0.30	0.31	0.20	0.21	0.40	0.41	0.00	0.00
Karnpryag	1.40	1.44	0.40	0.41	0.60	0.62	0.50	0.52	0.00	0.00
Pokhri	0.90	1.96	0.40	0.41	0.40	0.41	0.40	0.41	0.00	0.00
Gairsen	1.20	1.24	0.50	0.52	0.60	0.62	0.50	0.52	0.00	0.00
Narainbagad	1.10	1.14	0.40	0.41	0.20	0.21	0.40	0.41	0.00	0.00
Tharali	0.80	0.82	0.40	0.41	0.40	0.41	0.50	0.52	0.00	0.00
Devaal	0.70	0.72	0.30	0.31	0.30	0.31	0.40	0.41	0.00	0.00
Total	9.60	10.92	4.10	4.22	4.20	4.33	4.00	4.13	0.00	0.00
Uttarkashi										
Bhatwari	0.20	0.05	0.20	0.00	0.00	0.00	0.02	0.00	0.00	0.00
Dunda	0.10	0.03	0.00	0.00	0.00	0.00	0.08	0.04	0.00	0.00
Chinyalisad	0.10	0.03	0.00	0.00	0.00	0.00	0.05	0.02	0.00	0.00
Naugaon	0.60	0.06	0.00	0.00	0.00	0.00	0.02	0.01	0.00	0.00
Parola	0.15	0.75	0.05	0.12	0.00	0.00	0.06	0.14	0.10	0.3
Mori	0.50	0.95	0.50	0.95	0.00	0.00	0.30	0.60	0.10	0.2
Total	1.65	1.86	0.75	1.07	0.00	0.00	0.53	0.81	0.20	0.50
Hardwar										
Narsan	47.00	41.00	3.10	2.70	0.00	0.00	2.70	2.40	0.00	0.00
Bhagwanpur	3.10	2.70	2.80	2.50	0.00	0.00	0.50	0.50	0.00	0.00
Roorkee	13.00	14.00	3.80	3.40	0.00	0.00	1.80	1.60	0.00	0.00
Bahadrabad	63.00	56.00	5.00	0.50	0.00	0.00	17.00	15.00	0.00	0.00
Laksar	21.00	18.00	9.00	8.00	0.00	0.00	3.60	3.20	0.00	0.00
Khanpur	5.00	6.00	3.00	2.70	0.00	0.00	0.90	0.80	0.00	0.00
Total	152.10	137.70	26.70	19.80	0.00	0.00	26.50	23.50	0.00	0.00
Rudraprayag										
Agustmuni	2.30	3.20	0.23	0.56	0.26	0.60	0.56	0.60	0.00	0.00
Ukhimath	1.05	1.30	0.33	0.55	0.55	1.05	0.56	0.55	0.00	0.00
Jakholi	1.05	1.25	0.22	0.35	0.30	0.60	0.40	0.45	0.00	0.00
Total	4.40	5.75	0.78	1.46	1.11	2.25	1.52	1.60	0.00	0.00

District/ Block	*Marigold*		*Gladiolus*		*Dahlia*		*Rose*		*Halihack*	
	Area	*Production*	*Area*	*Production*	*Area*	*Production*	*Area*	*Production*	*Area*	*Production*
Tehri										
Chamba	0.05	0.05	0.00	0.00	0.00	0.00	0.00	0.00	0.00	0.00
Narendranagar	0.20	0.20	0.00	0.00	0.00	0.00	0.00	0.00	0.00	0.00
Bhilangana	0.10	0.10	0.80	0.80	0.00	0.00	0.00	0.00	0.00	0.00
Thauldhar	0.10	0.10	0.65	0.65	0.00	0.00	0.00	0.00	0.00	0.00
Jaunpur	0.25	0.25	1.30	1.30	0.00	0.00	0.00	0.00	0.00	0.00
Jakhnidhar	0.00	0.00	0.00	0.00	0.00	0.00	0.00	0.00	0.00	0.00
Kirtinagar	0.10	0.10	0.80	0.80	0.00	0.00	0.00	0.00	0.00	0.00
Pratapnagar	0.00	0.00	0.00	0.00	0.00	0.00	0.00	0.00	0.00	0.00
Devprayag	0.20	0.20	0.00	0.00	0.00	0.00	0.00	0.00	0.00	0.00
Total	1.00	1.00	3.55	3.55	0.00	0.00	0.00	0.00	0.00	0.00
Pauri										
Pauri	0.00	0.00	0.00	0.00	0.00	0.00	0.00	0.00	0.00	0.00
Kot	0.00	0.00	0.00	0.00	0.00	0.00	0.00	0.00	0.00	0.00
Kaljikhal	0.00	0.00	0.00	0.00	0.00	0.00	0.00	0.00	0.00	0.00
Khirsu	0.00	0.00	0.00	0.00	0.00	0.00	0.00	0.00	0.00	0.00
Pabaon	0.00	0.00	0.00	0.00	0.00	0.00	0.00	0.00	0.00	0.00
Thalisen	0.00	0.00	0.00	0.00	0.00	0.00	0.00	0.00	0.00	0.00
Ekeshwar	0.00	0.00	0.00	0.00	0.00	0.00	0.00	0.00	0.00	0.00
Pokhra	0.00	0.00	0.00	0.00	0.00	0.00	0.00	0.00	0.00	0.00
Birokhal	0.00	0.00	0.00	0.00	0.00	0.00	0.00	0.00	0.00	0.00
Nainidanda	0.00	0.00	0.00	0.00	0.00	0.00	0.00	0.00	0.00	0.00
Rikhnikhal	0.00	0.00	0.00	0.00	0.00	0.00	0.00	0.00	0.00	0.00
Yamkeshwar	0.00	0.00	0.00	0.00	0.00	0.00	0.00	0.00	0.00	0.00
Jaiharikhal	0.00	0.00	0.00	0.00	0.00	0.00	0.00	0.00	0.00	0.00
Dwarikhal	0.00	0.00	0.00	0.00	0.00	0.00	0.00	0.00	0.00	0.00
Dugadda	0.00	0.00	0.00	0.00	0.00	0.00	0.00	0.00	0.00	0.00
Total	0.00	0.00	0.00	0.00	0.00	0.00	0.00	0.00	0.00	0.00
Dehradun										
Doiwala	8.00	9.00	14.00	15.00	1.00	1.00	0.05	0.05	0.00	0.00
Raipur	7.00	7.00	12.00	13.00	0.34	0.20	0.05	0.05	0.00	0.00
Sahaspur	0.50	0.50	3.00	3.50	0.50	0.50	0.40	0.25	0.00	0.00
Vikasnagar	0.50	0.50	4.00	4.50	0.16	0.30	1.50	0.65	0.00	0.00
Kalsi	0.00	0.00	0.00	0.00	0.00	0.00	0.00	0.00	0.00	0.00
Chakrata	0.00	0.00	0.00	0.00	0.00	0.00	0.00	0.00	0.00	0.00
Total	16.00	17.00	33.00	36.00	2.00	2.00	2.00	1.00	0.00	0.00
Grand Total	184.75	174.23	68.88	66.10	7.31	8.58	34.55	31.04	0.20	0.50

District/Block	*Rajnigandha*		*Other*		*Total*	
	Area	*Production*	*Area*	*Production*	*Area*	*Production*
Chamoli						
Joshi Math	0.00	0.00	0.80	0.72	4.00	4.01
Dasholi	0.00	0.00	0.70	0.63	4.00	4.03
Ghat	0.00	0.00	0.80	0.72	2.50	2.47
Karnpryag	0.00	0.00	1.00	0.90	3.90	3.89
Pokhri	0.00	0.00	0.80	0.72	2.90	3.91
Gairsen	0.00	0.00	0.80	0.72	3.60	3.62
Narainbagad	0.00	0.00	0.60	0.54	2.70	2.71
Tharali	0.00	0.00	0.80	0.72	2.90	2.88
Devaal	0.00	0.00	0.80	0.73	2.50	2.48
Total	0.00	0.00	7.10	6.40	29.00	30.00
Uttarkashi						
Bhatwari	0.00	0.00	0.00	0.00	0.42	0.15
Dunda	0.00	0.00	0.00	0.00	0.18	0.03
Chinyalisad	0.00	0.00	0.00	0.00	0.15	0.05
Naugaon	0.00	0.00	0.00	0.00	0.62	0.07
Parola	0.00	0.00	0.00	0.00	0.36	1.31
Mori	0.00	0.00	0.00	0.00	1.40	2.70
Total	0.00	0.00	0.00	0.00	3.13	4.30
Hardwar						
Narsan	0.00	0.00	0.00	0.00	52.80	46.10
Bhagwanpur	0.00	0.00	0.00	0.00	6.40	5.70
Roorkee	1.50	1.40	0.00	0.00	20.10	20.40
Bahadrabad	2.00	1.80	0.00	0.00	87.00	73.30
Laksar	0.20	1.80	0.00	0.00	33.80	31.00
Khanpur	0.00	0.00	0.00	0.00	8.90	9.50
Total	3.70	5.00	0.00	0.00	209.00	186.00
Rudraprayag						
Agustmuni	0.00	0.00	0.44	0.44	3.79	5.40
Ukhimath	0.00	0.00	1.01	1.06	3.49	4.51
Jakholi	0.00	0.00	1.15	0.90	3.12	3.55
Total	0.00	0.00	2.60	2.40	10.40	13.46

District/Block	*Rajnigandha*		*Other*		*Total*	
	Area	*Production*	*Area*	*Production*	*Area*	*Production*
Tehri						
Chamba	0.00	0.00	0.00	0.00	0.05	0.05
Narendranagar	0.00	0.00	0.00	0.00	0.20	0.20
Bhilangana	0.00	0.00	0.00	0.00	0.90	0.90
Thauldhar	0.00	0.00	0.00	0.00	0.75	0.75
Jaunpur	0.00	0.00	0.00	0.00	1.55	1.55
Jakhnidhar	0.00	0.00	0.00	0.00		
Kirtinagar	0.00	0.00	0.10	0.10	1.00	1.00
Pratapnagar	0.00	0.00	0.00	0.00	0.00	0.00
Devprayag	0.00	0.00	1.40	1.40	1.60	1.60
Total	0.00	0.00	1.50	1.50	6.05	6.05
Pauri						
Pauri	0.00	0.00	0.00	0.00	0.00	0.00
Kot	0.00	0.00	0.00	0.00	0.00	0.00
Kaljikhal	0.00	0.00	0.00	0.00	0.00	0.00
Khirsu	0.00	0.00	0.00	0.00	0.00	0.00
Pabaon	0.00	0.00	0.00	0.00	0.00	0.00
Thalisen	0.00	0.00	0.00	0.00	0.00	0.00
Ekeshwar	0.00	0.00	0.00	0.00	0.00	0.00
Pokhra	0.00	0.00	0.00	0.00	0.00	0.00
Birokhal	0.00	0.00	0.00	0.00	0.00	0.00
Nainidanda	0.00	0.00	0.00	0.00	0.00	0.00
Rikhnikhal	0.00	0.00	0.00	0.00	0.00	0.00
Yamkeshwar	0.00	0.00	0.00	0.00	0.00	0.00
Jaiharikhal	0.00	0.00	0.00	0.00	0.00	0.00
Dwarikhal	0.00	0.00	0.00	0.00	0.00	0.00
Dugadda	0.00	0.00	0.00	0.00	0.00	0.00
Total	0.00	0.00	0.00	0.00	0.00	0.00
Dehradun						
Doiwala	1.00	0.75	0.75	0.10	24.55	25.90
Raipur	1.00	0.75	0.10	0.80	21.39	21.80
Sahaspur	0.50	0.25	0.80	0.05	5.15	5.05
Vikasnagar	0.50	0.25	0.05	0.05	6.91	6.25
Kalsi	0.00	0.00	0.00	0.00	0.00	0.00
Chakrata	0.00	0.00	0.00	0.00	0.00	0.00
Total	3.00	2.00	1.70	1.00	58.00	59.00
Grand Total	6.70	7.00	12.90	11.30	315.58	298.81

Source: Directorate of Horticulture, Ranikhet (Uttarakhand).

6

Marketing and Storage of Horticulture Products

Agrarian system is well adapted to the rural mountain environment and economy. Due to relatively lesser production most of produce is locally consumed. Although use of inputs such as HYV seeds and fertilisers has positive impact on the agricultural productivity but the desired result could not be achieved mainly due to rugged topography. However the use of improved quality inputs is more profitable for horticulture sector. Like subsistence agriculture, subsistence horticulture, traditionally prevailing in the hilly area may perform without additional infrastructure but commercial horticulture needs strong foundation of necessary infrastructure for its development. It may be noted that subsistence nature of prevailing economy is semi-self-reliant and hardly there is any scope for produce and import of inputs. Moreover, areas of horticulture production are generally far off from the motorable road and the demand market and fruits are grown in the area which require relatively more technical and economic resources. In order to earn high income, heavy investment is needed, on the other hand fruit crops are more sensitive to adverse climate like forst, hailstorms etc. Moreover, horticulture produce is highly perishable and fragile which means in order to maintain it in a suitable cool state over a long period of time and distance, the biological changes to which it is subjected, must be thoroughly studied and known to those involved in the cultivation and trade. This state of affairs poses problem of balance between supply and demand, which make the market for horticultural produce specially sensitive not only at the level of individual producer, but also at regional, national and even international levels.

The demand for horticultural produce on the whole, is elastic depending on a number of reasons including changes in population and it is composition, changes in income, particularly disposable income of the people, and prices of individual fruits and their possible substitute and supplements. The production can considerably be enhanced by properly phased supply of required inputs at the right time and in the right quantity. In case of high marketable surplus fruit need quick disposal and for which grading, packing, transportation etc. are the important prerequisites. A little delay may adversely affect the profits of the growers.

Keeping all these factors into consideration, an attempt has been made to put sincere efforts to analyse these aspects so that a suitable strategy could be developed for marketing and storage of horticulture produce from the region.

Grading and Packing

Facilities during disposal: After the establishment of a separate H.R.C. at Srinagar cold storage has been constructed at Gwaldom and Pipalkoti (under construction) and community fruit preservation centres (CFPCs) have also started functioning in the different parts of the entire region. The Government of Uttarakhand has made sincere efforts to encourage this industry and attempt was also made to sort out the problems of the fruit growers, which would ultimately solve the problems of the growers resulting in substantial increase in their income. Garhwal Mandal Vikas Nigam (GMVN) also make efforts to encourage the preservation of fruits by organising preservation camps at different locations. Though the farmers do take part in such preservation camp, however it is yet to take momentum. Nevertheless construction of cold storage would encourage the growers to participate in the government scheme in a big way.

Grading and standardization: Even under ideal conditions, fruits produced in an orchard or even on a tree cannot be uniform in all characteristics (Organization for Economic Cooperation and Development, 1970). Genetic factors, attack of pests and diseases, variations in soil structure, place of a tree in the orchard and that of a fruit on the tree etc. all lead to differences in quality and size. It has been realised that the growers can fetch better prices of their products if it is graded according to the well prescribed standards. It is most likely that the farmers may not earn expected returns to their crops if adequate attention is not paid while grading the fruits. It has also been realised that a large number of growers generally do not appreciate the significance of this particular process. The objective of the growers is to maximise the profits by avoiding the grading of their products. There are variety of reasons which forced the growers to avoid the grading including cheating the buyers successfully by mixing grades or by putting superior quality fruits in the upper few layers and the inferior ones in the lower layers. The fact is that the quality of fruits in a box is determined by the fruits of the poorest quality contained in it, is the same thing as the strength of a chain in the strength of its weakest link. We should not forget the consumers and traders are bound to made the critical cost benefit analysis before purchasing the fruits from the growers.

Grading means the sorting of fruits into different lots each with substantially the same characteristics with respect to market quality and each bearing its own label or name. In case of fruits such characteristics may be in terms of size, shape, colour, degree of ripeness, flavor etc. Standardization implies the establishment of uniform quality specification for various grades so that every body in the trade speaks the same language. Grading loses much of its value in facilitating exchange if the same specifications are not observed and understood in all sections of the market. Therefore, effective grading requires that specifications be formulated in precise terms, be agreed upon and made known to all concerned. Employment of skilled and experienced persons for the job is important. A good grader should be able to identify the variations and understand fully well the requirement of size, quality and size. Fresh fruits have many characteristics which make their post-harvest handling (picking, packing, and transport) very specialized and often expensive. Thus, a quality product is significant. Factors determining the quality of fruits include shape, stage of maturity, colour, freedom from injuries, blemishes, disease, spot, bruises etc.

Packing of fruits: Unlike the practices prevalent in the fruits and vegetables producing countries of the West, there are no set standards for types of packaging and methods used for packing. Since packaging with whatever materials are available is not only unsuitable but sometimes even harmful, rather than protective to the produce. Packing practices need greater attention for size of packaging, structural design, methods of packing, proper cushioning and stacking durability during transit and storage.

In the mountains, softwoods such as silver fir and pine (chir) are used for packing the fruit boxes. It has been estimated that if Silver fir used for packing about 0.85 million cubic meters of wood is required annually for packing apples and the demand will increase when additional areas are involved in commercial fruit production. The use of such large amounts of forest timber for packing fruit boxes will have greater influence on the ecological balance of the mountains and resulting in indirect impact on the growth of the horticultural industry in the area. Various task forces for integrated development in the Himalayas, constituted in India, have made a strong case for the need to preserve the environment and check deforestation. In order to encourage horticultural development and maintain ecological balance, alternative packing will have to be introduced.

The use of right type and size of packing fruit cases is essential when the consumers and producers are located at a long distance. The packages, particularly for perishable fruits should be convenient to handle, as well as attractive and acceptable for the traders. The type of containers employed varies widely with the character of the commodity, the physical and climatic environment and the phase of marketing. Therefore attempt should be made to develop suitable and convenient packing. This will reduce the chances of adulteration or substitution to a great extent. With the development of horticulture, the demand for packing cases will increase substantially leading to a great burden on the forests. Corrugated cardboard should be used to replace traditional type of packing material. Efforts in this regard are being made by Horticultural Research Centre at Srinagar and Garhwal Mandal Vikas Nigam (GMVN).

The horticulture produce particularity apples have market at a considerable distance. The apples are packed in a box in regular layers. The layers may be diagonal or rectangular depending on the choice and convenience of the traders and size of the boxes. Normally each fruit is wrapped in a paper. Padding is also provided both in the bottom and top of the box by pine needles, dry grass and wood wool.

Transportation

Transportation: Transportation is the key link in the marketing chain, between geographically specialized farmers and an urbanized consumers population (Nichols, 1969). Thus, transportation adds 'place utility' to good and commodities. Owing to special product and production characteristics, agriculture has unique transportation needs. Thus, transportation is an important nerve in fruit marketing not only as an integral link in the marketing chain but also because it has strategic implication for the cost involved in the process. Moreover, in the region where the producing areas are located in interiors with high altitudes and difficult road conditions, the role of transportation becomes highly important for the efficient marketing of these perishable and fragile commodities.

It has been realised that while transporting perishable commodity like fruits, the chances of damage due to breakage of containers are considerably higher. In the event of road blockage caused by variety of reasons including, landslides, traffic congestion etc. the chances of spoilage are likely to increase. Further the orchards being not connected by roads, the fruits are carried from orchard to road head by animal or human being on their back involving more jerks and thereby causing spoilage. The circuitous roads in hilly regions not only restrict the speed of vehicles but also jerks to the goods which is transported to other places. Transport of commodity may be for short or long distance but both involve proper care for the commodity being transported. For transporting the produce from the points of production up to the ultimate consumers, different modes of transportation were involved including human labours, pack animals, rope ways according to the terrain and distance of the destination. Thus, the transport of fruit from hilly areas of the region to the terminal markets of the country takes place involving two stages such as, from the point of production to road head, and from road head to the market.

Transport up to road head: Before sending dispatching fruits to the market, the produce is brought to certain strategic points on motorable road which may be called forwarding points. Most of the farmers/ orchards in the region are situated away from the road side and the produce has to be carried either by human labour or by pack animals up to the nearest road head. This involves not only heavy expenses but also a lot of time besides, rough handling of the produce. The introduction of rope-ways may be installed for this purpose as being used in Himachal Pradesh. GMVN has been recently constructing ropeway in Joshimath region. In case these ropeways are used for transporting the fruits and also constructing more such ropeways in the region, particularly in the hilly terrain where construction and maintenance of roads is too expensive, the marketing of horticulture produce will catch a new height.

Transportation of fruits by trucks, through costlier, is becoming more popular because of speed, economy and efficiency of the system. Road transport consists of trucks owned by transport companies or by State Govt. Corporation. Transportation cost influences both producers and consumers and it is the consumers who ultimately bear the burden because the traders generally shift the burden of increased cost to the consumers. It has also been observed that the burden of increased cost fall primarily on farmers in the short run and increase in freight rates reduces the price of the fruits considerably forcing the farmers to cut their profit. However, in the longer run, as farmers make necessary adjustment and transport costs are partially shifted on the consumers. This sharing of a freight rate increase between farmers and consumers depends upon the elasticity of the supply and demand.

Regulation of Supply and Storage

Storage is important for efficient marketing. There should be a definite time for harvesting fruits and vegetables because after the peak harvesting period the quality and texture of the produce deteriorate. Storage at low temperatures maintains the quality of the fruits for a certain period by retarding the physiological deterioration and reducing water loss (Anand and Grower). Cold storage is often not viable as the produce will be transported ultimately over long distances to different markets. Field-located cold storage facilities can be used for two to three months in a year. For longer storage periods, facilities are to be located in consumers' areas. Such facilities are expensive and require financing from cooperative or government organizations.

Since the sector is not fully developed in the region, therefore there is lack of coordination between supply and demand, seasonal production and demand and seasonal production and perishable nature of fruits. Access to suitable storage can help greatly in the marketing of perishable fruits and vegetables. Deterioration and wastage can be reduced considerably if the storage facilities are available which in turn reduces the impact of short-term gluts and facilitates a more even flow of produce to consumers. Storage exerts a standing influence on price and makes efficient use of transport and other marketing facilities. Conversely, lack of storage opportunities may lead to heavy losses by spoilage which will result in fluctuation of prices to a great extent.

During the harvesting season, apples, pears, and peaches move from cold Himalayan region to the hot plains where the major terminal markets are located. There is a wide variation in the surrounding temperatures between producing areas and the terminal markets. Temperature in the producing areas ranges between 15^{0}C during August, while in Delhi - a major terminal market the mercury moves between 30^{0}C and 40^{0}C. Most fruits get rapidly spoiled by exposure to temperatures beyond 38^{0}C after harvest (Rana, 1987). It will not be possible to keep the fruits in their fresh state unless they are moved to the markets in refrigerated containers.

It is also not easy to provide economic and convenient storage facilities for such highly perishable and seasonal products. Optimum storage temperature and humidity vary to a great deal according to the type of fruits and a minor deviation can cause deterioration, which may not be noticed normally. This is turn, may also vary with production zones, seasonal and atmospheric conditions, cultural and spraying practices, maturity at picking, care taken in handling, time between picking and storing, storage practices, etc. Therefore temperature and humidity play crucial role and it is important to take proper care of these factors while transporting the fruits and vegetables from the hilly areas. It is also suggested that the produce to be stored should be as free as possible from skin breaks, bruises and decay, and it should be neither too green nor over-riped.

The Horticultural Research Centre (HRC) has made a beginning, in setting up a chain of cold storage in the producing areas like Gwaldam and Pipalkoti and cold storages have also been established in terminal markets like Delhi, Mumbai and Chennai. These cold storages are specially designed for storing temperate fruits. Therefore in time to come the marketing and storage problems will be addressed more effectively.

Institutional Facilities

Institutional finance also plays important role for over-all development of any sector. It has been realised that institutional facilities for larger production and also for its efficient marketing are not available. However, attempts are being made to provide institutional facilities for development of horticulture in the area. Horticulture Research Centre, Srinagar and its micro level branches located at different places including Kothiyalsen served extensively for the over-all development of this sector.

Infrastructure facilities play important role to ensure the development of any sector particularly in the areas which are socially and economically backward. It has been estimated that production as well as productivity of agriculture produce is significantly low in the hilly areas of Uttarakhand region primarily due to hilly terrain and climatic conditions. However there is tremendous scope for high production and productivity in horticulture sector. Though sincere efforts have been made to create enough infrastuctural facilities in the areas yet, it is felt that development of such facilities was remained in close proximity of block headquarters. Though District Horticulture Departments (DHD) and Valley Fruit Research Centre (VFRC) provide the facilities of inputs and training to the producers yet the actual benefit are yet to be derived. It is also realised that most of horticulturists could not maintain inputs level as required. Now it is needed that the branch of research centres should be established in each and every tributaries of the region.

Supply of Inputs: Production of horticulture crops is a capital-intensive venture requiring intensive use of inputs. With technological changes, the nature and intensity of the inputs have undergone tremendous changes in the region during the last two decades. As the production has become more and more dependent on the use of purchased inputs like fertilizers, insecticides, seed/fruits plants etc., the farmers have also become more conscious in this regard. The Horticulture Research Centre (H.R.C.) Srinagar is engaged in supplying agricultural inputs to the farmers in this region. Plant protection measures have assumed added importance in plantation crops (Tiwari, Sharma, and Vashist, 1973) because without their timely and adequate application and expected returns may not come to farmer's expectations.

Marketing Management

There are no regulated markets for fruit and vegetables. Transactions are carried out in wholesale markets, which are managed and operated by associations, fruit, and vegetable merchants, or commission agents. In some wholesale markets, transactions are carried out by open auction, whereas in other markets they are done 'under cover'. In the prevailing marketing system, neither the grower nor the consumer derives appropriate benefits. If horticulture is to be profitable for growers, and if consumers are to buy fruits and vegetables at reasonable prices, in comparison to the cost of production, then the present marketing system is needed to be revamped.

Unless an alternative system is developed, it will be difficult to replace the middlemen who are already ingrained in the fruit and vegetable trade. Marketing perishable fruits and vegetables is expensive because of the need for facilities such as post-harvest operations, storage, and transport. These are beyond the financial capacity of the individual farmer. At this stage, an alternative to the current system would be to establish cooperative marketing centers for fruits and vegetable farmers and to establish government-run wholesale marketing organisations across the state. This involves long-term perspective because of the problems involved in handling perishables. In addition, a price forecasting system for horticultural crops would help stabilize crop production (Nasol).

Marketing and management activities involve in getting goods from the producer to the consumer. The producer is responsible for the design and manufacturing of goods. Marketing follows production is responsible for moving goods from the manufacturer through every subsequent phase to the point of final sale (Funk and Wangal, 1987). Marketing concentrates primarily on the buyers, or consumers, determining their needs and desires, educating them with regard to the availability of products and to important product features, developing strategies to persuade them to buy and, finally, make them satisfied with the purchase. Marketing management includes planning, organising, directly and controlling decision-making regarding products lines, pricing, promotion, and servicing. In most of these areas marketing has complete control: in product line development, its function is primarily to give advice. In addition, the marketing department of a business firm is responsible for the physical distribution of the products, determining the channels of distribution that will be used and supervising the profitable flow of goods from the factory or warehouses.

Producers may often consider marketing as just selling, or in other terms finding a buyer willing to exchange a satisfactory amount of money for their product. While middlemen may consider marketing of products as a way to earn a living. But consumers, on the other hand, consider marketing as little more than the frequent trips to the market to buy goods etc. and they are interested in low prices, the availability of a good selection of quality products and its performance. Each of these groups sees or is most familiar with only one position of the total marketing system (Darrah, 1967). But marketing in the present control concentrates meeting the needs of the ultimate producer through disposal of these products involved and the services added thereto.

In fact, efficient market strategy specially for horticultural produce, depends mainly on the decision on where, when, how and how much to market. In the process of marketing, a product has to pass through a number of marketing agencies and make use of the services of several functionaries. Each of the functionaries and services have to be paid for. The fruits pass through different channels of their way to the ultimate consumer and share of consumers money received by the producer depends upon the channel followed. The difference between the price paid by the consumers and that received by the producers consist of marketing costs and margins. Thus, it protects the interests of producers as well consumers, and it is essential to integrate the role of intermediaries. Keeping all these factors in view an attempt has been made in this chapter to find out the various marketing channels through which the horticultural produce of the region is marketed, price spread margins over a period of time and space and problems faced by the producers in the marketing of the fruits.

The region is highly characterised by inaccessibility from the motorable road and also low consumption of fruits in the domestic and local level. Therefore, the need of marketing management for alternation of fruits marketing in the regional level obtains a remarkable place.

Marketing Channels and Functionaries

Marketing is basically the process of movement of goods from producer to consumer at the desired time, place and form. Concentration of fruits production in specialized pockets coupled with their consumption dotted all over the country renders fruit marketing essentially a matter of skill, specially when J&K and H.P. have control on the horticulture markets. Vigilance is equally essential for reasons of the higher perishability of horticulture produce. A small mistake in the marketing decisions may lead to a low revenue for the hard toiled produce. A farmer has generally a number of alternative marketing channels to choose from.

The main channels, through which the produce of region reaches market are presented in Table 6.1. Among the eight channels listed, the first six channels are important through which the fruits are marketed. Out of these, the sixth channel is most important for apples, stone fruits and citrus.

Table 6.1. Marketing Chain

Marketing Chain	*Functionaries*
•	Producer- commission agent/ wholesaler-retailer-consumer.
•	Producer- pre harvest contractor- commission agent/ wholesaler-retailer-consumer.
•	Producer- retailer-consumer.
•	Producer- producer- dealer- retailer- consumer.
•	Producer- forwarding agent- commission agent/ wholesaler-retailer- consumers.
•	Producer- local trader- commission agent/ wholesaler- retailer-consumers.
•	Producer- cooperative societies- commission agent (consuming market)- consumer.
•	Producer- depot holder- commission agent (local market) - commission agent (consuming market)- consumer.

Agencies Involved in Marketing of Fruits

Pre-harvest contractor: Among the fruit growers of the region, a pre-harvest contractor is generally a welcome visitor. He purchases standing crops and perform all the functions necessary for the disposal of produce. To an outsider the pre-harvest contractor might appear as a superfluous agency or an avoidable intermediary but a close study of the functions performed by him would reveal that at times the services rendered by him are more valuable than what he factually gets out of the deal. Main reasons for which the fruit growers contract out their orchards are:

- Small orchards and hence small production.
- Lack of time during marketing season due to their pre-occupation in other agricultural operations.

- Lack of finances necessary for marketing.
- Ignorance about marketing practices.
- Preference to shift the risks of price changes and the inconveniences of undergoing the various marketing operations.

Pre-harvest contractors are generally the efficient marketers of fruits. The contractors are mostly belonging to the same region where the orchards are established. They are generally unemployed youth from the citrus fruits belts of Gopeshwar Mandal and, Mansoona, Narainkoti, they send fruits to the market of Rudraprayag and Srinagar.

Commission agents/wholesalers: In market generally the same firm acts both as a commission agent as well as a wholesaler. Irrespective of the channels followed, the major portion of all fruits pass through commission agents/ wholesalers. Normally it is expected that a commission agent will sell the produce on behalf of the seller and charge a fixed percentage of the value of transaction from the seller. But in practice, it was observed that (though with business motto), the commission agents/wholesalers were performing something more than this.

Garhwal Mandal Vikas Nigam (GMVN): Garhwal Mandal Vikas Nigam (GMVN) was set up in 1977, with the headquarters at Dehradun with the objectives to ensure the speedily development of the region thereby improving the living standard of the people in the area, and also creating an environment to attract tourists in the entire region of Garhwal Himalaya. The main thrust of GMVN is to get the better prices and efficient services to fruit growers and quality fruit at reasonable rates to consumer as their interests are not being taken care of by the middlemen. The major objectives of the Nigam are:

- To expand marketing in new cities and diversification of new trade.
- To improve marketing efficiency.
- To reduce marketing costs in all respects including transport, intermediary margins etc.
- Utilisation of large quantity of culls.
- To improve fruit quality and its public usage by introducing quality control.

- To establish competent and efficient marketing organisation engaged in trading of fruits and its products by creating an alternative to existing unsatisfactory wholesale channel of commission agents with their malpractices.

Price Spread/Market Margin

The two basic components that affect product pricing are costs of manufacture and competition in selling. It is unprofitable to sell a product below the manufacturer's production costs and not feasible to sell it at a price higher than that at which comparable merchandise is being offered. The marketing margins as used in relation to the marketing of agricultural commodities refers to the difference between the price paid by the ultimate consumer and that received by the farmer. Marketing margins include all costs of assembling, grading, packing, transportation, handling, processing, storage, wholesaling and retailing in the whole process of marketing. The study of marketing margins is very essential in the formulation of an appropriate marketing policy. On the one hand, producer deserve legitimate share in the consumers rupee (Azad, Swaroop and Sikka, 1988), and on the other hand consumers have to be safeguarded against excessive prices. There twin objectives can best be achieved by ensuring the services of intermediaries and functionaries at reasonable costs.

The main idea behind this is to ascertain from time to time the share of producer and the margins of various intermediaries involved in the sale and purchase of fruits under study and thereby to study the variations in producers' price and components of marketing margins in important markets. This would also throw light on the incidence of fiscal and other measures e.g. imposition of taxes, increase in freight rates, etc. on the volume and pattern of cost of marketing and consequently on prices. The price spread and margins were worked out for various fruits and vegetables grown in the region and market in the plains. The market selected for this purpose were purposive keeping in view the importance and bulk of the commodity marketed.

The method of measurement of marketing margins is the most important aspects of price spread and the most difficulty too, as on its accurate measurement will depend on the study of agencies who perform various marketing services. There are three methods generally used for the calculation of marketing margins (Mirchandani, 1965) which are:

(a) following specific lots of consignments through the marketing system and then assessing the cost involved at each of different stages, (b) submission of average gross margins obtained by dividing money value of sales minus money value of purchases by the number of units transacted for each type of marketing agency and (c) comparison of prices at different levels of marketing over the same period of time.

None of the above listed three methods is regarded as perfect and each has merits and demerits of its own. However, for this study the first method was adopted because in case between the time the commodity enters the marketing system and the time within which it is consumed in rather narrow, whereas in the non-perishables like grains it is not so. The study of price spread and marketing margins could be a valuable indicator provided comparable and reliable time series is available. It is, however, difficult to measure the price spread in an absolute way, firstly because the agencies involved are too many and consequently, the costs involved are too numerous. Accurate prices have to be obtained from specific markets which are never easy to determine and to obtain. Thus marketing margin (F.A.O. 1986) can be computed by two ways: (i) cash margins and (ii) percentage margins. The percentage margins indicate the relative cost of marketing and production at a particular time, but can be misleading such as a rise in the percentage marketing farm price. Similarly, high farm prices may make the marketing margins look small even though there has been no cost saving measures in the marketing efficiency. But, on the other hand, the cash margins are a good indicator of the trend of marketing costs. In the study both types of margins have been calculated to compare the margins in an absolute as well as in proportions for important markets under study. Since the fruits are produced in hill areas, while they are consumed all over the country, it has to be carried over long distances. The perishable nature of the produce, the seasonality of production and the long distances separating the producers from the consumers are some of the factors which are important in the assessment of marketing margins.

Problems Connected with Marketing

This region has traditionally been an agricultural region, but due to concerted efforts made by the people and the horticulture department, the area and production of fruits has increased significantly during post-independence period. This has brought in many problems with regard to the marketing of horticultural produce. The main characteristics of horticultural produce have made the marketing difficult and delicate. The reach of the produce from producing areas to ultimate/intermediate markets is difficult and cumbersome job, as such it poses great problems to every body involved with this task. In the absence of any planned marketing programme, the fruit producers are often deprived of getting reasonable returns and at the same time the consumers suffer by not getting the produce at a reasonable price. Here the problems faced by the growers, who are the ultimate sufferers required due attention.

Grading and packing problems: Grading is a process of sorting out the produce into different uniform lots each substantially of the same characteristics. In the absence of definite grade specification, the returns are lower. The main problems like higher wage rates, shortage of skilled labour and non-availability of labour for grading and packing are faced by the growers.

Problems of packing material: Another important function in the process of marketing is that of packing. If the commodity reaches the markets well packed the purchase offer is always better than the un-packed lot. Thus, the packing is to be done carefully so as the efforts put in packing and grading of fruit do fetch high remuneration. The problems such as shortage of packing boxes and packing material, high prices, non-availability of packing materials in time, lack of credit, etc., are generally faced by the growers.

Storage problem: Most of the fruits produced in the Garhwal Himalaya reach the market during monsoon season. Since storage facilities near the orchard sites are not available there is always danger that the fruit may get rotten due to its perishable nature. Generally the fruits are left in open for a day or two or kept in shady place or in ventilated cattle sheds etc., for some times before finally disposed off. This bring down the quality of produce. The main problems regarding storage of produce is that the growers have no shortage facilities and if they have some, that is inappropriate as well as inadequate. The absence of shortage facilities at farm the farmers have got no choice but to sell the cost at whatever rates they get from the traders.

Problem of Transportation: Transportation plays an important role in the marketing of fruits. The movement of the produce from the producing areas of the region to other consuming states of the country involves long way and complicated transport operation. In the Garhwal

Himalaya, one of the major problems in the marketing of horticultural produce has been and still remain to be is the lack of efficient and cheap transport for the movement of these commodities from the interiors to the distant markets of the country. Another problem in this regard is that most of the villages are not linked with any kind of motorable road and thus the growers have to pay higher charges because the transporters generally hesitate to come to such places and therefore charge more for unmetalled roads. The problem is aggravated due to excessive rain during monsoon seasons, which generally result in road blockage due to landslides and non-movement of trucks for number of days. Consequently the growers have to incur huge losses.

***Market information*:** Market information is a facilitating marketing function, and is essential for a smooth, efficiently operating marketing system. Accurate and timely market information facilities, marketing decisions, regulates the competitive market processes, and lubricates the marketing machinery. Every one who produces, buys, or sells agricultural products is continuously amassing, revising and writing market information on prices, supplies, demand, and other market conditions. Market intelligence plays an important role in marketing of produce. The prices of produce are mainly dependent on the market situation. If the grower does not have proper information regarding the market, he cannot take the advantage of high prices whenever those be prevalent. Problems faced by the farmer in this regard are late information, information available for limited markets only, inadequate information, misleading information, etc.

***Problem of malpractices*:** The fruit growers reported that if they sell their produce through middlemen, sometimes they get very little of the sale value because of malpractices by commission agents and other market functionaries, etc. Majority of the farmers revealed that the commission agents generally quote lower price than the one at which the produce has actually been sold. The other problems as reported, are that the commission agents deduct more charges than the prescribed ones, deduct undue charges, payments in installment and delay in payments.

Thus, the marketing system besides the creation of utilities gives an indication of consumer preferences, which serves as guideline to the allocation of resources in production and marketing. Also, price spread as a major of efficiency of marketing system rates on the assumption that the prices are reflectors of consumers choice which may not always be valid. In the present marketing system particularly for upper Chamoli district most of the benefits are fetched by the affluent growers. It is suggested that an attempt be made to strengthen the marketing system by organising cooperative societies particularly for small growers and suitable policy measures e.g. provision of suitable substitute to the presently used wooden packing boxes, availability of timely the better transportation facilities and strict enforcement of market regulation, will go a long way in roving marketing efficiency for the Garhwal Himalaya.

Garhwal Himalayas has tremendous potential for growth of horticulture, provided suitable mechanism is developed. The issues of storage, packing, grading, marketing and transportations are very crucial considering the nature of the horticulture produce and inaccessible hilly terrain, which may ruin the efforts put in by the growers in no time. Therefore serious thinking is required to tackle these issues effectively in order to ensure that the ultimate growers fetch suitable compensation for the efforts put in by them. The state machinery can also play important role by making the venture hassle free and promoting and protecting the small and marginal farmers which are the ultimate strength for the overall growth of this sector. The state Government should come forward to provide storage facilities by constructing cold storage of lesser capacity with reduced distance and easy accessibility in the entire region, which is inevitable.

7

Processing and Preservation of Horticulture Products

Fruits and vegetables are available as a seasonal surplus in production areas and large quantities of it is wasted due to the absence of facilities and know-how for proper storage, transportation, handling, distribution, processing and marketing facilities. A massive amount of perishable fruits and vegetables produced during a particular season result in a glut in the market and becomes scarce during other seasons. Neither can they be all consumed in a fresh condition nor sold at economically viable prices. Only adoption of improved storage facilities and processing facilities can help increase shelf life of perishable commodities.

Total production of fruits and vegetable in the country was recorded 45.5 million tonnes and 90.8 million tonnes respectively (1999-2000). On the other hand the per capita availability of food and vegetable was significantly lower than the recommended level (80g/day for fruits and 150g/day for vegetables). As per the estimate available with Government of India, 40 percent of the total production is lost in post harvest and the same is much higher in the in accessible hilly region of Uttarakhand. With creation of proper storage and processing facilities near the production area the post-harvest losses can be reduced significantly. The processing plants in the country have the capacity of processing 1.5 million tonnes of fruits and vegetables which is less than 2 percent of the total production. The location of processing plants also plays crucial role, unfortunately most of the processing plants in the country are installed far from the catchment areas near the towns and cities. Presently processing of fruits and vegetables in rural areas is very minimal and mostly in the form of pickle and drying of seasonal vegetables for household consumption in the off-season. In the state of Uttarakhand preserved products are usually kept for future use and often not intended for sale. Thus, farmers are often forced to sell their produce in local markets at a very low price. In order to prevent the seasonal glut in market as well as to reduce storage and transportation requirement there is a large scope for adoption of home scale processing of fruits and vegetables in rural areas.

It has also been observed that most of the preserved horticulture produce are at the reach of elite urban class and the actual producer are deprived of its uses which in turn deprive them of better nutritional availability. As per estimate 90 per cent commodity are produced by the rural farmers. Therefore there is a need to establish processing plants at the farms level which will not only ensure additional income to the farmers but also open up the avenues of employment. The sector harnessed properly may provide opportunities of employment not only in the processing areas but also in trade and marketing and transportation.

Principle of Preservation

In order to avoid the spoilage of consumable items preservation is the main condition to store material in perfect condition. Moisture, microorganisms, enzymes etc. are major factors responsible for spoilage of fruits and vegetable. Fruits are mostly acidic in nature. Acidity naturally controls some types of microorganisms like mould and yeasts, which are likely to be developed during storage. Generally fruits can be preserved by drying or by using preservatives such as sugar, salt and vinegar. But due to low acidity content a wide range of microorganisms grow in vegetables, which may lead to spoilage and food poisoning. To prevent this vegetables can be preserved by pickling, salting, heating or drying. Basic principles of preservation involve heating to destroy enzymes and microorganisms combined with a high acidity and sugar content to prevent recommendation.

Depending upon the length of storage of this finished product, preservation techniques can be categorized as temporary preservation and permanent preservation. Further classification of preservation techniques is presented below:

Temporary Preservation	*Permanent Preservation*
• Protection from infection	• Sterilisation
• Low temperature Cold storage Freezing	• Drying and Dehydration Sun Drying Machine drying
• Exclusion of Moisture	• Freeze drying
• Exclusion of Air	• Using preservatives
• Pasterurization	• Bottling and canning
• Fermentation	• Ionizing radiation

Important Vegetables and Fruits and their Preservation

In Uttarakhand the varied climatic and soil conditions encourage the cultivation of different types of fruits and vegetables. The acreage and production of vegetable and fruits is directly influenced by the climatic conditions to a large extent. The vegetable cultivation in Doon Valley, plain and fertile land of Hardwar district and narrow strip of Bhabar is highly remunerative and productivity of potato, cabbages, cauliflower, peas, carrot, jack fruit, tomato, onion, garlic etc. is considerably high. Similarly in the middle altitudes the cultivation of garlic, *arbi,* onion and potato can be promoted. On the other hand high altitudes are best suited for cultivation of potato. The production of vegetable is primarily demand driven, however cultivators sometimes produced more than the actual demand in the market. Since the cultivators have very less information of the actual market situation, sometimes they get very less reward for their produce.

Due to absence of preservative techniques they have got no choice but to sell the produce at the much lower price. Therefore, there is a need to develop fruits and vegetables preservation trade in the region in order to save the cultivators from recurring loss for the hard work they have put. The region also provide suitable climatic conditions for cultivation of fruits. Different types of fruits are grown in the different agro climatic zones. Major fruits suitable for cultivation in the region include apple, plum, cherries, peach, guava, apricot, mango, lemon, *zamun, kaphal, burash, malta, santra,* litchi etc. A suitable preservation and processing strategy is required in order to develop the industry. The sector may provide ample opportunities of trade in all the sector of the economy vis-a-vis primary, secondary and tertiary.

Fruit and vegetable preservation processing industry have yielded desired results in the hilly and inaccessible region. In Jammu and Kashmir and Himachal Pradesh the bumper production of apple has open up doors for its processing and preservation at a large scale. Similarly in Darjiling area of West Bengal the fruit juice of water melon is sent to the plains have fetched lucrative prices. However proper techniques of processing and packing is essential in order to fetch higher prices. In the western countries and America high priority has been given for preservation and processing of fruits and vegetables grown in the hilly area which have laid solid foundation for the up-liftment of the local economy. Unfortunately processed product of fruits and vegetables are considered as luxurious consumable items and the cost of the product is increased many folds due to heavy taxation. As a result this industry has suffered badly over a period of time as it do not fetch desired benefit to the actual growers. As per estimate about 40 per cent production and other taxes are levied on the processed juice of apple. This do not include the profit margin of wholesaler and retailers and other expenditure involved in processing. The fruits are perishable items and even with due care the wastage in terms of decaying etc can not be ignored. If the fruits are not processed properly the intensity may decrease considerably. Therefore holistic picture of the industry be looked at before any policy is framed in terms of levying of taxes.

In order to boost the processing industries in the state the issues such as production, orchard management, marketing management need careful attention with integrated approach. Uttarakhand has tremendous potential for harvesting this enterprise, and same may provide platform for the economic prosperity of the region.

Potential Processed Products

In order to make the industry a viable and sustainable comprehensive approach is required and due attention should be paid for developing the network at the regional level. The cultivation of fruits and vegetables should be promoted in hot and humid valleys to the high altitude villages. Promotion of crop diversification is essential prerequisite for the growth and development of the industries in the region. Priority should be given for multiproducts and multifruit products so that the industry may get the raw material throughout the year. Production of variety of products should be primarily demand driven. An indicative list of product and usages of fruits is given in the following Table.

Table 7.1. Processed Product Based on Fruits

Product	*Raw Fruits used*
Cold Drinks (beverages)	Apple, Santra, Malta, Lemon, Litchi, Rhododendron (Burash) Kaphal, Guava, Mango, Narangi
Squash/Juice	Kaphal, Burash Flowers, Ginger, Mango
Jams and Jelly	Apple, Apricot, Peach, Adu, Khumani, Guava, Awala
Pickle	Mango, Lemon, Awala, Garlic, Ginger, Chilly, Peas
Sauce/Chatni	Apple, Mango, Cherry, Tomato, Awala, Chilly, Jamun,
Chips	Potato, Pudina

Identification of Potential Areas for Establishing Processing Units

In the state of Uttarakhand the overall development of the horticulture industry can be ensured by establishing a network of processing units at the micro level particularity in the fruits and vegetables belts. While establishing such units attempt should be made to promote cottage and small scale industries as it require low investment and may provide employment to a large number of people besides being suitable and sustainable for the environmentally fragile region. Even attempt should be made to promote farmers cooperatives at a large scale. As per the observations of the research team and interaction with the different sections of the society in the region district-wise identification of suitable locations is given in Table 7.2.

Fruit Preservation and Processing Industries

As discussed earlier fruits and vegetables preservation and processing industries has tremendous potential to grow considering the agro-climatic conditions, geo-physical nature and environmental situation of the region. However, considering the national and international industrial development trend and emergence of free market economy, proper policy framework is required, where due consideration should be given to the past experience and future challenges, besides giving due importance to local factors. Privatization has not yet spread its roots in Uttarakhand, primarily due to inaccessible hilly terrain and involvement of risk. Moreover the entrepreneurs are also reluctant to invest in the state because of its geo-physical conditions. Therefore,

Table 7.2. Districtwise Potential Places for Establishment of Processing Units

District	*Area suitable for establishment of Processing Units*
Chamoli	Talwari, Mundoli, Dewal, Tharali, Nauti, Gewar, Jangalchatti, Diwalikhal, Gairsain, Mehalchauri, Nandprayag, Ghat, Mandal ghati, Pipalkoti, Pakhi, Urimath, Urgam, Salangaon, Kimda Tapovan, Reni, Nagnath, Pokhri, Kandhul, Khandura, Bacher, Gauchar,
Rudraprayag	Ratura, Rudraprayag, Gulabrai, Fata, Gholtir, Ukhimath, Guptakashi, Agustmuni, Chopta, Jakholi
Pauri	Pauri, Khanda, Srinagar Kliasor, Khirsu, Pabon, Uprenkhal, Dudhatoli, Pokhara, Khidsain, Bhosar, Gumkhal, Bhosar, Satpuli, Kandai, Dugadda. Beronkhal, Yamkeshwar, Kot, Rikhnikhal Lansedown, Kotdwar.
Tehri	Tehri, Chamba, Thatud, Dhanolti, Kaddukhal, Ghansali, Chikhatia, Lambgaon, Agrakhal, Khadi, Gaja, Maletha, Mangron, Badiyar garh, Mangron, Silkakhal, Paukhal, Kanatal, Naredranagar, Tapovan.
Uttarkashi	Bhatwari, Harshil, Gawela, Nogaon, Purela, Muri, Dhontari, Jarmola, Mori, Nahakhar, Arakot, Raithal.
Dehradun	Kalsi, Shaiya, Korba, Chakrota, Punahpokhari, Magtipokhari, Koti Kanasar, Minus. Nagthath, Lakhwar, Magtipokhri, Chausal, Birotha, Tuni, Kathiyan, Ethan Herbertpur, Langha, Sahaspur, Thano, Ranipokhri
Hardwar	Bhagwanpur, Rampur, Mangolore, Laxur, Hardwar, Roorkee

for the overall development of the sector, public investment should poured in, unfortunately, public sector undertakings such as Garhwal Mandal Vikas Nigam has primarily made investment in the sectors such as Petroleum and domestic gas, where least risk is involved. On the other hand KVIC is also not working to its potential and has become a mere loan sanctioning authority.

Therefore KVIC should promote and protect units being established in the field of processing and preservation. Attempt should also be made to develop marketing network which may take the responsibility of purchasing the horticulture products from the region. Marketing cooperative should be promoted in the region.

In the fruits and vegetables belt 'Processing and Preservation cooperative' should be established with the overall responsibility of packing, grading, quality control, marketing and management. The units should be established in the following manner: The attempt should be made to develop community fruit preservation centres at the village level with the objective to develop the industrial chain from village level to state level.

Quality Control Units (Top Level)
↓
Processing Units (at Middle level)
↓
Ancillaries (Cottage and Village Industries)

Due importance should be given to the grading of horticulture products as the market preferences are always for the better quality product. Therefore the proper grading of fruits and vegetables is essential before they are finally sent for sale. The remaining fruits and vegetables should be sent to processing units through the cooperatives. In the inaccessible areas where means of transport are not available or scarce attempt should be made to establish the farmers cooperatives and these cooperatives should be given responsibility of grading, packing, transportation and marketing. Even on the road heads cold storage, sheds and rest houses should be established. Importance of grading should not be ignored and poor quality fruits should be sent for processing with the help of mobile community fruit preservation team. Attempt should also be made to establish community fruit preservation and training team at the grass–root level so that people may utilize the remaining produce in the production of pulp, juice, sauce, squash, jelly etc. Equipments required at the community level should be supplied by the government initially on loaning basis.

Training should also be imparted to village youth for establishing cottage industry in the area. For establishing cottage industries convergence with rural development departments is essential as these departments implement a large number of employment and income generating schemes in the rural areas which may be beneficial to fruits and vegetable growers of the region.

Integrated approach should be adopted for promotion of production, processing, preservation, transportation, storage and marketing of horticulture products. Fruits and vegetable preservation and processing federation should be a certainty and success of Anand Milk Federation should be replicated in Uttarakhand in the field of horticulture development, for which suitable agro-climatic conditions are available.

Employment Prospects

As stated earlier there is tremendous potential for growth and development of horticulture industry based on fruits and vegetables. It is estimated that considering the existing production, in the entire state more than one thousand units can be established, providing average employment to 6-8 people. Therefore in the initial stage of processing and preservation about 6 to 8 thousand people can be absorbed. In addition to storage, packing, marketing (wholesale, retails and sale agents), grading research and training are the another areas where the requirement of manpower is inevitable. The industry may become self-reliant, provided due attention is paid for the over-all growth and development during plan period. There is urgent need from the government side to harness the sector to its full potential. In time to come the sector may ensure the process of cyclical development in the region.

Development of Horticulture in the state is primarily rooted in subsidy culture with the role objective of taking benefit from the government grant/loan. For the overall development of the sector self adaptation by the farmers of state is essential. It should reach to the remote and inaccessible region, not with the government initiatives but with the sole initiatives of the farmers, who will ultimately reap the benefit of the sector. It is essential that the farmers should understand the importance of this sector in providing employment opportunities and as well as the sector has an edge over traditional agriculture system being followed in the region. The role of state is to ensure proper price of the produce to the farmers at their farms. In place of having dependence of economics of statistics a realistic evaluative system should be followed. The industry should evolve in the state and those who wish to associate with the sector should have confidence in themselves and the state machinery should ensure security to them in place of subsidy.

Since the region is climatically highly fragile, therefore combat efforts should also be ensured so that the farmers are not denied with the ultimate benefit of their produce which they are expected to get after each crop cultivation. In place of involving middlemen proper marketing cooperatives should be established with the objectives of ensuring minimum support price.

In order to ensure high quality training and research the role of Pantnagar Agriculture University and the other state level training and research institutions should be diversified and it should give greater emphasis on the development of Agriculture and Horticulture Industry in the state of Uttarakhand so that cultivators of the region can take advantage of their presence in the region. There more focus research covering wide range of subject is essential. The issues of fruit preservation, processing, financial management, marketing management, transportation management should also be given due importance, besides providing basic research input for improving the production of horticulture produce.

Fruit processing and preservation sector may provide enough opportunity of employment in the region, provided basic input is ensured by the state machinery. Proper forward and backward linkages will encourage a large number of farmers to cultivate the healthy enterprising in place of traditional one. However proper policy document is required which guarantee hassle free environment in the state. The subsidy free culture should be developed in the state. Commitment is not only requirement from the government but also from the other stake holders in order to ensure the cyclical growth and development of this sector in the state of Uttarakhand.

8

Status and Prospects of Floriculture in Uttarakhand

Floriculture activity mainly deals with cutting of flowers cultivated under controlled conditions. These flowers are grown primarily for export purpose. Cultivation of cut flowers is growing in the world at a rate around 6-10 per cent per annum. Increase in these activities worldwide is supported by the demand in the developed countries of Europe, America, Australia, Japan and Singapore. However, the climatic condition in most of these countries does not favour year around cultivation of these flowers and many of them import flowers from other countries. The major importing countries of Cut Flowers are Netherlands, USA, Germany, France, UK, Switzerland, Italy and Japan. The major exporting countries include Netherlands, Columbia, Ecuador, Israel, Spain and Kenya. Being a major market for floriculture, Netherlands on the other hand both imports and re-exports the flowers. Rose flower occupies an important place in the field of flower trade in the international market, nevertheless, others like Chrysanthemum, Carnation, Gerbera, Dahlia, Poinsettia, Orchids, Lily etc. are also marketed in a large quantities in these countries.

In spite of a long tradition of Agriculture and Floriculture, India's share in the international market for these flowers is negligible. However, during the last two decades, Government of India provided incentives for floriculture development. Taking advantage of the incentives offered by the Government, a number of Floriculture units were established in India for producing and exporting flowers to the developed countries. However, most of them were placed near Mumbai, Bangalore and Delhi and obtained the technical know-how from Dutch and Israeli Consultants. Almost all of them were capital intensive and made large investments in greenhouse and other infrastructure. Several of them are at present non-working. The major reasons for their failure were lack of experience, inadequate research support, inadequate market knowledge and infrastructural and procedural problems. Floriculture industry in India comprises florist trade, nursery plants and potted plants, seed and bulb production, micropropagation and extraction of essential oil from flowers. Even though traditional flower cultivation has been going on in India for centuries together, Indian cut flower industry for export purposes has been of recent origin. The policy of economic liberalization since 1991-92 had given an impetus to the Indian entrepreneurs for establishing 100 percent export oriented floriculture units under controlled climatic conditions. However, by their very nature, these units require high cost investments and hence these units have come up mostly under the corporate sector. The expert committee set up by Govt. of India for promotion of export oriented floriculture units has identified Bangalore, Pune, New Delhi and Hyderabad as the major areas suitable for such activity especially for cut flowers. APEDA is the registering authority for such units.

Floriculture in India: Emerging Issues

The units established during last two decades are running into losses today, mainly because of infrastructural weaknesses like lack of cold storages and handling facilities at farms, fields and the airports, high air freight charges, frequent disruption in time schedule of flights and lack of round the week cargo clearing facility at the airports. Moreover the banks are also reluctant to fund projects because of poor past performance and high risk involved in the cultivation and trade. Ironically, experts consider the quality of flowers produced in India excellent and having tremendous export potential.

The other demand for cut flower in India is for ornamental plants. Ornamental plant research in India is of recent origin. During early years, research in floriculture has not been given due attention. In India floriculture research was strengthened with the establishment of a Division of Floriculture and Landscape Gardening at the IIHR, Bangalore, in 1969 and a Division of Vegetable Crops and Floriculture at the IARI, New Delhi, in 1971. The All-India Co-ordinated Floriculture Improvement Project was also started by the ICAR during 1970-71. The Division of Floriculture and Landscaping was established in 1983 at the IARI, New Delhi. Simultaneously research work on ornamental crops was started in different agricultural universities and research institutes with an objective to provide better input for the overall development of floriculture in India.

However, there was a great challenge to survive in the market and those who have survived the initial difficulties and are working have increased the export of floricultural products of India and enabled the country to become, although still small, an important player in the world market. They have also diversified their exports and, besides Europe, have reached to the countries of Singapore, Japan and Australia. It has also been observed that there is also an increasing tendency of the Indian growers to directly send flowers to the European countries rather than through Netherlands. In spite of this achievement, the present health of the floriculture units is not exactly sound and many of them are facing both routine problems as also long term financial and marketing difficulties.

To enable these units to function more efficiently and competitively and to increase the volume of India's exports, it is necessary to orient this activity entirely from a new angle. The first and the foremost policy change dictated by the past experience are to treat the entire floriculture activity, whether it is catering to local demand or to the international demand, as an agricultural activity and not as an industry. The only difference between Agriculture and Floriculture is that the latter uses high technology like poly-houses and refrigeration. But quite soon, the technological inputs in the entire Agricultural activities will have to be upgraded and modernized on more scientific lines. By declaring Floriculture as Agriculture, we will not only take a logical step, but also we will ensure it certain benefits like income tax relief and would free the cultivators from many procedural hassles and unnecessary regulatory provisions. The second most important step will be to encourage a "consortium" approach among the units for branding, grading, packaging, transporting, quality control, supply assurance, market development, market promotion, and research and development. For this purpose, it is necessary to encourage some of the successful and experienced entrepreneurs to take a lead in forming such consortia. They can also develop satellite farms and operate the existing closed or semi-closed units with a suitable waiver or postponement of their liabilities. This would also necessitate the relief from Land Ceilings Act.

The present chapter seeks to analyze the potential of floriculture as an income generating activities in the state of Uttarakhand. Therefore the chapter mainly deals with issues pertaining to the prospects and problem of floriculture in the state by taking the interest of cross-section of people into consideration. In order to accomplish the task a series of visits were undertaken to the various villages of district Dehradun and Almora and Pithoragarh. Interaction was held with the farmers, scientists engaged in the fields, traders and general public. Main objective of the chapter is to assess the potential of floriculture sector in the state of Uttarakhand and to find out emerging issues and problems and to suggest remedial measures for the same. Therefore the study primarily focuses on the issues which have substantial role to play for the overall development of this sector in the state.

IMPORTANT CUT FLOWERS CULTIVATED IN INDIA

India holds a very rich germplasm collection of different ornamental crops, which consists of both indigenous and exotic plants. Work on varietals improvement has been carried out utilizing large diversity in germplasm, and significant achievements have been made in developing new ornamental varieties with many superior qualities. Various flowers, their varieties and varietals improvements are given below.

Rose breeding has received highest importance in India, and as a result about 545 rose varieties were evolved during the last 55 years. The main objective of rose improvement has been to evolve varieties with attractive flower colour, form and fragrance, floriferousness, disease and pest resistance, and suitable for growing under tropical and subtropical conditions. There are three types of commercially grown roses. They are Hybrid Tea, Floribundas and Spray roses. Only hybrid tea and floribundas are grown under green house for export in India. The hybrid tea types are having a long stem that varies from 50-120 cms and big size blooms from 3.02-3.5 cms. These flowers are bigger and more often tender than the floribunda type under ideal conditions. This type is expected to yield about 140-180 stems per sq. mtr. But under Indian conditions the average yield obtained by many units is 100-130 stems per sq. mtr. These flowers are liked mainly in USA, Japan and other European countries. They fetch higher price as planting is done with a close density it inhibits branches and such plants grow up to a height of 2mtrs.

Floribundas or sweethearts type produces flowers with stem length of 35-60 cms. and bud size from 2.0-2.5 cms. They yield much higher than hybrid teas producing as many as 300 flowers per sq. mtr. per year but the average yield obtained under Indian conditions is around 130-150 stems per sq. mtr. These types of flowers are much popular with the Dutch and German consumers. These flowers fetch around 30-40 percent less price than the hybrid tea. According to the Department of Agricultural Research and Education, ICAR, Government of India, in 1999-2000, rose varieties Dr. B. P. Pal, Blue Delight, Anurag, Ashirwad, Ico, Ambassador, Blue Ocean and Aditya were promising at the national level; Ashirwad, Anurag and Siddhartha for exhibition purpose; Black Delight, Blue Ocean and Aditya for garden display and Ico, Ambassador and Kanchi for cut and loose flowers at Hyderabad (htpp://www.tifac.org.in/pffer//;np/rep).

Gladiolus: Gladiolus is one of the most important bulbous flowering crops grown commercially for cut-flower trade in India. The main emphasis on gladiolus improvement has been on the development of varieties having attractive colour and large size of florets mainly for cut-flower, long spikes, more number of well spaced and large-sized florets, good corm multiplication ability and field resistance to diseases, particularly Fusarium wilt. The success of G. psittacinus hybrid at the NBRI inspired research in evolving different coloured varieties suitable for growing in the plains and resulted in the release of 11 cultivars. Notable among these are Jwala, Priyadarshini and Gazal, all of which are open-pollinated selections. Further, through systematic hybridization involving gladiolus Friendship (2n = 60) with G. tristis (2n = 30), 8 new triploid (2n = 45) cultivars were evolved.

According to DARE, Gladiolus Shagun and Shringarika were released by Delhi centre. Hybrids Amal and Tambri performed well at Vellanikkara. Gladiolus Snow White, Suchitra, Punjab Morning, Jester, Aldrion, Golden, Wave and Thrombolina were promising at Hyderabad.

Chrysanthemum is recognized as a potent flower crop in India. It is used as a cut flower for interior decoration and as loose flowers for making garlands, wreaths and for religious offerings. Work on evolving new chrysanthemum varieties has been underway mainly at the NBRI, Lucknow, and the IIHR, Bangalore. The aim of breeding chrysanthemum has been to evolve exhibition, cut-flower and garland types. A new approach has also been adopted to breed varieties, which naturally bloom in different months without light and temperature control. At the IIHR, Bangalore, emphasis had been on breeding high-yielding cultivars for garland and pot-culture and 5 new cultivars have been developed. The PAU, Ludhiana, and TNAU, Coimbatore, each has evolved 4 cultivars. Apart from institutional efforts, some amateur and professional growers have also developed a good number of chrysanthemum cultivars.

According to DARE in 1999-2000, at Lucknow, a new small-flowered, red, Anemone type, mini chrysanthemum variety, Diana, was released. A desirable natural mutant was isolated and multiplied in Nilima and a promising hybrid 87-17-1 was identified for future release at Hessaraghatta.

New varieties, Mutant No. 9 (for cut flower and loose flowers) and Hybrid No. 10, Hybrid No. 11, Hybrid No. 12, Hybrid No. 13, Sunil, Indira, Sonaly, Tara, Selection 5 and Shyamal (for loose flowers) were suitable for commercial flower production. Shyamal, Baggi, IIHR Sel. 5 and Indira were promising at Pune, whereas Basanti, Sharadmala, Baggi, Red Gold, Co 1, IIHR 13 and Vasantika at Hyderabad. Indira, IIHR Sel 6, Meera and Red Gold performed well in respect of flower yield at Udaipur.

Carnation is an important cut-flower crop in the world florist trade. However, commercial cultivation of carnation in India is in infancy. Systematic work on the production of new cultivars has not yet been taken up. At the IARI, New Delhi, mutation-breeding experiments of different lines of carnation resulted in some interesting mutants with variegated leaf.

Gerbera is an attractive cut-flower crop, and the flowers last for a longer duration in vase. The magnitude of the genetic diversity has been studied in 31 strains of Gerbera utilizing 9 characters. Significant differences exist between varieties for all the 9 characters. The study indicated the presence of wide genetic diversity among the strains.

Bougainvillea is an important and popular flowering plant grown widely throughout the country. Through hybridization, sports and mutation breeding, about 150 varieties have been developed in India. The Division of Floriculture and Landscaping, IARI, New Delhi, has been designated as the International Registration Authority for Bougainvillea Cultivars, and the first checklist described more than 300 cultivars of bougainvillea. However, breeding work is hampered largely because of the extensive pollen and seed sterility or both. The choice of female and male parents is limited only to relatively fertile types, which more often are not good cultivars. However, fertility can be restored by the colchicine-induced polyploidy which has given a wider choice for breeding bougainvillea cultivars. Thus a number of very promising, colourful and floriferous, often bicoloured, hybrid bougainvillea (triploid, tetraploid and aneuploid) ideal for pot-culture have become handy. Bloched-bract varieties like Begum Sikander, Wajid Ali Shah and Mary Palmer Special provide a visual feast in pots.

Five varieties of bougainvillea developed by Dr B P Pal in 1959, viz. Dr R R Pal, Sonnet, Stanza, Spring Festival and Summer Time, are popular even today. At Bhaba Atomic Research Centre (BARC), Bombay, several varieties were developed through mutation breeding with the use of gamma rays. The IIHR, Bangalore, has also released 6 cultivars, viz. Chitravati, Dr H B Singh, Jawahar Lal Nehru, Purple Wonder, Sholay, and Usha. A colchicine-induced mutant with bright magenta bracts has been isolated from cv Zakariana. A number of promising seedlings and bud sports with variegated leaves are now under evaluation.

In **Hibiscus** hybridization and selection work at the IIHR, Bangalore, has led to the release of 25 varieties which are floriferous and bear attractive flowers. The TNAU, Coimbatore, has developed an inter-generic hybrid (*Hibiscus rosasinensis* x *Malvaiscus arboreus*) named Thilagum (Carmine red) in addition to a seedling selection Punnagai. Another hybrid named Co 1 hibiscus has also been released by the TNAU. It is floriferous and produces apricot-yellow flowers with signal-red throat. Lalbagh, Bangalore, has also developed 22 attractive varieties.

Jasmine. Systematic research work on jasmine breeding was first started at the TNAU, Coimbatore, in early seventies, and at the IIHR, Bangalore, in mid-seventies. *J. auriculatum, J. sambac* and *J. grandiflorum* are commercially important sources of fresh flower and perfume. The objective of breeding for high essential oil content in jasmine differs from that of the fresh flower market. For essential oil extraction, the objective is high oil productivity. Flowers with short corolla tube and high yield are preferred, since the corolla tube contributes mostly plant waxes. The objectives for breeding of jasmine for fresh flower market are high yield of lower buds spread over many months of the year, long and soft corolla tube, bolder buds and better keeping quality.

The TNAU, Coimbatore, has released 3 varieties of *J. auriculatum* and 2 varieties in *J. grandiforum*. Initially, work carried out in *J. auriculatum* led to the identification of a high-yielding, gall-mite-resistant clone Parimullai. The clone is characterized by long flowering season of 9 months with flower bud yield of 7,800 kg/ha and concrete recovery of 0.34 percent. Subsequently, the university released Co. 1 Mullai and Co.2 Mullai. The yield of flower buds in Co. 2 Mullai is reported to be 8,800 kg/ha with 0.34 percent concrete recovery. Co. 2 Mullai is a cross between a mutant (s1) x Long Point (JA 1). It yields 1, 100 kg flower buds/ha accounting for an increase of 26.88 percent over Co. 1 Mullai. In *J. grandiflorum,* Co. 1 Pitchi is a clonal selection from Lucknow type which yields 10,000 kg flower buds/ha with concrete recovery of 0.29 percent. Co. 2 Pitchi is an induced mutant from Co. 1, which yields 11, 600 kg of flower buds/ha, and concrete recovery is of 0.30 per cent.

Surabhi a high-yielding variety from *J. grandiflorum* has been developed by clonal selection at the IIHR, Bangalore. The potential flower yield is 10,000 kg/ha with high concrete recovery.

Orchids produce remarkably attractive flowers with long lasting quality. Conventional plant breeding has contributed to the generation of wide range of hybrids in orchids. In India, breeding work on orchids was started at the IIHR, Bangalore, during mid-seventies. The institute has developed 2 hybrids, viz. IIHR 164 and IIHR 38, in Vanda and Dendrobium respectively.

Dahlia with their most gorgeously coloured flowers is very popular in the Indian gardens and is widely used for garden display and indoor decoration. In dahlia, several varieties have been developed under giant decorative (11), medium decorative (6), small decorative (6) and cactus group (1), all by amateur growers.

Hippeastrum is an important cut-flower, grown in beds, borders and pots. Several varieties have been released by the NBRI, Lucknow. They include cv. Kiran a triploid, cv. Samrat a tetraploid and Jyoti a semi-double. The IARI, New Delhi, has released variety Suryakiran. A variety named Anjali has been developed from an inter-varietal cross between Bouquet and White Favourite.

Tuberose: In India, tuberose occupies a prime position in floriculture industry. Two mutants, viz. Rajat Rekha and Swarna Rekha in single flowered a double flowered tuberose, respectively, were obtained through gamma irradiation (1 to 5 kr) at the NBRI. In Rajat Rekha there are silvery white streaks along the middle of the blade, whereas in Swarna Rekha golden-yellow streaks are present along the margins of the blade.

Croton are popular ornamental shrubs with colourful and attractively shaped leaves. Most of the breeding work on varietal development of this crop has been carried out at Lalbagh, Bangalore, and at the IIHR, Bangalore. At the IIHR, Bangalore, 15 hybrids of crotons have been developed.

Barleria is an evergreen shrub and is commercially grown for production of loose flowers. The TNAU has released a variety Co. 1 Barleria. It is a clonal selection from the local type, and bears attractive pink flowers, producing on an average 2.11 kg of flowers/plant/year.

Amaranthus: Systematic hybridization and selection programme in amaranthus has resulted in the development of 8 cvs, viz. Amar Kiran, Amar Poet, Amar Prithu, Amar Parvati, Amar Suikiran, Amar Tarang, Amar Raktab and Amar Mosaic. These represent various combinations of leaf shape and colour, and are entirely new to floriculture trade. A telraploid cultivar Amar Tetra was evolved through colchiploidy. Amar Shola, a hybrid Amaranth, is a selection from a cross within *Amaranthus caudatus* complex involving a grain type and an ornamental type.

Antirrhinum: Tetra giant snapdragons were raised at the NBRI, Lucknow, from some F1 hybrids. The resultant tetraploids are hardier, sturdier, stockier and shorter than corresponding diploids. They have generally more flowering stems with conspicuously larger, deeper-coloured flowers, that are long-lasting than their diploid counterparts.

China Aster: From the germplasm collections at the IIHR, Bangalore, 25 pure lines were developed by a single plant selection. Of these AST 1 and AST 2 were found very promising. Hybridization followed by repeated selection resulted in 6 promising pure lines, which were numbered IIHR 35, IIHR 18, IIHR 19, IIHR 26, IIHR 31 and IIHR 35. According to DARE in 1999-2000 China aster Kamini,

Poornima, Phule Ganesh Pink and Phule Ganesh Violet were recommended for release at the national level.

In **Marigold,** a F1 hybrid triploid has been developed at the NBRI, Lucknow, by using male-sterile African diploid marigold (*Tagetes erecta*) and male-fertile French tetraploid (*T. patula*). The F1 hybrids are dwarf, highly floriferous and free flowering with uniform golden-yellow heads that bear nearly one-and-a half times more flowers by weight per unit area. At the IARI, New Delhi, a F1 hybrid of French marigold obtained from crosses between Petite Orange x Rusty Red and Naughty Marrieta x Pygmy showed increase in the weight and number of flowers respectively than that of parents. In African marigold, F1 hybrids between Hawaii x Cupid Orange and Alaska x Spungold were superior to parents.

Hollyhock at the IARI, 4 F1 hybrids have been developed from intervarietal crosses in hollyhock. These are Pusa Apricot Supreme, Pusa Pastel Pink Supreme, Pusa Pink Beauty and Pusa Yellow Beauty.

Zinnia by recurrent selection from the irradiated seeds of *Zinnia elegans*, a mixed coloured variety resistant to leaf-curl virus, has been evolved at the IARI, New Delhi.

The state of Uttarkhand has tremendous scope in the field of cut-flower. Lessons learnt elsewhere on strategies for low cost production, marketing channels and systems are expected to benefit the growers in Uttarakhand. The state has already made some inroads in this field. As evident from the following Table 8.1 the important floriculture crops grown in the state of Uttrakhand include marigold, gladiolus, dahlia, rose, hollyhock, and rajnigandha. The total area under floriculture in Garhwal region was 315.58 hectares and total production was reported 298.81 metric tonnes during 2004-05. While looking at the spatial distribution of area it has been noticed that Hardwar has 186 hectares land under flower cultivation followed by Dehradun district (59 hectares). It is also noticed that the coverage of floriculture in the hilly districts was relatively low. Among the various crops, area under marigold was highest (184.75 ha) followed by gladiolus (68.88 ha). Similar pattern has been noticed for the production of various crops.

On the other hand, total acreage for the state as a whole was 525 hectares, and production of cut-flower was 558 mt. The acreage and

Table 8.1. Area and Production Under Various Crops (Ha./Mt.)—2004-05

District	*Marigold*		*Gladiolus*		*Dahlia*		*Rose*		*Hollyhock*		*Rajnigandha*		*Other*		*Total*	
	A	*P*	*A*	*P*	*A*	*P*	*A*	*P*	*A*	*P*	*A*	*P*	*A*	*P*	*A*	*P*
Chamoli	9.60	10.92	4.10	4.22	4.20	4.33	4.00	4.13	0.00	0.00	0.00	0.00	7.10	6.40	29.00	30.00
Uttarkahsi	1.65	1.86	0.75	1.07	0.00	0.00	0.53	0.81	0.20	0.50	0.00	0.00	0.00	0.00	3.13	4.30
Hardwar	152.10	137.70	26.70	19.80	0.00	0.00	26.50	23.50	0.00	0.00	3.70	5.00	0.00	0.00	209.00	186.00
Rudraprayag	4.40	5.75	0.78	1.46	1.11	2.25	1.52	1.60	0.00	0.00	0.00	0.00	2.60	2.40	10.40	13.46
Tehri	1.00	1.00	3.55	3.55	0.00	0.00	0.00	0.00	0.00	0.00	0.00	0.00	1.50	1.50	6.05	6.05
Pauri	0.00	0.00	0.00	0.00	0.00	0.00	0.00	0.00	0.00	0.00	0.00	0.00	0.00	0.00	0.00	0.00
Dehradun	16.00	17.00	33.00	36.00	2.00	2.00	2.00	1.00	0.00	0.00	3.00	2.00	1.70	1.00	58.00	59.00
Total	184.75	174.23	68.88	66.10	7.31	8.58	34.55	31.04	0.20	0.50	6.70	7.00	12.90	11.30	315.58	298.81

Source: Directorate of Horticulture and Fruits Processing Department, Ranikhet, (Uttarakhand).

production under marigold and gladiolus was significantly higher than the other flower crops. It may also be noted that the net cropped and gross cropped area for the state as a whole comes roughly to 784117 and 1259391 hectares respectively. Therefore the share of flower crops comes to 0.067 and 0.042 percent respectively, which is negligible. However, in the recent time it has captured the attention of the farmers and floriculture can be exploited in a bigger manner through proper planning and orientation.

Table 8.2. Area and Production of Various Crops

dz0la0	*Name of the Crop*	*2005-06*	
		Area	*Production*
1.	Rose	56.00	59.00
2.	Gladiolus	195.00	225.00
3.	Marigold	225.00	237.00
4.	Carnation	3.50	4.00
5.	Dahlia	10.50	12.00
6.	Rajnigandha	10.00	6.00
7.	Other flowers	25.00	15.00
	Total	525.00	558.00

Source: Directorate of Horticulture and Fruits Processing Department, Ranikhet Uttarakhand.

Management of Floriculture in Uttarakhand

In Uttarakhand, focus on the development of floriculture has been emphasized as a result attempt has been made to have a well-developed hierarchy of support system. The overall activates of the sector is monitored by the horticulture department, however for the World Bank funded project a state unit has been established at the top level. Under the state unit, there are separate district units in the potential districts which are supported by the District Project Coordination units. At the block level there is a block coordination unit, which is supported by technical supervisors, community organizers and block level facilitators. The number of functionaries in these units depends on the volume of work; however, facilitators include both male and female. Their main objective is to form self help group, who actually regulate all the activities of floriculture including marketing. The facilitators also conduct base line survey and chalk out the activities of the farmers.

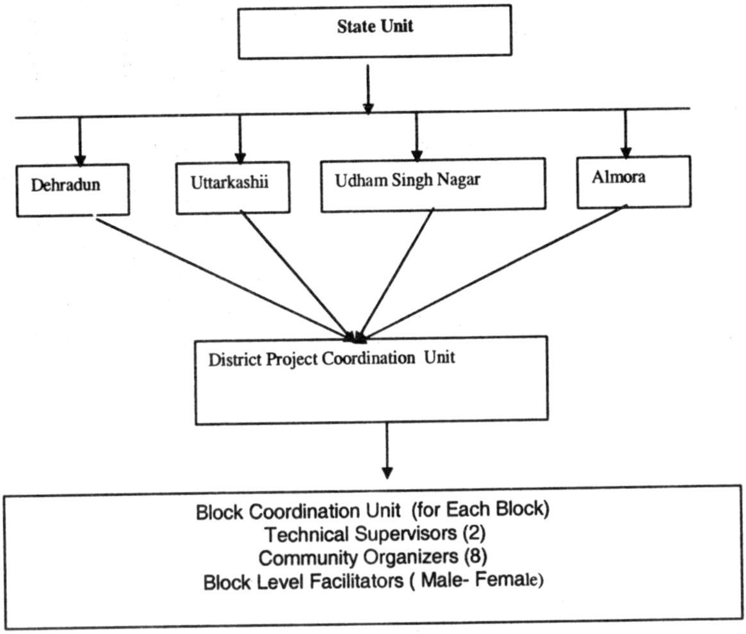

Floriculture Production

Economics of Floriculture: Farmers' Perceptions

While visiting various villages in the Uttarakhand region attempt has been made to make a comparative analysis of floriculture crops and cereal crops as a profit earning venture. During the interaction with the villagers at Haripur kalan, Nagal Brahmpuri in Raipur Block, Kyrkuli-Bhatta in Sahaspur Block, Balawala, Haripur,Shyampur and Gumaniwal in Doiwala block and with the traders at Dehradun and Pithoragarh an interesting picture has emerged.

Comparative analysis of rice and marigold in one bigha land is given in the Table 8.3. It is evident to note that profit on cultivation of rice in one bigha has been worked out to Rs. 390 only, whereas marigold can fetch a profit of Rs. 5350 on the same piece of land. Though the operation cost on cultivation of marigold is marginally higher, however considering the profit margin it is negligible. During the discussion with the villagers it has been pointed out that the traders encourage them to grow more crops, but the risk involved in cultivation of marigold is relatively higher which discourages the farmers to put more land on cultivation of cut flowers. Nevertheless farmers are ready to take risk in order to fetch more profit. It is also reported that yield of rice depends on the climatic conditions, as failure of monsoon may also lead to substantial loss to their farm products. Therefore, government policy should concentrate on providing irrigational facilities to the farmers.

Table 8.3. Comparative Analysis of Rice and Marigold

	Crop- Rice		*Crop- Marigold*		
Activities	*Mandays*	*Expenditure*	*Activities*	*Mandays*	*Expenditure*
Preparing the field including ploughing	3	3xRs 80= Rs 240	Field preparation including ploughing	1	5xRs 80 = Rs 400
Weeding	3	3xRs 80= Rs240	Plant Generation	1	1xRs 80= Rs 80
Irrigation	21/2	21/2xRs 80= Rs 200	Sowing	1	1xRs 80= Rs 80
Harvesting	4	4xRs 80 = Rs320	Plantation	5	5xRs 80= Rs400
Urea	5 kg=	Rs 130 Rs 130	Manure	1	1xRs 80= Rs 80
Manure	1	1xRs 80= Rs 80	Weeding	2	2xRs 80= Rs 160
Average Yields	2.5 quintal	2.5xRs650= Rs 1500	Insecticide/urea Plucking (5 Plucking)	2 1/2	Rs 250 21/2x Rs 80 = Rs 200
			Average yield	Rs 5 Per calam x 1500 x Rs	Rs 7500
Income		Rs 1500	Income		Rs 7000
Expenditure	—	Rs 1110	Expenditure		Rs 1650
Loss/Profit		Rs + 390			Rs +5350

Source: Based on the discussion with farmers including Miram Devi, Maya Bhutola and Dhan Singh.

On the other hand while comparing wheat with rose plant it has been noticed that operational costs of wheat comes to Rs 1110 whereas same is Rs 1760 for rose which is marginally higher. Nevertheless net profit from wheat is Rs 140, which is negligible. On the other hand the net profit on production of rose is Rs 5740, which is significantly high. This shows that the cultivation of rose is profitable ventures for the farmers and they can earn relatively higher cash income from this crop.

Table 8.4. Comparative Analysis of Wheat and Rose

Crop- Wheat			*Crop-Rose*		
Activities	*Mandays*	*Expenditure*	*Activities*	*Mandays*	*Expenditure*
Preparing the filed including ploughing	2	2xRs 80= Rs160	Field preparation including ploughing	2	2 x Rs 80 = Rs 160
sowing	1	1xRs 80= Rs 80	Plant Generation (kalam dalana)	4	4xRs 80= Rs 320
Irrigation	4	4x 80= Rs 320	Manure	1	1xRs 80= Rs 80
Harvesting	2	2xRs 80= Rs160	Weeding	5	5 x Rs 80 = Rs 400
Urea/ die		Rs 170	Insecticide	—	Rs 240
Manure	1	1xRs 80= Rs 80			
Average Yields		1.5 x Rs 800	urea		Rs 500
		Rs 1250	Plucking (5 Plucking)	2 1/2	21/2 x Rs 80 = Rs 200
			Average yield	Rs 5 per kalam x 1500 x Rs	Rs 7500
Income		Rs 1250	Income		Rs 7500
Expenditure	—	Rs 1110	Expenditure		Rs 1760
Loss/Profit		Rs + 140			Rs +5740

Table 8.5. Problem Matrix: Preferences for Cultivation

Medicinal plant name versus reasons for growing it	*Availability of Planting material*	*Labour requirement rial*	*Storage*	*Market Accessibility*	*Sale of planting material*	*Total score*	*Rank*
Marigold	5	5	3	4	1	18	II
Gladiolus	4	5	4	3	3	19	I
Dahlia	4	4	3	2	2	15	IV
Rose	5	2	5	4	1	17	III
Hollyhock	3	4	4	4	2	17	III
Rajnigandha	2	4	2	2	2	14	V

During the field visit farmers were also asked to give their perception on various problems associated with cultivation of different variety of floriculture crops. The major problem include availability of planting material, labour requirement, storage, market accessibility, illegal transportation, non-availability of flower collection centers, lack of government support, poor technical know-how, high risk and sale of planting material. Farmers were asked to give value judgment on these problems awarding more points to flower crop where they think the problem is least. It has been noticed that gladiolus has obtained first rank with 19 points followed by marigold 18 points, which indicate that farmers faced least problems in cultivation and sale of gladiolus as compared with other crops. On the other hand rajnigandha has been ranked last with 14 points. It was also reported that gladiolus, rose and marigold are always in demand and marketing of these flower crops is not a big problem. However the demand for marigold may vary in Indian market particularly at the local market during festival season.

Table 8.6. Issues of Floriculture: Value Judgement by the Key Informants

Indicators	*Cultivators*	*Researchers/ Academicians*	*Traders*	*Government Officials*
Illegal Transportation	2	1	3	1
Refrigerated Mobile Van	1	1	1	2
Flower collection centre	1	1	3	2
Planting Materials	1	1	3	2
Market	1	1	1	1
Government Support	3	2	3	1
Technical support	2	1	3	2
Risk	3	3	3	3
Storage	3	3	3	3
Illegal Marketing	2	3	2	2
Price Uncertainty	3	3	3	2
Future Potential	1	1	1	1
Role of Self Help Groups	2	2	3	2

Note: 1 =High, 2 =Moderate, 3 =Poor.

Similarly attempt was also made to identify various problems after having detailed discussion with the cross-section of people including cultivators, researchers, traders and government officers, which are presented in a coherent framework in the above table. While looking at the various problems identified by them it has been observed that the researchers feel that there was illegal transportation of crops from Uttarakhand to the other parts of the country in order to save taxes and same were the opinion of the government officials also. However, the traders and cultivators do admit the problem of illegal transportation of the product while, same has not been reflected when they were asked to give their judgment on three point scale. The researchers, traders and cultivators have opined that refrigerator mobile van is essentially required as crops are perishable and would not last long if such facilities were not available.

Researchers as well as cultivators and traders feel that there is urgent need of flower collection centers to reduce the burden on cultivators who are always apprehensive about the sale of their crops. Cultivators as well as researchers feel that planting material should be made available to the farmers in time. Farmers are some times discouraged to grow flower crops mainly because of non-availability of planting material. Farmers in village Gumaniwal, Ṣhyampur have reported that some times quality planting material is not available as a result the production of crops is also poor. Cultivators, researcher as well as traders feel that though, the government of Uttarakhand has declared ' Uttarakhand as an Herbal State', the desired support to the farmers and traders is not provided yet. Declaration of state as an herbal state will not yield desired result unless concentrated strategy to grow cut flowers is not designed. As expected cultivators, researchers, traders and government officials have expressed that flower cultivation is a risky venture and crops should be insured so that the burden of risk would be minimum on cultivators. Problem of storage was also paramount in the state of Uttarakhand. Therefore this issue needs special attention on the part of the government. Traders, cultivators and government officials had rated that problem moderately; the researcher has opined that the problem is significantly high in the state of Uttarakhand. However researchers, traders, cultivators as well as government officials feel that floriculture has tremendous scope in the state.

Emerging Problems

Disease and Pest Management: The sector is likely to capture movement in time to come. Therefore, research on the identification, diagnosis and management of viruses occurring in carnation, chrysanthemum, dahlia, gladiolus, hippeastrum, hollyhock, narcissus, petunia and zinnia is essential. Attempts should also be made to produce virus-free plantlets in gladiolus as it may cause considerable economic losses. Some new agro-technologies such as the cropping system approach, new fertilizer regime and irrigation schedule is also required to enhance production.

Research and Development: It has been realized that close linkage should be established between governments, research institutions and flower growers for assistance for market development, provision of infrastructure (which is extremely critical for Floriculture), reduction in air freight charges, reduction in interest rates by banking institutions, waiver of excise duties on domestic sales and much focused research on key areas is essential.

Training and Orientation: Training and manpower development is also another important area, which also need proper attention in order to enhance the skill of the growers. The use of information technology and, particularly, Internet for trading should also be promoted as the demand for same is more in the foreign market.

Planting Material: Government has made attempt to supply planting material to the farmers. District Horticulture Department supplies planting material to the villagers from time to time. However the supply is not proper, therefore villagers germinate planting material in the nurseries to meet their day-to-day requirement. It has been suggested that private agency should be involved for supplying planting material to the farmers.

Poor Technical Support: Uttarakhand has a suitable climatic condition for cultivation of flower crops. It produces high quality crops and demand for the crop is significantly higher in domestic and foreign market. It has been realized that cultivators should be provided technical know-how for proper farming. It has been reported that cultivation of flower crops is a highly risky business, therefore farmers should be aware of risk involved and they should also be provided contingency plan to meet out the exigencies.

Cold storage: It is surprising to note that the cold storage facilities are not available in and around Dehradun city. Farmers have no choice but to store the seeds at Saharanpur, which is quite costly affairs. It may also be noted that to break the dormancy of seeds 10 days room temperature is required. Besides for transportation of planting materials refrigerated mobile vans are also required even at the grass-root level.

Price uncertainty: Most of the traders as well as cultivators have reported there is price uncertainty. Even some times due to unsuitable climatic conditions the curve and stem of the plants get affected as a result the growers do not fetch desired benefit of their crops. Therefore a suitable insurance policy should be introduced for cut-flower growers.

***Illegal Marketing and transportation*:** Though government of Uttarakhand has taken some steps to explore the marketing facilities for flower crops, however, most of the traders have made their own arrangement to export the material.Traders from Balawala, Gumaniwal and Rishikesh have reported that flowers are exported illegally to Delhi through night buses plying between these places and is sold at Flower Mandi in Hanuman Mandir area in Delhi which take place in the morning hours. It was also reported that during summer season the demand for Uttarakhand Cut flowers is more in Dehli mandi and only competitor is Himachal Pradesh.This is primarily due to longer sustainability of cut flowers.

From the above analysis it is clearly evident that Uttarakhand has a tremendous scope for development of floriculture. Creation of new state has given the sector-desired momentum. However it has been realized that concentrated efforts are required particularly in field of infrastructure development to achieve desired result. The problems of cultivators and traders should also be given due attention so their interest could be sustained. Though the state government has formed guidelines, however, more focused policy regarding marketing and preservation of cut flowers should be designed. Nevertheless state has incredible scope for development of floriculture sector.

9

Medicinal Plants: Production and Perceptions

The combination of other geographical features that determine the climatic conditions are favorable for many species of medicinal, consequently, nearly all types of medicinal plants ranging from tropical to temperate to alpine are grown across the region (Bhakuni 2002). The State is spread in a geographical area of 53484 sq. km, accommodating 847million people with 74.40 percent rural population, primarily engaged in agriculture and allied activities. 72.67 percent workers were reported engaged in primary sector (Census 2001). The region also has diversified agro-climatic and soil conditions which are best suited for the cultivation of medicinal plants. The irrigational facilities, particularly in the hilly region is scanty. However, in the irrigated land, cultivation of vegetables, specially of off-season vegetables, flowers and seed production of vegetables are more profitable than agriculture and fetch high return to the farmers. Uttarakhand is a kind of natural habitat for many medicinal and aromatic plants. A rich medicinal flora flourish in the valley and ridges of Uttarakhand hills. It is estimated that more than 1000 species of documented medicinal values grow in the region. The estimated production of commercially used plant produce is about 1400 MT and cost earned was about Rs. 1,21,000 during the year 1991-92. However, the true figures are many-many times more because most of the valuable produce is being sold out through illegal channels (Mehta 1998). Presently all this production mainly comes from forests and alpine areas.

The present chapter is an outcome of a series of field visits undertaken across the Uttarakhand. This Chapter aimed to investigate various dimensions of medicinal plant sector by analyzing the perceptions of key informants including farmers, researchers, traders and government officials, thereby dealing with a variety of issues pertaining to this sector in the state of Uttarakhand. The efforts of state government in developing Uttarakhand as a herbal state also motivated us to capture the various dimensions of medicinal plants sector, which ultimately contributes to the income generation and gainful employment, thereby making the state economically prosperous and ensures sustainable development.

In the fragile and difficult conditions of the Himalayas, agriculture is a traditional but uneconomic occupation. Agriculture in hill areas has primarily been uneconomic due to hilly terrain and poor infrastructural and irrigational facilities, which are unable to cope-up with the increasing demands due to ever increasing population. Alternatively, the diversification of agriculture in the region may give a momentum to the development process. Although the diversification in terms of horticulture is as ancient as the animal husbandry and grain cultivation in Uttarakhand. However, the interest in medicinal plants cultivation has captured the attention of the farmers mainly during the last decade, owing to its higher returns.

This chapter mainly analysees the problems and prospects of cultivation of medicinal plants in Uttarakhand; to identify the main opportunities and constraints; to suggest policy measures and plan of action to support the sector. It also focuses on analysing the perceptions of the cultivators with regards to the cost- economics of select crops, besides dealing with the following points:

- traders view points on the prospects and problems of medicinal plants cultivation;
- to synopsize the perceptions of cross-sections of people, emerging through interaction during the course of the field visits; and
- to suggest policy measures for the development of medicinal plant sector in the state.

Medicinal Plants and Traditional Cash Crops: A Comparative Analysis

This section presents an analysis of the perceptions of the farmers of Munsyari area to cultivation of medicinal plants and problems faced by them while cultivating and marketing the produce. The cultivators were persuaded to compare some of the traditional crops such as potatoes with Kutki, Gandhryni and Atis. Accordingly they were asked to compare and analyse the advantage of replacing medicinal plants with traditional cash crops. Table 9.1 presents an analysis of Kutki and Seed Potatoes. Interpretation of table are as follows:

Kutki (Picrorhiza kurooa): Kutki is grown at an altitude of 2745-4575 m. Its roots as well as whole parts of the plant are used. The plant is generally useful for cathartic, somachic, fever, Dyspepsia and purgative (Purohit 1997).

- Conditioning of production site in terms of soil selection, terracing and fencing is required for kutki as it has longer gestation period, even new land is required for cultivation of kutki, whereas potatoes have slight edge over kutki for conditioning of production site.
- Planting material of seed potatoes is easily available and can be stored in the pits during winter. Kutki, however, is not easily available as its roots are collected from the forest, which is a time consuming process and skill is required for uprooting the planting material.
- Kutki does not require humus, compost and manure, whereas 8 to -10 bags of manure is applied in each Nali[1]of potatoes, which require the services of ¼ mandays.
- Manual labour is required for land preparation of kutki, whereas for seed potatoes land preparation is carried out by oxen which required 2.5 mandays for preparing one nali land involving at least three ploughing.
- Planting of Kutki as well as potatoes require manual labour and planting of kutki is more complicated than potatoes. However seeds/roots to be planted at proper spacing for both potatoes and kutki. Potatoes in alpine region do not require irrigation, whereas at least one irrigation is essential for kutki.
- Kutki does not require weeding as its roots are very sensitive and it grows better with the weeds. Whereas potatoes require at least two weedings, with the services of two maydays. After

the first weeding potatoes also require two mandays per nali for earthing.

- Both Kutki and potatoes have to be protected from animals, the problem is more acute in case of potatoes as it can be easily destroyed by wild animals such as monkeys, porcupines for which constant watch on the fields is required.
- Kutki has long gestation period and it takes at least three to four years for getting crops ready for harvesting the first crops. Nevertheless harvesting of kutki is easier than potatoes, as potatoes require two mandays for harvesting, whereas one nali kutki can be harvested by ¼ mandays.
- Processing of kutki is slightly difficult and it is to be dried up for seven days after making small pieces, whereas potatoes can be sold immediately after harvesting.
- Storage of Kutki is easier and can be stored for longer periods, even for ten years, without any problem. However for potatoes, a pit is to be dug. The risk of damage is always higher as wild animals such as rats may destroy the potatoes. Once the air passes through the pit potatoes are rotten and of no use.
- Transportation of potatoes is also costly affairs as it has market at the road heads for which 3-4 days journey from alpine villages of Johar valley is involved and 50 percent potatoes are given to the shepherd for transporting the potatoes to the road heads which makes cultivation of potatoes an uneconomic venture.
- At summer residence potatoes is sold @ Rs 2 per kg and Kutki @ Rs 60 per Kg. In one nali 100 kg kutki and 500 to 600 kg potatoes are produced. The total income from potatoes would be Rs. 1000.00 to 1200.00 per year. The total income for a period of four year is estimated between Rs. 4000.00 to 4800.00 by the cultivators. On the other hand kutki may fetch Rs 6000.00 per nali. As analysed earlier seed requirements for potatoes was estimated 40 kg per nali which means the income from potatoes would further go down (40kgx4yearsxRs.2=Rs 400)

Table 9.1. Comparative Analysis of Kutki and Seed Potatoes

Cultural practice	*Kutki (Picrorhiza kurrooa)*	*Seed potato*
1. Conditioning of the production site (fencing, soil selection, terracing etc.)	Fencing would be required to avoid grazing, not in terraced land (not fertile). New land is needed.	No fencing is required during crop growth terraces are guarded
2. Procurement of planting material	Roots are collected from the forest	Seed potatoes are stored in pits during the wintertime.
3. Manuring (timing, labour and cost)	No humus, manure or compost is applied	8-10 bags of manure (sheep, goats, cows) is applied in each nali. One person applies manure in 4-5 nali in a day
4. Land preparation (hand-hoe, plough)	Shallow land preparation in deep sandy soils with a hoe.	Ploughing with oxen: 2.5 day/ person/nail
5. Planting (cost, labour, timing)	July with small whole roots (2.5 cm) at 15 cm spacing. Despite the water shortage the crop is irrigated once at planting time.	30 kg per nali2 nali/day/ person in May/June
6. Weeding (timing, frequency, labour)	Weeding is never done, since kutki is extremely sensitive to root damage and with weeds it grows better.	Two weedings two days for one nali.
7. Earthing-up (timing, labour, frequency)	Not done	Not at planting but after first weeding 2 days/nali
8. Plant protection (pests and diseases, treatments)	Eaten by goats	No pests and diseasesEaten by goatsIn winter rats can enter in the pits if not well made. Thieves can steal potatoes from the pit.
9. Harvesting (Timing, labour)	September after four years. No 'milking' of the roots. Harvesting kutki is easy	Two persons for one day in September/October
11. Processing (drying, chopping etc.)	Chopped into small pieces, dried for seven days at home, cleaning (no water).	No special treatment apart from pit making.
12. Storage	Can be stored for ten years without problems	Potatoes are stored in pits for seed and sale in May (tourists, soldiers etc.) at 4 IR/kg. Pit has to be very well made
13. Transport (labour, costs)	Not yet applicable	50 % of the potatoes is paid to the shepherd who transports potatoes to nearest roadhead
14. Production and prices (yield per nali, seasonal prices)	No real data, in the forest with larger roots: 1 quintal per nali.In Summer residence sold for 60 IR /kg	5-6 bags/nali. Bag at 60-70 kg (? Seems high)High: 2 IR/ kgMunsiyari: 8 IR/kg

Table 9.2. Operating Cost for Potatoes Per Nali

Operation	*Description*
Planting material	Of last year.
Land preparation	Ploughing, animal. 1 person, 1 day.
Manure	2 people, 1 day.
Sowing	3 people, 1/2 day.
Weeding	1 people, 2 days.
Earthing-up/furrowing	3 people, 1 days.
Harvesting	5 people, 1/2 day. All in village assist, all is harvested in 1 day. In September/October.
Making pits	For sale when back, if possible.
Transporting	IR 4 / kg. 54 km.

Pests and diseases are a problem (not at bad as in lower altitude), not treated. Yield 5 – 7 quintal / nali. Price IR 4 /kg. Not always sold.

Total number of mandays required for cultivation of per nali potatoes are presented in the Table 9.2. As estimated in the table, 12 mandays are required for cultivation of one nali potatoes. The existing labour rate in the villages vary from Rs. 70 to Rs 100 per day. It may also be noted that while harvesting potatoes the services of children are always taken for collecting potatoes. The operational cost of potatoes cultivation is estimated a maximum of Rs. 1200 and a minimum Rs. 840.00 per nali per year.

***Gandryani (Angelica glauca)*:** Another important medicinal plant of alpine area is gandryani which is also known as Chippi. The operation cost for the same is presented in Table 9.3. Its root decoction used is to cure dysentery and relieve body pain due to cold (Maikhuri et.al. 2001). It is found in an altitude of 2400 -3500 m in the alpine area. It is harvested during the month May- July. The planting material of gandryani is developed in nurseries. Farmers also purchase the planting material from other farmers at very minimal price. The collection of planting material from the forest can not be ruled out. It takes two years to grow and pest and diseases problem is also common in the plant. It is estimated that for cultivation of one nail gandryani 10 mandays labour is required. The plant is productive for 5 to 6 years and it needs a lot of rain. In one nali of land 100 kg gandryani can be produced. Nevertheless, the production depends on the monsoon conditions. The plant has huge local demand as well as outside demand. The rate varies from Rs. 120 per kg to Rs 150 per kg.

Table 9.3. Operating Cost for Gandryani Per Nali

Operation	*Description*
Planting material	Either raised in nurseries or taken from other farmers. Usually it is for free. Price IR 1 plant 5 years ago.
Land preparation	3 days, 2 people. Manure is not purchased, one month before land preparation sheep and goat are allowed to graze on the fields.
Planting	Distance 6 x 6 inch. 3 days, 3 people
Weeding	Done 2 times. 1 day, 2 people.
Harvesting	2 days, 2 people.
Drying	Make 'garlands' to hang for drying. 1 day, 2 people.
Transporting	IR 1,000 / 100 kg. Takes 4 days, 54 km. By mule.

Yield: 50 – 100 kg/nali, depending on rain. Takes 2 years to harvest. No pests, no diseases reported. For the first week, every day 1 hour watering. Planting season: June – July or September – October. Harvest: September. Daily labour rate: IR 80 – 100.

Aits (*Aconitum hetero phyllum*): This medicinal plant is found within the altitude of 2240-4200 m. Its tuber and roots are used for tonic, aphrodisiacs, diarrohoea, dyspepsia, cough (Purohit 1997). Roots decoction also used to relieve headache and tuber used for gastric disorder and fever (Maikhuri et al.). Planting material is primarily collected from the forest. Sowing starts in the month of September before the cultivators leave for winter villages and in April – May when they return to summer villages seedlings are ready. Cultivators take care of seedlings for another three months and transplantation starts in the months of August. Manure is not applied and no pests and diseases are reported. It takes three years for crops to be ready for harvest. In one nali land 10 kg atis is grown and the existing price for the same was reported Rs. 700.00 per kg. Table 9.4 presents the operating cost for cultivation of Atis per Nali.

Table 9.4. Operating Cost for Atis (One Nali)

Operation	*Description*
Planting material	Own seedlings (sell to Cooperative when surplus this year). 250 gr seeds/Nali.
Land preparation: seedlings	1 people, 2 days. Done in September (little before they leave).
Watering/weeding	Every 3rd day.
Land preparation	1 people, 7 days to prepare land. Manure is ploughed in the land.
Transplanting	1 people, 4 days for transplanting.
Watering	Critical issue: need H2O for transplanting. Every week water; if no irrigation than max. 1 nali. When established, every second week needs H20
Weeding	1 people, 3 days. Once a month.
Harvesting	1 people, 4 days. September-October.
Cleaning	1 people, 1 day.
Drying	4 days.
Transporting	IR 10 / kg. 54 km. In October.
Permit	IR 5 / kg (to Cooperative).

Cost Benefit Analysis

Table 9.5 presents cost benefit analysis of traditional crops with medicinal plants grown per nali of land. From the Table 9.5 it is evident that cultivation of kutki, atis and Gandrayni is more profitable to the farmers. They are likely to fetch profits even if these crops are sold at their summer villages.

Table 9.5. Simple Cost – Benefit Analysis of Traditional Crops with Medicinal Plants (For one Nali Land)

	Potato	*Kutki*	*Atis*	*Ganhrayan*
Total income (Rs)	4000.00 to 4800.00	6000.00	10500.00	24000.00-30000.00
Expenditure				
Seed	Rs 400.00	Nil	—	—
Operational Cost	Rs .840.00 to Rs.1200.00	Rs. 420.00 to Rs.600.00	1050-1500	1400.00 to 2000.00
Total Profit	Rs. 2760.00 to 2600.00	5580-5400	9000-9500	22600-28000.00

Among the three medicinal plants analysed, gandryani seems to be highly profitable, as in one nali of land farmers may get a profit of Rs. 22600 to Rs. 28000. Similarly cultivation of atis is also profitable venture as it may fetch them profit in a range of Rs. 9000 to 9500 per nali, whereas Kutki may yield relatively low profit with Rs 5500 per nali. Nevertheless all the three species under reference has comparative advantage over Potatoes. It may also be noted that the operational hazards are least in cultivation of medicinal plants. The transportation of produce from summer villages to the winter villages may influence the profit margin to some extent.

Preferences for Cultivation

In order to understand the preferences of the farmers they asked to name some of medicinal plants species commonly cultivated or collected from the region. The species identified by them included Jambu, gandryani, kutki, kuth, atis, kalazira, mitha vish, nirvish, salampanja, jatamashi, jhula yarssagambhu Kira, Cater pillar), pudina, vantulsi, gingri, bankakri, dolu, hattajari, laljari, chiraiyata, guchhi (*Cucurmutta*), ratanjoti etc. For understanding the difficulties involved in collection and cultivation of medicinal plants farmers were asked to prepare a matrix giving possible reasons for growing different types of medicinal plants. For this purpose they themselves identified ten species and ranked them accordingly on a scale of one to eleven, where one represents highest preference and 11 least.

While preparing the matrix the farmers were asked to identify some indicators for their preference, which plays crucial role in selection of a particular species for cultivation and rank them accordingly. The indicators identified by them include ease in selling, domestic use, labor requirements, difficulty in collection and sale of planting materials. It is interesting to note that cultivators have given first preference to cultivation of Atis, followed by Kutki. Cultivation of Atis is labour intensive, but it certainly has an edge over other medicinal plants as far as other indicators are concerned. Out of five indicators identified by them for making a certain choice or preference Atis has got first preference for easiness, domestic use and sale of planting materials and ranked 2 for difficulty in collection after kuth. Gandryani and kuth have scored equal points, and both have obtained third rank. Attempt was also made to persuade the farmers to make clear distinction between kuth and gandryani regarding their preference and the comparative advantage they see. However they strongly supported the tie citing both has advantages as well as disadvantages. It may be noted that the market for Kuth has decreased substantially over a period of time, as a result it has got considerable low rank. Our interaction with the farmers in Mana and Tapovan villages, where Herbal Research Institute, Gopeshwar through Bhaisaj Sangh provided seeds and credit to the farmers to cultivate Kuth with a buy back guarantee, tells the plights of the farmers. Unfortunately cooperative could not buy it from the farmers as it could not find the buyers. As a result the hard work put in by the farmers in cultivation of kuth turned into serious loss for them (KIT-IAMR-CSD 2002). Further investigation of demand for kuth in the market was analysed and it was revealed that:

- Large supply of kuth reduced prices considerably.
- Kuth grown by the farmers of the region had relatively poor medicinal gradients.
- Supply at relatively cheaper rates from other parts of country and Nepal induced sharp decline in the prices of kuth produced from the region.

Although kalajira occupies IVth rank, however it has been rated considerably higher in terms of labour requirements, on the whole other indicators have performed moderately for this plant. On the other hand Ganjerí (Khakjari is *Polygonum rumicifolium*) occupies sixth rank in terms of farmers preference. The domestic use, and difficulty in collection has been rated significantly higher by the farmers and occupies second last preference. Since it is less labour-intensive, it has an edge over other MPs and farmer's preference is highly skewed for its cultivation. The sale of planting material is also easy. The overall analysis of the plants makes it farmers preference for cultivation. Hatazari is another plant which captures the attentions of the farmers as well as researchers. The plant has no problem in finding the market as it occupies second rank for the same. However domestic use of the same is limited. Though the crop is labour intensive, but the demand for the plant in the market nullifies it. The collection of the plant is also not very difficult and the sale of planting material is also moderate.

Relatively poor ranking in most of the indicators have placed dolu at VII, Bankaari VIII and Laljira and Chiriata IX. The analysis of above matrix also shows that farmers do exhaustive analysis before cultivating and collecting any medicinal plant. The demand for the material and price for the same plays critical role in selection of species for cultivation.

Table 9.6. Problem Matrix: Preferences for Cultivation

Medicinal plant name versus reasons for growing it	*Ease in selling*	*Domestic use*	*Labour requirement*	*Difficulty in collection*	*Sale of planting material*	*Total score*	*Rank*
Atis (*Aconitum hetero phyllum*)	1	1	10	2	1 (seed)	15	I
Ganjerí (Khakjari is Polygonum rumicifolium)	4	10	1	10	3 (root)	28	VI
Gandryani (*Angelica glauca)*	5	5	6	5	2 (root)	23	III
Kala jeera (*Carum carvi*)	6	8	2	6	5 (seed)	27	IV
Kutki (*Picrorhiza kurooa)*	3	2	3	4	8 (root)	20	II
Dholu (*Rheum australe*)	9	4	6	7	8 (root)	34	VII
Kuth (*Saussurea costus*)	8	3	5	1	6 (root)	23	III
Hatazari (*Dactylorhiza hatagirea*)	2	10	9	2	4 (root)	27	V
Laljira *Arnebia benthamii)*	7	7	8	9	8 (root)	39	IX
Bankakri (*Podophyllum hexandrum)*	10	9	4	8	7 (root)	38	VIII
Chiraita (*Swertia-chirata*)	11	6	nk	11	11 (seed)	39	IX

Medicinal Plants: Problems and Prospects

In the course of our discussion with the key players associated with the medicinal plant sector a variety of issues ranging from illegal collection to government interventions and policy measures were cropped up and accordingly, attempt was made to put them at three point scale of grading. A comparative table was prepared and the issues identified by the key informants were put under four categories. The perceptions on a particular issue obtaining 67 above percent was rated good for that particular group, the score between 34 -66 was rated moderate and less than 33 as poor (i.e. out of total farmers interacted during field visits 64 percent say that collection is not done, since the score obtained for this category falls in a range of 34 to 66, grade 2 is awarded for this issue under cultivators category). Similarly grades were obtained for other issues/categories also. All the view points of key informants are presented in the Table 9.6.

Issues of Collection: An analysis of the Table 9.7 reveals that collection of medicinal plants in the area has been traditionally practiced, as a result fragile Himalayan eco-system is facing serious problems. Government initiatives to categorize the plant species as rare, endanger and extinct has also not served the purpose. An analysis of above table also indicates that the cultivators do agree that the collection of MP from the reserve forest is taking place in the region. However they strongly defend that the local farmers make all efforts to preserve the plant species. It is also apparent that cultivators are more knowledgeable not only about medicinal values of a particular species but the environment required for its growth. In Mana village, headman narrates, in high altitudes particularity, in *bugyals*[2] the entry of all the villagers is restricted upto a particular period. This is because of two reasons. Firstly if medicinal plants are collected before they mature fully the seeds will not fall down and there is always danger of species becoming extinct. Secondly, excessive grazing may cause huge damage to the seedlings of rare species. The villagers have to enter in the bugyals bare foot as some of the species grown in the bugyals are so sensitive, that the seedlings may get destroyed with the rash walking. The entry period is clubbed with a religious[3] ceremony organized by the villagers during August end or early September when the process for harvesting starts. Similar views were expressed by Indira Kabhal and her husband in Darkot village of Munsyari block in Pithoragarh district. They are highly knowledgeable about cultivation, marketing and other aspects of MP business. The premature harvesting is never done as it is associated with many problems. Therefore no professional collector will prefer the extensive collection resulting in extinction of species. Species are rather preserved by them, as they go for collection only after flowering. The species which germinate from fibrous roots, while uprooting the plants, it is ensured that a part of the root or fiber is left underneath, so that it may grow the following year also. This practice is followed since generations. However, in the recent years this system is not being followed and excessive extraction of MP species is taking place, admits Indira Kabbal.

On the other hand, researchers have strongly opined that collection at a large scale is taking place. The cultivation of the same is possible but it is time consuming and long gestation period which is the main hurdle to make farmers skewed towards cultivation. However, the evidence of illegal collections are not available. Though collection at a large scale cannot be ruled out. On the other hand, traders are least bothered about the legality issues and have different view points. Farmers have authentic permits issued by government; therefore, whatever produce is bought by them is legal, says a trader in Ramnagar. Government officials do agree that illegal collection is possible but the same has reduced considerably due to intervention of government by issuing permits to them and getting them registered with the herbal cooperatives.

Table 9.7. Issues of Medicinal Plants: Value Judgement by the Key Informants

Indicators	*Cultivators*	*Researchers/ Academicians*	*Traders*	*Government Officials*
Illegal Collection	2	1	3	2
Cultivation	2	2	2	2
Permit	2	2	3	1
Planting Materials	3	2	2	2
Market	1	1	1	1
Government Support	3	2	3	1
Technical support	2	1	3	2
Transportation	3	3	3	3
Restrictions	3	2	3	2
Illegal Marketing	2	2	2	2
Price Uncertainty	3	2	3	1
Future Potential	1	1	1	1
Role of Cooperatives	2	2	3	1

Note: 1 =Good, 2 =Moderate, 3 =Poor.

Problems and prospects of Cultivation: The evidences show that the farmers of Niti and Mana valleys of Joshimath Block and Johar valley in Munsiyari have made sincere attempts to cultivate medicinal plants despite all associated problems. Uttam Singh Sayana has 40 nali land in Milim. He cultivates jamboo, kalajira, kutki, kuth bankakri, sweet atis, gandrayani etc. He started cultivation in 1972 because of high returns for the medicinal plants and search for alternative employment due to closure of Indo-Tibetan border. However, poor irrigational facilities could not yield desired result and the efforts put in for 3-4 years ended in mere frustration. However, he continued, his efforts, despite being discouraged by the villagers, and provided similar ecological surroundings on the farmland for germination of seeds and growth of plants therein. Finally his attempt was successful, and he grew 5-6 kg atis in 0 .5 nali and sold the same in Delhi for Rs. 250 per kg at that time. As a result farmers of the area started growing MPs. As evident from table, all the interest groups have indicated that moderate cultivation of MP is taking place.

Issuance of Permit: A Challenge: It has been observed that no uniform policy is adopted to issue the permits to the cultivators. Our earlier findings in Tapovan and Mana village suggest that there has been confusion regarding the procedure and eligibility for obtaining the permits. Forest Departments, Baishaj Sangh and Herbal Research Institute are primarily involved in issuance of permits(KIT-IAMR-CSD 2002). In Munsyari the situation is more clear as farmers have to register themselves with the Supervisor of Baishaj Sangh for getting permits. They furnish information regarding the species they are likely to grow and total acreage for a particular species. The supervisor has to visit the area to assess the ground realities before issuing the permit, clarified J C Pandey, Supervisor, Bhaishaj Sangh. However, he admits that due to his age and health problem he does not visit the farmland to verify the information furnished by the farmers. Therefore the permits are issued without physical verification. There is a need to follow the procedure more strictly, and farmers when contacted are also comfortable with this procedure laid down for issuing permits.

On the other hand, the landless poor and Scheduled Castes also play crucial role in the business of MP in the region. They are the one who actually collect the MP for the big farmers and small traders. Since majority of them are landless labourers, they solely depend on collection of MPs. However they also have issues to share. They take advance in cash and kind from the big farmers and small traders before they actually migrate to the summer villages. They are engaged in extensive collection of MP primarily from the Alpine region but deprived of the ultimate benefit as they are bound to sell the collection to the petty traders or big farmers from where they have taken the advance. Since they are landless permit can not be issued to them. However they feel that a large amount of land in the alpine region is uncultivable due to considerable reduction in trans-human migration to high altitude villages.[4] The main reason for reduction in migration is, increasing interest of new generation in government jobs. Therefore the Scheduled caste strongly feel that they may be allowed to cultivate on this land which will substantially contribute to uplift their economic conditions. It is suggested that such type of land can be leased out to them. However the issue is very sensitive as there is always possibility of loosing lands to actual cultivators. A farmer in Mala Dummar village says that he had about 900 nali of land at Barfu, Middle altitude village but same is lost to the actual cultivators during Implementation of Land Resettlement Act. The danger of loosing land to actual cultivators will never be supported by them. Nevertheless if settlement is made the landless may also obtain permits for cultivation of MP and will not be deprived of the benefit of hard work put in by them. This was pointed out by a resident (Malla Dummar, winter village and Barfu Summer village).

The analysis of table clearly indicates that the farmers do not face problems in getting the permits as their lands have to be verified before permit is issued to them. Researchers have rated the problem moderately. However government officials are quite satisfied with the current practice of issuing the permits to the farmers. Traders on the other hand do not agree with the current practice and indicate this as a main hurdle for the growth of the sector.

***Planting Material: A Big Challenge*:** Planting material is not easily available and this is the area where researchers have to take initiatives. The initiatives taken by HAPPRC, by developing a research lab at Tugnath and the Nurseries developed by Forest department near Munsiyari and at Milam, Martoli and Pachu is likely to benefit the farmers to a great extent. However the successful transfer on the farmland have to be seen in times to come. But the role of these nurseries is definitely going to be crucial. Farmers seems to be committed to cultivate MPs in their farm land but the availability of planting material is always questionable. This is a policy issue which needs serious deliberation, otherwise, it will be another futile exercise. The farmers in Darkot, Malla Dummar, Laspa, Sarmoli do show the sample of planting material but it is insufficient. Cultivators, researchers, traders and government officials do agree with the view points.

Market: A proper linkages: In India, only 20 MAP's are under commercial cultivation in a few states, which means that nearly 90 percent of medicinal plant raw material is harvested both illegally and in a destructive and unscientific manner from the wild. In Uttarakhand, except for a few crops which are grown as garden crops, the cultivation of medicinal plants is not even in an initial stage. Nevertheless, as state wishes to be recognized as a herbal state, massive scale cultivation of wild, threatened MAP's is needed urgently for the commercialization of these crops. Most of the population in Uttarakhand lives at middle to high altitude (1000-2500m) and people are still looking for the alternative crop options because their traditional crops are less productive. They get little benefit from growing cash crops like apple, potato and rajma because there is a lack of cheap transport, and technology for the cultivation of high altitude species has not been available before 5-7 years. Cultivators, researchers, traders and government officials agreed that there is tremendous potential for marketing of medicinal plants. However, a proper marketing channel has to be identified and developed where suitable price of produce is ensured to the farmers. Farmers are not happy with the current practice of selling their produce to the Bhaisaj Sangh. The need for developing forward and backward linkages is felt by all the groups. Credit facilities should be provided to those taking advance from the traders while going to the summer villages.

Table 9.8. Export-Import Data of MAP during 1997-98 to 2000-01

		1997-98	*1998-99*	*1999-2000*	*2000-2001*	*% increase over 90-91*
Medicinal Plants	Quantity in Tonnes	43,523.17	44,437.35	41,711.35	50,081.48	20.06
Exported in Tonnes	Values in Rs Lakhs	30,209.98	28,908.35	22,741.38	40,819.24	79.49
Medicinal Plants	Quantity in Tonnes	3,855.10	6,573.84	6,746.54	7,846.7	16.30
Exported in Tonnes	Values in Rs Lakhs	1,779.37	4,052.27	5,908.84	7,979.48	35.04

Source: Export-Import Report.

The information presented by statistics of foreign trade (table) reveals that during last four years (1997-98 to 2000-01) export has fluctuated both in terms of quantity and value, nevertheless import had increased regularly both in the term of quantity and value. There was an increase of 20.06 per cent in the quantity of export and the same was 79.49 per cent for value of export and 16.30 per cent in quantity of import and 35.04 percent in value of import during the year 2000-2001 over previous year 1999-2000.

The study of trade data (Table 9.9) of last four decades indicates that quantity of export decreased during the decades 2000-01 over the previous decade, but value of export has increased regularly even after decrease in quantity of export which become possible only due to increase in market rate of MAP, whereas quantity as well as value of import increased regularly. Thus, it is clear from these data that internal demand of MAP is increasing.

Table 9.9. Export-Import Data of MAP during Last Four Decades

		1970-71	*1980-81*	*1990-91*	*2000-2001*	*% increase over 90-91*
Medicinal Plants	Quantity in Tonnes	15057.21	68673.10	71485.21	50081.48	-29.94 D
Exported in Tonnes	Values in Rs Lakhs	552.32	5452.74	18755.95	40819.24	117.63
Medicinal Plants	Quantity in Tonnes	827.37	3304.70	3473.70	7846.7	125.88
Exported in Tonnes	Values in Rs Lakhs	29.77	214.15	1188.66	7979.48	572.43

Source: Export - Import report.

Government support: Flexible approach: It is estimated that the world demand for medicinal and aromatic plant products is growing at the rate of 7 per cent per annum and if this trend continues it is expected that by 2005 AD India's export would be of the value of Rs. 5000 crore. In Uttarakhand approximately 500 plant species are being traded. However nearly 160 species have been identified as threatened, and if these are not saved, nearly 10 percent reduction in the present turnover can be expected during the next five years. Furthermore, according to cumulative estimate, Uttarakhand has nearly Rs. 1.5 billion per annum trade through the hidden market, as most species collected from the wild are already banned, and there is no proper trade price controlling authority. Our concern is therefore to conserve these plants in the wild and to identify means for their sustainable utilization.

Constructive government support is required for the overall development of the sector is essential. A uniform policy is to be adopted throughout the state. Farmers view points should also be taken into consideration while designing the policies. Since the farmers have taken initiatives to cultivate the medicinal plants in the state the policies intervention needs to be more flexible and best suited in the interest of the farmers. Traders as well as cultivators have rated government support moderately.

Technical support*: *Need of the hours: Need of concentrated technical input is felt throughout the region. Therefore research institutions operating in the region should provide proper input to the farmers from time to time. More demonstration labs should be set up to augment the requirement of the cultivators. The prevailing doubt in the minds of farmers regarding the loss of gradients and poor price for the plants once cultivated in the farmland should be removed by establishing the demonstration lab at different places.

Transportation: Transportation of produce from the alpine region is a major hurdle and farmers have to loose a considerable amount of their earning while transporting the produce. Even accessibility to the region is not easy. Therefore, proper road network should be developed in the region.

Illegal marketing: *Policy Interventions:* At number of places while discussion with the key informants it has been pointed out that a large volume of the produce is being illegally exported under different brands. Therefore policy interventions are required to tackle the issue. The government should come forward with clear cut policy in this regard.

Price uncertainty: Price uncertainty is also a cause of concern for the cultivators. The Buy back policy adopted by HAPPRC in case of Ghes village is the best suited policy to ensure minimum support price for the cultivators for their produce. In some of the deliberations with the researchers it has also been revealed that some of the pharmaceutical companies have buy back agreements with the farmers. Since the cultivation has recently started, any such type of arrangement will certainly boost the morale of the cultivators. Government policies should be designed in such a way that minimum prices are ensured to the farmers.

Future potential: *Need Assessment:* In the analysis it is also revealed that this sector has tremendous potential to provide gainful employment, thereby increasing the income opportunities. The systematic cultivation and collection in an organized way will lead to both the economic betterment of the people and the region, and the maintenance of biodiversity and ecology. The cultivators and people involved in the sectors should be trained on extensive scale.

***Role of Cooperative: ensured Policy*:** The role of cooperative has been rated poor both by the farmers and traders. The need for forming self help group was felt in the villages. In Bela village farmers of alpine region have taken initiatives by forming a grower's association to protect their rights. Nevertheless the instances of exploitation of cultivators by the middlemen under such organization can not be ruled out, if the real farmers are not made aware of the economic potential of the sector and at the same time, in case of unsystematic harvesting, the harmful effects of the same on the ecological balance of the region.

The sector has tremendous potential and may provide a platform to boost the economic development of the state. However, variety of issues as discussed above should be tackled carefully. More flexible approach, best suited to the actual cultivators should be adopted by the government. Role of research and training in this regard is crucial to provide proper inputs to the farmers. Close cooperation between various agencies is desirable, only then the aims of the sustainable economic development, maintaining the ecological balance, can be achieved.

NOTES

1. In Uttarakhand *Nali* and *Muthi* are used for measurement of land 20 nalis are equal to one hectare.
2. *Bugyals* are the green patches of grass in alpine region.
3. Religious function organized in the villages during late August or early Septembers is known as Nanda Austmi. The harvesting of new crops starts from Nanda *austmi*. The villagers of alpine region used to worship goddess by offering *Brahmkamal* (A kind of medicinal plant of alpine meadows).

4. Between 1947-62, there were 600 households residing at Milim and it was the largest village of undivided Almora District and the number of households were also large in other villages of Johar Valley. However over a period of time the number of households migrating to summer villages have reduced considerably and currently out of 120 households only 30 are migrating.

Bibliography

Abbott, J.C. (1958): *Marketing Problem Improvement Programmes,* Food and Agriculture Organisation of the United Nations, Rome, p. 19.

Aditya Purohit, R.K. Maikhuri, K.S. Rao and S. Nautiyal, (2001). Impact of bark removal on survival of Taxus Baccata L. (Himalayan Yew) in Nanda Devi Biosphere Reserve, Garhwal Himalaya, India. *Current Science,* Vol. 81, No. 5, 10 September 2001.

Agro-Economic Research Centre (1975): *Fruit Industry of Himachal Pradesh in Restrospect and Prospect,* Occasional Paper No. 3. A.E.R.C., H.P. University, Shimla.

Agro-Economic Research Centre (1977-78): *A Comprehensive Study on Marketing of Apple of Himachal Pradesh,* Vol. iii, AERC, H.P. University, Shimla, (mimeo).

Airi, S., R.S. Rawal, U. Dhar and A.N. Purohit (2000). Assessment of availability and habitat preference of Jatamansi, a critically endangered medicinal plant of west Himalaya. *Current Science,* Vol. 79, No. 10, 25 November 2000.

Alderman, W.H. (1962). Development of Horticulture on the Northern Great Plains. *Region American Society for Horticultural Science.* Chapter 8, Minnesota.

AMDD, (1995): *Food Balance Sheet of Nepal,* Lalitpur, Nepal.

APP (1995) *Agriculture Prospective Plan,* NPC/ADB/APROSC, Kathmandu, Nepal.

Armitage, A.M. and Laushman, J.M. (2003) *Specialty Cut Flowers, The Production of Annuals, Perennials, Bulbs, and Woody Plants for Fresh and Dried Cut Flowers,* Second Edition. Timber Press, Portland, 586 pp.

Atkinson, E.T. (1973): *Himalayan Gazetteer,* Reprinted Cosmo Publications, Delhi, Vol. 11, p. 369.

Azad, K.C. (1985): *Packing and Transport of Horticultural Produce in H.P.*, Paper Presented at the first workshop on Science and Technology in H.P. October 29-31, Shimla.

Balge, R., Gill, S., Blessington, T., Ross, D., Butler, B., Rosenkranz, G., and Bosmans, R. (2000). Production of Alliums as Cut Flowers, *University of Maryland, College of Agriculture & Natural Resources Extension Publication FS-767.*

Banskota, K.; and Sharma, B., (1999): *Traded Resource Flows from Highland to Lowland: Understanding Economic Linkages.* Kathmandu: ICIMOD, 110 pp.

Barooach, Anudo Ram (1971): *Ancient Geography of India,* Publication Board, Assam, Gauhati, pp. 48-50.

Bhakharu, H.M. (1985): Nutritional Value of Fruits, *The Economic Times,* 1st June, New Delhi.

Bhakhuni, DS: Medicinal Plants of Commerce of Uttarkhand: Problems of Phytopharmaceutical industries, in Nautiyal et al. (Ed.) *Harvesting Herbs 2000: Medicinal and Aromatic Plants: An Action Plan of Uttrakhand.* 1997.

Carson, B., (1992): *The Land, the Farmer and the Future,* A Soil Fertility Management Strategy for Nepal. *ICIMOD Occasional Paper No. 92/21,* Kathmandu, Nepal.

CBS (1991): *Agricultural Statistics*, Kathmandu, *Population Censces,* (1991) Kathmandu, Nepal.

Census of India, 2001.

CGIAR, (1999): *CGIAR Research Priorities for Marginal Lands,* CGIAR Document No. SDRITAC: IAR/92/12.

Chand, S.P., (1999): *SSSP Report. Proc. Regional Seed Production and Marketing* Workshop, 4 March 1999. SSSP/SEAW, ARS, Lumle Nepal.

Chandra Shekhar Silori and Ruchi Badola, (2000). Medicinal Plant Cultivation and Sustainable Development: A Case Study in the Buffer Zone of the Nanda Devi Biosphere Reserve, Western Himalaya, India . Wildlife Institute of India, India Mountain Research and Development Vol. 20, No. 3, Aug 2000 272-279.

Chitra, Phadnis, (2002), Floriculture units caught in a pincer, *Financial Daily.*

Dabral, Shiv Prasad (1965): *Uttarakhand Ka Itihas* (in Hindi), Part I, Veergatha Prakashan, Dogada (Garhwal), p. 84.

Dimri, Anil K (1994) Impact of Male Migration of Women: A Study of Garhwal Himalayan Region, *The Administrator*, July-Sept., 1994, Vol. XXXIX No. 3.

Dimri, Anil K (1996): *District Planning: A Case Study of Dehradun District UP,* Unpublished D. Phil Thesis.

Dobhal, G.L. (1987): *Development of Hill Areas*, Concept Publishing Company, New Delhi.

Encyclopedia of Americanna (1984): Vol. 9.

F.A.O., (1982):*Marketing and Its Role in Increasing Productivity, Freedom from Hunger Campaign*, Basic Study No. 4, F.A.O. Rome.

Faroquee Niheal A. and Krishna G. Saxena, (1996). Conservation and utilization of medicinal plants in high hills of the central Himalayas. *Environmental Conservation* 23 (1) 75-80, 1996.

Funk and Wagnalls (1988): *New Encyclopedia*, Vol. 11.

Gardner, G. (1996): *Shrinking Fields: Crop land loss in a worlds of eight billion*. World Watch paper 161. World Watch Institute, Washington DC.

Gittinger, J. Price (1971): *Economic Analysis of Agricultural Project*, The Economic Development Institute, ISBRD, Washington, D.C., U.S.A.

Goldman, M. (ed.), (1998): *Privatizing Nature: Political Struggle for Global Commons*. London: Pluto Press. 257 pp.

Gupta, G.S. and George, P.S. (1974): Profitability of Nagpur Santra (Orange) Cultivation, *Indian Journal of Agricultural Economics,* Vol. XXIX, No. 3, July-September pp. 134-142.

Gupta, R.P., and Pandey, U.B. (1983), *Apple Diseases with Special Reference to Doab -in India*, paper presented at the National workshop on India Apple industries at NAFED, New Delhi, on 19-21 January.

Hemant Pandey, Shyamal K. Nadi, Bhuwan Chandra, Mohammed Nadeem and Lok Man S. Palni, (2001). GA3 induced flowering in Podophyllum hexandrum Royle: A rare alpine medicinal herb. Acta Physiologogiae Plantarum Vol. 23, No. 4, 2001:467-474.

htpp://www.tifac.org.in/pffer//;np/rep.

http://en.wikipedia.org/wiki/Tomato#Modern_uses_of_tomatoes

http://indianfood.indianetzone.com/spices/1/seeds_spices.htm

http://www.agnr.umd.edu/MCE/Publications/Publication.cfm?ID-85&cat=C>

http://www.caca.essortment.com/useforlemon_rtbf.htm

http://www.gardensablaze.com/HerbGarlicMed.htm

http://www.google.co.in/search?hl=en&q=Spice+cultivation+in+Uttaranchal

&btnG=Google+Search&meta=

http://www.spice-trade.com/fenugreek.html

ICIMOD (1997): *Districts of Nepal: Indicators of Development*, ICIMOD, Kathmandu, Nepal.

IFAD (1993): *Providing Food Security for All*, IFAD, Rome, Italy.

Jodha, N.S., (1997): *Highland - Lowland Economic Linkages: Issues in Mountain Development* 97/8. Kathmandu: ICIMOD, 6 pp.

Jodha, N.S. (1998): *Reviving the Social System Ecosystem Links in Himalayas*. In F. Berkes and C. Folke (eds.) *Linking Social and Ecological Systems: Management Practices and Social Mechanisms for Building Resilience*. Cambridge: Cambridge University Press, 285-310 pp.

Jodha, N.S. (1999): *Enhancing Food Security in a Warmer and More Crowded World: Factors and Process in Fragile Areas*. In *Climate Change and World Food Security* (ed. T.E. Dowing).

Jodha, N.S. and Shrestha, S. (1994): *Towards Sustainable and More Mroductive Mountain Farming. Proc. International Symposium of Mountain Environment and Development: Constraints and Opportunities*. ICIMOD, Kathmandu, Nepal.

Jodha, N.S., (1993): *Perspective on Property Generating Process in Mountain Areas,* Proceeding of International Forum on 'Development of Poor Mountain Areas' 22-27 March, Beijing, China 1993, pp. 38-46.

Jones, J.E., Tripathi, B.P., Joshi, K.R., and Pant, B.B. (2002): *Results from a Household Survey with Emphasis on Rural Livelihoods and Soil Fertility Management Undertaken in the Mid-hills of Nepal*, SRI/UK-ARS Lumle/NARC Collaborative Project Report.

Joshi & Pandey, (1980): *A Backward Region Within an Underdeveloped State*, The problem of Uttarakhand, Himalaya, *Man and Nature,* Vol. 3, No. 9.

Juyal R.P., Amitava Mukherjee and A.K. Dimri (1994): Pattern of Seasonal Unemployment, *Agrarians Move,* Vol. I, No. 1, Dehradun.

Juyal, RP and Dimri, Anil K (1995) *Demographic Pressure And Urbanisation: A Case of Dehradun Urban Agglomeration,* In Agnihotri, V.K. (Ed), *Public Policy Analysis and Design*, Concept, New Delhi.

Juyal, R.P. (1985): *Micro Level Planning for Integrated Rural Development in Garhwal Himalaya*, Unpublished Ph.D. Thesis, Garhwal University, Srinagar, Garhwal.

Kala, Chandra Prakash and Mathur, Vinod B., (2002). Patterns of plant species distribution in the Trans Himalayan region of Ladakh, India. Journal of Vegetation Science 13: 751-754, 2002.

Kausic, S.D.: Climatic Zones and their Related Soio-economic in Garhwal Hiamalaya, *Geog. Rev.* Vol. 24.

KIT Netherland, IAMR. New Delhi AND CSD Dehradun (2003): *Cultivating A Healthy Enterprise: Developing A Sustainable Medicinal Plant Chain in Uttaranchal — India, A Joint Project Report.*

Kohls, R.L. (1955): *Marketing of Agricultural Produce*, Macmillan Co., New York.

Koirala, G.P. and Thapa, G.B. (1997): *Food Security Challenges, Where does Nepal Stand ?* Research Report Series No. 36. HMG-Ministry of Agriculture and Winrock International, Kathmandu.

Kreutzmann, H. (1995). Globalisation, Spatial Integration, and Sustainable Development in Northern Pakistan. *Mountain Research and Development* Vol. 15 (3), pp. 213-227.

M. Nadeem, H.C. Rikhari, Anil Kumar, L.M.S. Palni and S.K. Nandi, (2002). Taxol content in the bark of Himalayan Yew in relation to tree age and sex. *Phytochemistry* 60 (2000) 627-631.

Maikhuri, R.K. and A.K. Gangwar (1993) 'Ethnobiology of some tribal societies of Arunachal Pradesh in northeast India', *Economic Botany* 47(4): 345-357.

Maikhuri, R.K. and P.S. Ramakrishnan (1992) 'Ethnobiology of some tribal societies of Arunachal Pradesh in northeast India', *J. Econ. Ta. Bot. Addl. Ser.* 10: 61-78.

Maikhuri, R.K., K.S. Rao and K.G. Saxena (1996a) 'Traditional crop diversity for sustainable development of Central Himalayan agroecosystems', *International Journal of Sustainable Development & World Ecology* 3: 8-31.

Maikhuri, R.K., S. Nautiyal, K.S. Rao, and K.G. Saxena (1996b), *Ecology and socio-economy of transhumanse communities of Garhwal Himalaya. Final progress report.* DST, New Delhi.

Maikhuri, R.K., S. Nautiyal, K.S. Rao, and K.G. Saxena (1998a), 'Medicinal plants cultivation and biosphere reserve management: a case study from Nanda Devi Biosphere Reserve, Himalaya', *Current Science* 74: 157-163.

Maikhuri, R.K., S. Nautiyal, K.S. Rao, and K.G. Saxena (1998b) 'Role of medicinal plants in traditional health care system: a case study from Nanda Devi Biosphere Reserve', *Current Science* 75 (2): 152-157.

Mazumdar, D.N. (1960): *Himalayan Polyandry*, Asia Publishing House, Bombay, p. VII-VIII.

Mehta, G.S. (2008), *Towards Improving Livelihoods in Mountains: Options and Strategies,* Zenith, Delhi.

Mehta, G.S. (2007), *Backward Area Development Through Rural Industrialisation,* Zenith, Delhi.

Messerli, B. and Ives, J.D. (eds), (1997). *Mountains of the World: A Global Priority*. New York: The Pathenon Publishing Group. 495 pp.

MOA, (1992): *National Sample Census of Agriculture*, Ministry of Agriculture, Nepal.

MoAC, (2000): Statistical Information of Nepalese Agriculture, Ministry of Agriculture and Cooperatives, 1999-2000, HMG, Nepal.

Mohan Deepender (1982): *Economics of Tree Verses Annual Crops on Marginal Agricultural Lands*, Oxford and IBH Publishing Co., New Delhi-Bombay-Calcutta.

Myrdal, Gunnar (1963): *Economic Theory and Under-Developed Regions*, Metheun & Co., London.

Myrdal, Gunnar (1968): *Asian Drama: An Inquiry into the Poverty of Nations*, Vol.I. II and III, Pantheon, New York.

Nagar, PS, (2005), Floristic Biodiversity of Barda Hills and Its Surroundings Jodhpur, *Scientific Pub.* Jodhpur, xxiv, 325 p.

Nagpal, S.,(1999): Self Sufficient Slopes in K. Dixit, A. John and B.

Subba (eds). *Tough Terrain: Media Reports on Mountain Issues*. Kathmandu: PANNOS and APMN pp. 27-37.

Nakata, T. (1972): *Geomorphic History and Crustal Movement in Himalaya*, Sci. Rep. Japan, 7th Series (Geology), Vol. 22.

Nand, Nitya and Kamlesh Kumar(1989): *The Holy Himalaya, (A Geographical Interpretation of Garhwal Himalaya)*, Daya Publishing House, New Delhi.

Nandi Shyamal K., Lok Man S. Palni and H.C. Rikhari, (1996). Chemical induction of adventitious root formation in Taxus baccata cuttings. *Plant Growth Regulation* 19: 117-122, 1996.

Negi, P.S. (1990): *Horticultural Produce Marketing Technology and Marketing Management*, Himachal Pradesh Horticultural Produce Marketing and Processing Corporation Ltd., Shimla.

Nichols, T.E. (1969): Role of Transport in Agricultural Marketing and Development, *American Journal of Agricultural Economics*, Vol. 51, No. 5, December, p. 4555-1463.

Nurkse, Ragnar (1966), *Problem of Capital Formation in Under Developed Countries*, Oxford University Press.

Oldham, R.D. (1883): *Note on the Geology of Jaunsar and Lower Himalaya*, Record, Geological Survey of India, Calcutta.

Organisation for Economic Cooperation and Development (1970): Standardization of Fruit and Vegetable Technological and Economic Aspects, Paris, pp. 9-28.

Pal, Devendra and S.C. Shah (1984): *Doon Environments: Its Geological Setting, Mineral, Wealth and Landuse,* Doon Science Forum, Dehradun.

Pandey, H., S.K. Nandi, M. Nadeem and L.M.S. Palni, (2000). Chemical stimulation of seed germination in Aconitum heterophyllum Wall. And A. balfourii Stapf: important Himalayan species of medicinal value. *Seed Sci. and Technol,* 28, 39-48.

Pandey, B.K. and V.K. Verma (1983): *A Study of Shiwalik Sediments (Garhwal Himalaya)*, *Geo Science Journal,* Vol. 4.

Papola, T.S., (1998): *High Value Enterprises for Sustainable Livelihood: Trends, Experiences and Policies in Hindu Kush-Himalayan Region*. Paper Presented at Mountain 2000 and Beyond-International Conference on Sustainable Development of Hindu Kush-Himalayan Region. Wildbad Keuth, Federal Republic of Germany 22-24 June.

Pratap, T. (2001): *Mountain Agriculture, Marginal Lands and Sustainable Livelihoods: Challenges and Opportunities,* International Symposium on Mountain Agriculture in HKH Region, 21-24 May 2001, ICIMOD, Kathmandu, Nepal.

Pratap, T., (1995): *High Value Cash Crop in Mountain Farming: Mountain Development Process and Opportunities,* Kathmandu: ICIMOD.

Pratap, T., (1999): Sustainable Land Management in Marginal Mountain Areas of the Himalayan Region, *Mountain Research & Development*, Vol. 19, No. 3 pp. 251-260.

Purohit, A N Medicinal Plants—Need for Upgrading Technology for Trading the Tradition in Nautiyal et al. *Harvesting Herbs 2000: Medicinal and Aromatic Plants: An Action Plan of Uttrakhand.* 1997.

Purohit, SS and R Ranjan, (2002) Flowering: Physiological, Biochemical and Molecular Aspects, *Agrobios*, viii, 187 p.,

Raj Desh (2005), *Floriculture in Hills,* Agrotech Publishing Academy, Udaipur, 200 p.

Ramachandran, Nira and A K Dimri (*1996*): Participating in the Planning Process - A Must For Sustainable Development, *Social Change,* March, Vol. 36, No. 1.

Rikhari, H.C., L.M.S. Palni, S.S. Sharma and S.K. Nandi (1998). Himalayan yew; stand structure, canapoy damage, regeneration and conservation strategy. *Environmental Conservation* 25 (4): 334-341.

Rongsen, L. (1998): *Enterprises in Mountain Specific Products in Western Sichuan, China.* Discussion paper No., 98/7, ICIMOD, Kathmandu, Nepal.

Rongsen, Lu (1998): *Enterprises in Mountain Specific Products in Western Sichuan*, China. MEI Discussion Paper 98/7. Kathmandu: ICIMOD, 51 pp.

Roy, Babul, Nehal A Faroquee, S. Sharma and L.M.S. Palni (2002), Indigenous knowledge of wool dyeing: A Bhotiya practice on its way out in the higher Kumaun Himalaya. *Indian Journal of Traditional Knowledge.* Vol. 1(1), October 2002 pp. 40-46.

Roy, S., (1997): Globalisation, Structural Change and Poverty: Some Conceptual and Policy Issues. *Economic and Political Weekly* Vol. 32 (33 & 34), pp. 2117-2135 pp.

S. Nautiyal, R.K. Maikhuri, K.S. Rao and K.G. Saxena (2001). Medicinal Plant Resources in Nanda Devi Biosphere Reserve in the Central Himalayas. *Journal of Herbs, Spices and Medicinal Plants.* Vol. 8(4) 2001. Haworth Press.

Sah, R.P. (2001): *Socio-economic Issues and Options of Marginal Farms in the Hills of Mountains of Nepal: An Experience in the Western Hills.* International Symposium on Mountain Agriculture in the HKH Region, 21-24 May 2001, ICIMOD, Kathmandu, Nepal.

Samant, S.S. and L.M.S. Palni, (2000). Diversity, distribution and indigenous uses of essential oil-yielding medicinal plants of the Indian Himalayan region. *Journal of Medicinal and Aromatic Plant Sciences* 22 (2000) 671-684.

Sati, MC and R.P. Juyal, (2008) "A Gender Approach to Sustainable Rural Development of Mountains," *Mountain Research and Development,* Vol. 28, No. 1, Feb. 2008.

Seeley, J.G. (1982). Advancements in Commercial Floriculture. *Southern Florist and Nurseryman.* p. 45.

Semwal, R.L., R.K. Maikhuri (1996) Agroecosystem analysis of Garhwal Himalaya. *Biological Agriculture and Horticulture.* Vol. 13: pp. 267-289.

Sharma, H.R. (1999). *Issues and Options for Horticulture based Marginal Farms and Lands.* (Paper presented at Planning Meeting on Investigating Issues and Options for Improving Livelihood of marginal Mountain Farms). Kathmandu: ICIMOD, 17 pp.

Sharma, H.R. (1996): *Mountain Agricultural Development Process and Sustainability – Micro-level Evidence from Himanchal Pradesh,* Discussion Paper, Series No. MFS 96/2, ICIMOD, Kathandu, Nepal.

Sharma, P. (ed), (1999). *Mountain Tourism and Local Development: Case Studies from the Hindu Kush-Himalayas,* Verlag, Austria: Himal Book & Studies, (In Press).

Sharma, U., (1998): *Development of Micro-enterprises - Ilam and Bhojpur Districts,* Discussion Paper No. MEI 98/4,: ICIMOD, Kathmandu, Nepal.

Sud, Ramesh Kumar and Sudhir Kumar, (2004), Flowers and Vegetables of India, *Scientific, viii, 276 p.*,

Sumit Manjkhola and Uppeandra Dhar (2002). Conservation and

utilization of Arnebia benthanii (Wall. Ex G.Don) Johnston, a high value Himalayan medicinal plant. *Current Science,* Vol. 83, No. 4, 25 August 2002.

Tripathi, B.P. (1999): *Soil Fertility Status in the Farmers' Fields of the Western Hills of Nepal, Lumle* Seminar Paper No. 99/4, SAS/N Convention, 9-11 June 1999, Kathmandu, Nepal.

Tripathi, B.P. Gardner, R.; Mawdesley, K.J.; Acharya, G.P. and Sah, R.P., (1999): *Soil Erosion and Fertility Losses in the Western Hills of Nepal: An Overview.* Workshop on *Enhanced Farming Livelihood the Hills of Nepal through Improved Soil Fertility,* Dhulikhel, 25-26 July 1999, Kavre, Nepal.

Tulachan, P.M., (1999): *Trends and Prospects of Sustainable Mountain Agriculture in the Hindu Kush-Himalayan Region. Issues in Mountain Development,* No. 2, ICIMOD, Kathmandu.

UNDP (1999): *Human Development Report 1999.* New York: Oxford University Press.

Vaidya, A.K. and Floyd, C.N. (1997). *From Recommendation Domains to Providing Basis for Research Prioritisation and Locating Representative Sites for Technology Generation and Verification in the Hills of Nepal.* LARC Occasional Paper No. 97/3, Kaski, Nepal: Lumle Agricultural Research Centre.

WDR, 1996. *World Development* Report (1996): World Bank.

World Bank, (1999): *Entering the 21st Century—World Development Report 1999-2000.* New York: Oxford University Press.

Index

■■■